W9-BNO-662

Contemporary States and Societies

This series provides lively and accessible introductions to key countries and regions of the world, conceived and designed to meet the needs of today's students. The authors are all experts with specialist knowledge of the country or region concerned and have been chosen also for their ability to communicate clearly to a non-specialist readership. Each text has been specially commissioned for the series and is structured according to a common format.

Published

Contemporary Russia
Edwin Bacon with
Matthew Wyman

Contemporary South Africa
Anthony Butler

Contemporary America (2ed)
Russell Duncan
and Joseph Goddard

Contemporary China
Alan Hunter and John Sexton

Contemporary Japan (2ed)
Duncan McCargo

Contemporary Britain (2ed)
John McCormick

Contemporary Latin America (2ed)
Ronaldo Munck

Forthcoming

Contemporary India
Katharine Adeney
and Andrew Wyatt

Contemporary France
Helen Drake

Contemporary Spain
Paul Kennedy

Contemporary Ireland
Eoin O'Malley

Contemporary Europe
B. Guy Peters

Also planned

Contemporary Asia
Contemporary Germany
Contemporary Italy

Contemporary States and Societies
Series Standing Order
ISBN 978–0–333–75402–3 hardcover
ISBN 978–0–333–80319–6 paperback
(outside North America only)

You can receive future titles in this series as they are published by placing a standing order. Please contact your bookseller or, in the case of difficulty, write to us at the address below with your name and address, the title of the series and the ISBN quoted above.

Customer Services Department, Palgrave Ltd
Houndmills, Basingstoke, Hampshire RG21 6XS, England

Contemporary Russia

Edwin Bacon
with
Matthew Wyman

First published in 2006 by
PALGRAVE MACMILLAN
Houndmills, Basingstoke, Hampshire RG21 6XS and
175 Fifth Avenue, New York, N.Y. 10010
Companies and representatives throughout the world.

PALGRAVE MACMILLAN is the global academic imprint of the Palgrave Macmillan division of St. Martin's Press, LLC and of Palgrave Macmillan Ltd. Macmillan® is a registered trademark in the United States, United Kingdom and other countries. Palgrave is a registered trademark in the European Union and other countries.

ISBN-13: 978–0–333–77201–0   hardback
ISBN-10: 0–333–77201–6   hardback
ISBN-13: 978–0–333–77202–7   paperback
ISBN-10: 0–333–77202–4   paperback

This book is printed on paper suitable for recycling and made from fully managed and sustained forest sources. Logging, pulping and manufacturing processes are expected to conform to the environmental regulations of the country of origin.

A catalogue record for this book is available from the British Library.

Library of Congress Cataloging-in-Publication Data

Bacon, Edwin, 1966–
      Contemporary Russia / Edwin Bacon ; with Matthew Wyman.
          p. cm.—(Contemporary states and societies)
      Includes bibliographical references and index.
      ISBN 0–333–77201–6 – ISBN 0–333–77202–4 (pbk.)
      1. Russia (Federation). I. Wyman, Matthew. II. Title. III. Series.

DK510.23B33 2005
947.086—dc22   2005048845

10 9 8 7 6 5 4 3 2
15 14 13 12 11 10 09 08 07

Printed and bound in China

Contents

List of Figures, Tables, Boxes and Maps

Figures

Tables

Boxes

Maps

List of Abbreviations

CIS	Commonwealth of Independent States
CSTO	Collective Security Treaty Organization
EU	European Union
FDI	foreign direct investment
GDP	gross domestic product
KGB	Komitet gosudarstvennoi bezopasnosti (Committee for State Security)
LDPR	Liberal Democratic Party of Russia
MFA	Ministry of Foreign Affairs
NATO	North Atlantic Treaty Organization
OECD	Organisation for Economic Cooperation and Development
OSCE	Organisation for Security and Cooperation in Europe
PJC	Permanent Joint Council
RSFSR	Russian Soviet Federative Socialist Republic
UN	United Nations
USSR	Union of Soviet Socialist Republics
WTO	World Trade Organization

Acknowledgements

Edwin Bacon would like to thank those colleagues and friends who, at various points – some so long ago that they may have forgotten – took time to read through and answer queries on different sections of this book, notably, Rebecca Bull, Julian Moss, Mark Sandle, and Mark Webber. I am grateful too to my original co-writer Matthew Wyman; we conceived this project together and I am sure that the final version is all the poorer for the fact that Matthew had to withdraw from its later stages.

In so broad a work as this, many influences come to bear on the final text. I found myself surprised to be drawing at different times on memories of student days in the Soviet Union, on literature classes at the University of Sheffield in the 1980s, on months spent scouring the archives of the Soviet state in Moscow, on weeks spent in a small Russian town north-east of Mongolia, on periods of time working for the UK government and parliament, and on repeated trips over the past two decades to a Moscow which has changed dramatically but still retains its hold on me. There are too many people to name who have contributed to those times and to whatever accumulation of knowledge about Russia is distilled here; I am grateful to them all. I am grateful especially to colleagues in the Centre for Russian and East European Studies at the University of Birmingham, which has been my intellectual home for most of the period writing this book, and at Bishop Grosseteste College in Lincoln, where the book was finished during my leave of absence in that splendid setting.

This book is dedicated, however, to five people whose only connection to Russia is that they put up with my absences whilst I am there. To my wife, Deborah, and our daughters, Eleanor, Charlotte, Emily and Joanna, with love.

EDWIN BACON

Map 1 Russia and its neighbouring states

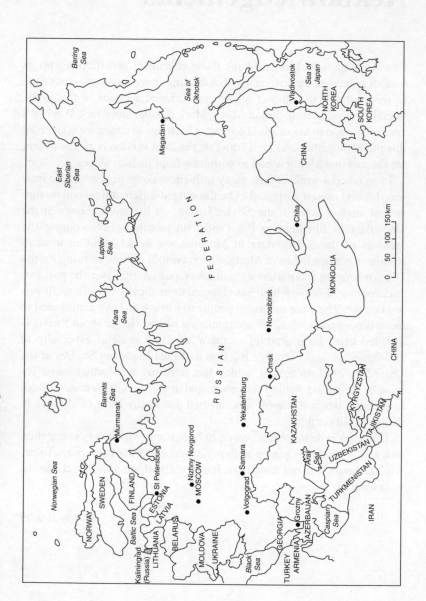

Introduction

Russia today is a country marked, some might say scarred, by a century of upheaval and radical change. Of course all countries experience change, but few in recent history have anything to match the path taken by Russia.

For most of the twentieth century Russia was ruled by the Communist Party of the Soviet Union. This did not simply entail autocratic, and occasionally totalitarian, domination of the country by the ruling regime, but rather the imposition of an entirely new form of government, the influence of which was felt the world over. Based on the premise that a benevolent, all-powerful, and scientifically rational state could guide the people to the paradise on earth of communism, the Party set about creating in Russia, and in the growing number of nations which came into the Communist bloc, a socialist system.

The Soviet economy was dominated by the state; virtually all forms of public communication were controlled by the state; the lives of citizens were directed by the state; the essentials of life such as accommodation, food and heating were subsidized by and in the gift of the state. The Soviet Union (as Russia and 14 other constituent republics were known) became one pole in a bi-polar global system. It represented 'the other', the alternative to the West, and as such developed a network of client states, armed forces of immense power, and a place at the top table – with the United States – as one of the two superpowers in global affairs.

Then, in 1991, the Soviet Union collapsed. And it collapsed with astonishing rapidity. Few had foreseen its demise, and from those who had, predictions usually entailed either lengthy decline or apocalyptic upheaval. As it happened, the break-up of the Soviet Union and the collapse of the communist system came remarkably peacefully and quickly.

In 1989 the countries of Eastern Europe which had been in the Soviet sphere of influence were allowed the freedom to choose their own direction, and swiftly did so, rejecting communism and looking to Western Europe. In 1991, the Soviet Union itself split up into its constituent parts. The more nationalist-minded republics – notably the Baltic states of Estonia, Latvia and Lithuania – led the way, and then by the end of the year Europe's two biggest countries, Ukraine and Russia, decided to leave the Soviet Union.

Of course, without Russia, there could be no Soviet Union, and so by the end of 1991 the Communist hammer and sickle flag was lowered over the Soviet seat of government – the Kremlin in Moscow – for the last time, and the Russian tricolour was raised. A new independent Russia emerged from out of the Soviet state.

Ostensibly Russia after 1991 has been built on an acceptance of those central elements of Western life rejected by the Soviet regime, namely, liberal democracy, a market economy and individual freedom. In other words, today's Russia represents an attempt at a sharp, historical 'about turn'. Contemporary Russia presents itself as a democratic regime with a growing market economy, and as an ally of the West in international relations. Its citizens are free to travel, its leaders are elected, and all shades of opinion can be found in its newspapers.

As noted above, there are very few states that can lay claim to such a roller-coaster of a ride in their recent history. We are not talking here of mere regime change, but of entirely differing approaches to and concepts of the identity and role of Russia. Furthermore, these changing approaches represent only the framework of recent Russian history. Within this framework we find catastrophic events – revolution, civil war, famine, state repression on an inconceivable scale, losses in the Second World War which dwarfed those of any other combatant nation, the collapse of empire, repeated economic collapses in the post-Soviet years, tens of millions of deaths as a direct result of the policies of the state or the horrors of warfare.

If this brief summary were the entire story, then that would perhaps be enough for most states. However, as this book makes clear, the immediate history of contemporary Russia, though immensely influential, is only part of what makes Russia what it is today. There are two other key themes which re-occur time and again over the following chapters.

First is the deep-seated Russian national identity. Both communism and, since 1991, Western liberalism can to some extent be accurately portrayed as a veneer applied over more influential and longer-lasting features of Russian life. Whatever the regime, there are elements of 'Russian-ness' which re-occur repeatedly, for example:

- An ambivalent relationship between the state and the people – the alleged desire of the Russian people for a 'strong hand' to lead them, and yet at the same time a deep distrust of those who operate on behalf of the authorities and a deep cynicism about the political process. At times it can appear as if there is a recurrent cycle of reform and reaction in Russian life, of the gaining of individual liberties and the reeling back in of the same by the state.
- A self-identity which often defines Russian-ness in relation to the West. For many centuries, Russian history has developed through cycles of

embracing and deriding Europe and 'the West' more generally, torn between adopting many of the West's advances in prosperity and technology, and at the same time believing in the inherent uniqueness of Russia and its superiority over the materialist, decadent West. Russia is – geographically and demographically, culturally and spiritually – both European and Asiatic. To understand Russia it is essential to recognize this fact.

The second theme which re-occurs throughout this book stands at odds to some extent with what we have so far outlined in this introduction. In order to gain a good understanding of what makes contemporary Russia the country it is, it is important not to buy too readily into the clichés of Russian history. One can recognize the importance and influence of history, without being blind to the inevitability of change.

Despite the predictions of some observers as the Putin regime has strengthened the Russian state in the early years of the twenty-first century, Russia cannot go back to what it was in the communist era. Russia is not locked into an unbreakable imperialist impulse or on an inevitable path back to an all-powerful authoritarian state. At least as influential as history are today's circumstances and today's Russians. Table 1.1 summarizes some key facts about Russia.

Contemporary Russia is a country replete with tensions and problems:

- The gap between the growing affluent middle class and the quarter of the population living below the poverty line is widening.
- More Russians travel and live abroad than ever before, and yet at home Russian nationalism and xenophobia is a growing political force.
- The generation entering adulthood in Russia today has no memory of the communist years, and yet those years were formative for Russia's ruling elite.
- Terrorist attacks, stemming from Chechen separatism but with an increasing element of radical Islam within them, have increased in recent years in terms of frequency and barbarity, and Russia remains unwilling to back away from its own hardline policy of brutal repression amongst alleged separatists in Chechnya itself.
- During the early years of the twenty-first century, the Russian economy has grown impressively, largely on the back of oil and gas production, but the actions of the state in overtly controlling such production flies in the face of a commitment to the free market.
- Despite over a decade under a democratic constitution, four parliamentary elections, and three presidential elections, there has still not been a democratic change of regime in Russia.

Table 1.1   Quick facts about Russia

Official name	Russia, or the Russian Federation
Capital	Moscow
Area	17,075,200 sq km (6,592,800 sq miles)
Population	143.78 million
Population density	8.4 per sq km (22 per sq mile)
Population growth rate	−0.45%
Languages	Russian, and other minority ethnic languages
Religions	Predominantly Russian Orthodox, with a significant Muslim minority. Christianity, Islam, Buddhism and Judaism officially acknowledged as Russia's historical religions
GDP (2003)	$1.282 trillion
Per capita GNP	$8,900
Distribution of GNP	60% services, 35% industry, 5% agriculture
Literacy	99%
Infant mortality	17 per 1,000 live births
Life expectancy	66.4 years
Government type	Federation with elected president and parliament
Administration	21 republics, 49 oblasts, 10 autonomous okrugs, 6 krais, 2 federal cities, 1 autonomous oblast
Executive	President, prime minister and government
Legislature	Bicameral Federal Assembly; Federation Council, two members appointed by each of the 89 regions, one by the regional legislature, one by the regional executive; State Duma, 450 members elected, 225 in single mandate constituencies, 225 by party list (from 2007 all 450 to be elected by party list)
Party structure	Multi-party with United Russia dominating parliament (2003–07) and the other main parties being the Communists and two nationalist parties – the Liberal Democratic Party of Russia, and Rodina (Motherland)
Judiciary	Constitutional Court, Supreme Court and Higher Court of Arbitration – judges appointed by the Federation Council on the recommendation of the President
Head of state	President Vladimir Putin (2000–)

In the following chapters, these issues and many others will be examined, presenting an introduction to Russia today, its society, politics, economy and culture.

Chapter 1 provides the historical background, briefly covering the tsarist period, the communist years, and then, in a little more depth, the events which brought about the collapse of the Soviet Union and the presidency of Boris Yeltsin. It ends with an account of President Putin's rise to power. Throughout the chapter, key elements of Russia's history are drawn out, notably the role of the state and Russia's relationship with Europe.

Chapter 2 introduces the Russian land and peoples. The first part deals with Russia's physical setting, environmental issues, borders and cities. The second part discusses the identity of the inhabitants of Russia, focusing particularly on the multi-ethnic nature of the Russian Federation. It considers, too, the notion of national values.

Chapter 3 looks at Russian society today. In particular it covers four areas of great significance to the inhabitants of Russia, namely, living standards, demographic and health issues, judicial policy and education.

Chapter 4 turns to the governance of Russia. Having set the scene with a brief overview of the Soviet system, it outlines Russia's approach to democracy and governance since 1991. It establishes the main features of the Russian constitution and deals with the tensions inherent in Russia's decisions surrounding the form of democracy chosen in the early 1990s. We then set out the powers of the executive, legislature and judiciary, and consider the major forces acting in Russian politics today, before concluding with an assessment of the political scene under President Putin.

Chapter 5 focuses on the economic transition of Russia, from the centrally planned command economy of the Soviet era, through the economically catastrophic transition period of the 1990s to the relative prosperity of the early years of the twenty-first century. The chapter ends by assessing three major challenges to the Russian economy today: balancing the benefits and disadvantages of resource dependence; establishing an appropriate legal framework for economic activity; and engaging with the wider global economy.

Chapter 6 deals with the subjects of rights, freedoms and civil society. The Soviet Union was marked out as much by its poor record in these areas as by its military might, political ideology and planned economy. It follows, then, that Russia's record in this regard serves as an indicator of its progress towards liberal democracy. The chapter outlines the progress made in the 1990s and points to negative trends emerging under Vladimir Putin.

Chapter 7 turns its attention to the more ephemeral aspects of Russian life – namely, ideas, culture and ideology. The 'Russian idea' is a distinctive, if partly mythical, aspect of national identity. This chapter draws out the provenance and central features of the Russian idea and explores the place of ideas and ideology in the national consciousness. It explores, too, the state of the arts, particularly literature, film and music, in today's

Russia, noting the challenges brought by the globalization of culture in the 1990s and beyond.

Chapter 8 turns its attention outwards, considering Russia's place in the world in the sphere of international relations. The global reach of the Soviet superpower was impressive, but since then Russia has effectively lost an empire and had to face many of the accompanying problems which this brings. At the same time, Russia remains a permanent member of the UN Security Council and has joined the G8 group of leading nations. This chapter pays particular attention to Russia's continuing ambitions to be a global player, considering especially its relative impotence in the face of events such as the expansion of Nato, Nato's action against Serbia, the war on terrorism, and the invasions of Afghanistan and Iraq in 2002 and 2003 respectively.

1
The Historical Context

Russia is the world's biggest country, nearly twice the size of China and more than one and half times the size of the United States. And yet the area which it covers in the early twenty-first century is smaller than at any time since the nineteenth century. At that time the Russian Empire was engaged in a process of expansion which had begun more than 300 years earlier, and was to continue until the invasion of Afghanistan by the Soviet army in 1979.

Twelve years later, in 1991, the Soviet Union – one of two global superpowers and to many critics merely the Russian Empire by another name – ceased to exist. Each of its 15 constituent republics, including Russia itself, declared independence from the Soviet state. Expansion gave way to an immediate loss of lands which had been under Russian rule for well over a century, be it the rule of a Russian Tsar or a Communist Party Secretary. When Russia emerged from out of the Soviet Union in 1991, the territory ruled from Moscow retreated by a third.

This geo-political introduction to contemporary Russia – or the Russian Federation, to use its other official name – serves to highlight a duality which is essential to our understanding of Russia today. There is a combination of decline and greatness which shapes much which goes on in the various areas of activity considered in this book. For most of the 1990s and into the twenty-first century the socio-economic and political dividing lines in Russia ran through the question of how far this great nation should open itself up to the West in terms of economic policy, international allegiance, cultural identity, governance and much more. The ancient question of whether Russia is a backward country trying to catch up with Europe, or a unique civilization carving out its own superior path through history still has a resonance in contemporary debate and remains a common theme in the pronouncements of President Vladimir Putin. Putin's view in his eve of the millennium statement in 1999 was that, 'our very future depends on the lessons we learn from our past and present'. One thing is clear, with Russia perhaps more so than with most other countries, it is impossible to correctly read the contemporary scene without knowing what has gone before.

What we are about in this chapter is introducing the past to help us understand the present, and to that end the aim of this chapter is to consider the development of ideas and moods in Russian history within the framework of key events. We will start our look at contemporary Russia with a *tour d'horizon* of its history over the past centuries, focusing on the tumultuous twentieth century. Box 1.1 provides a chronology of key events. This chapter then draws out the significant elements of Russian history in three phases: Russia before 1917, the Soviet period (1917–91), and the post-Soviet era.

Russia before 1917

The history of Russia is the history of a country on the edge of Europe. The 'semi-European-ness' of Russia is apparent in a number of key historical moments. First, there was the adoption of Eastern Orthodoxy as the religion of modern Russia's predecessor state, Kievan Rus, in the tenth century. Just like the countries of Europe, Russia has been predominantly a 'Christian nation' throughout most of its existence. Unlike most of Europe, however, the form of Christianity which Russia adopted was Eastern, not Roman. After Constantinople fell to the Turks in 1453 and hegemony in the Orthodox world shifted to Muscovy, the uniqueness of Russian civilization was emphasized still further. The faithful would refer to Moscow as 'the Third Rome'. According to this theory, ancient Rome fell because of heresy, and the 'Second Rome', Constantinople, was brought down by infidels. The 'Third Rome', Muscovy, would illuminate the world and never fall.

There is therefore an 'otherness' about Russia's cultural history, and this otherness was heightened by the fact that for most of the medieval era in Europe, from 1240 to 1480, the territories which make up contemporary Russia were under the control of the asiatic Mongol Khanates, or 'hordes', of Ghengis Khan and his successors. Therefore, as Europe moved into the reformation and renaissance of the sixteenth and seventeenth centuries, Russia, expanding from the principality of Muscovy, was a relative newcomer on the scene, undergoing the brutal and sadistic rule of Ivan the Terrible and the anarchic period of civil war and foreign invasion known as the 'time of troubles'.

The separation of Russia from the mainstream of European cultural developments and the imposition of Mongol forms of government have been seen by some historians as a key determinant of Russia's sociopolitical system subsequently. Only in 1613, with the establishment

Box 1.1   Key events in Russian history

c. 882	Establishment of first Russian state with Kiev as its capital (Kievan Rus)
1237–40	Mongol invasion of Kievan Rus
1480	End of Mongol rule in Rus
1547	Ivan IV ('The Terrible') becomes Tsar
1598–1613	'Time of Troubles' – civil war and foreign invasions, ends with founding of the Romanov dynasty
1682–1725	Reign of Peter the Great
1762–96	Reign of Catherine the Great
1812	Napoleon invades Russia and reaches Moscow before retreating
1861	Emancipation of the serfs, under the rule of reformist Tsar Alexander II
1905	'the 1905 revolution' – promise of limited parliamentary rights
March 1917	Tsar Nicholas II abdicates in the face of popular demonstrations
October 1917	Russian Revolution – Communists seize power under Lenin's leadership
1922	Formal establishment of the Soviet Union
1924	Death of Lenin
1928–29	Stalin's power consolidated
1930s	Industrialization, collectivization of agriculture, growth of labour camps
1937–38	The 'great terror' sees a wave of arrests and executions
1941	German invasion of Soviet Union
1941–45	Soviet Union fights on the allied side in Second World War
1945–48	Soviet Union consolidates control of Eastern Europe
1953	Death of Stalin
1964	Khrushchev replaced by Brezhnev as Soviet leader
1982	Death of Brezhnev
1985	Mikhail Gorbachev becomes Soviet leader
1989	Countries of Eastern Europe leave the Soviet bloc
1991	Collapse of Soviet Union. Boris Yeltsin elected President of Russia
1993	Presidential-parliamentary conflict resolved in Yeltsin's favour by military means. New Russian Constitution adopted
1999	President Boris Yeltsin resigns on 31 December
2000	Vladimir Putin elected president
2004	Vladimir Putin re-elected president

of the Romanov dynasty which was to last until the workers' revolution of 1917, did a degree of stability and 'normality' begin to appear. Nonetheless, the perceived separation of Russia from the European mainstream continued to play a key part in historical developments.

Peter the Great

Peter the Great (Tsar of Russia, 1682–1725) oversaw a period in which the Russian state was modernized and increased its power through a mixture of discipline and administrative reform (a combination of approaches which is repeated throughout Russian history up to the present day).

For Peter the Great the humiliating defeat of Russian forces by the Swedes at Narva in 1700 can be seen as the trigger for fundamental reforms which began by introducing foreign expertise and technology into the armed forces. This reform of the military demanded subsequent reform in many areas – notably tax rises and a social reorganization which affected both peasantry and nobility, with lifetime conscription into the army for one peasant from every 20 households and a strict 'table of ranks' for the nobility.

Nothing symbolized reform more in Peter's reign than the construction of a new capital city, St Petersburg, as a 'window on the West' (see Box 2.3, Chapter 2); nothing except perhaps his infamous tax on beards, whereby men who continued with the 'Slavic look', rather than adopting the clean-shaven Western fashion, would be singled out for the regime's fiscal disapproval. Alongside these symbolic representations of Peter's Westernizing intent, came the introduction to the Russian court and nobility of enlightenment philosophies which were then flourishing in Europe.

Catherine the Great

The influx of Western political thought continued throughout the eighteenth century and flourished particularly during the reign of Catherine the Great (1762–96). Intellectual life in Russia was transformed as knowledge of European languages grew and indicators such as the number of books published and the number of students studying in universities showed a dramatic increase. However, there was a duality present in the attitude of the regime to the influence of enlightenment thought. The desire to allow and benefit from a closer relationship with the European mainstream had to be kept in increasingly uncomfortable tension with the autocratic nature of the Russian state itself. Catherine's enthusiasm for enlightenment philosophy waned, for obvious reasons, after its contribution to the French revolution and the subsequent anti-royalist terror.

Russia's history over the first half of the nineteenth century was dominated by military and diplomatic, as well as intellectual, engagement with Europe. As the French Empire spread across the continent, under the leadership of Napoleon Bonaparte, Russia – led by Alexander I – at first reached an accommodation with the French which bought time before, in 1812, Napoleon attempted the invasion of Russia. Napoleon's efforts famously resulted in his army reaching Moscow, which had been set on fire by the retreating Russians, before succumbing to the ferocity of the Russian winter. In the retreat from Moscow in 1812, Napoleon's famous 'grande armée' was destroyed, and by 1814 Russian troops had entered Paris.

For years the Russian nobility had imported Western European ideas and customs into Russia without a great deal of experience of Western Europe itself. For many of those Russian officers who entered Paris in 1814, the first-hand experience was formative, and arguably played a role in the debates which were to dominate Russia over the next several decades. These debates can be summed up in two examples:

- Demands for the Tsar to cede some of his autocratic powers to representative bodies began to be put forward amongst the more liberal members of society's upper stratum. Most famously the Decembrist Revolt of 1825 entailed a group of military officers putting together a low-level, poorly organized revolt in support of a demand for some representation. Although the actions of the Decembrists in themselves posed little danger to the Tsar's powers, their symbolic significance as the first liberal challenge to autocracy was seminal.
- The intellectual debate between the Slavophiles and the Westernizers flourished in the years after the Decembrist revolt. In short, it developed the arguments of the Slavophiles who saw in Russia a unique, and superior, civilization, and the Westernizers who preferred to pursue Western examples and ideals.

Alexander II

It was not until the reign of Alexander II (1855–81) that further far-reaching reform in Russia was introduced. Alexander's reformist tendencies were arguably spurred on by the defeat of the Russian forces in the Crimean War, coinciding with his accession to the throne in 1855.

Military defeat highlighted the need for Russia to catch up with the West economically, technologically and socially. In simple terms, war was a huge burden to an already heavily indebted state, and the technological advances of a rapidly industrializing Europe were not being seen in a Russia whose social structure was still founded on serfdom. Alexander II gradually but radically reformed his realm, most notably overseeing the abolition of serfdom in 1861 (four years before the abolition of slavery in the United States). The Tsar, like Mikhail Gorbachev in the 1980s, faced the difficulty of conducting fundamental changes without bringing down the regime. He succeeded in the short term, in that the Tsarist regime remained in place into the twentieth century, although he himself was assassinated by revolutionary terrorists in 1881.

Each of the reform periods noted above was accompanied by a discourse of reform which implicitly, and sometimes explicitly, sought to import values from the West.

The development of political thought, with its roots in Europe, can be seen throughout the nineteenth century in Russia. After victory against the French armies of Napoleon, Russian troops, many members of the educated nobility amongst them, saw and experienced Western Europe. By 1825 the Decembrist uprising, led by such army officers, sought the beginnings of constitutional reform and representation in Russia, only to be met by the determined autocracy of Tsar Nicholas I (1825–55). During the reign of Alexander II (1855–81) the liberal movement, with its basis in enlightenment thought, saw a little progress with the creation of local representative bodies, *zemstva*, as the Tsar sought to widen debate on policy, if not grant direct decision-making powers.

The European enlightenment did not, however, give birth only to a weak Russian liberalism, it also led to a more robust and radical strain, the revolutionary socialist movements out of which the communists emerged. In Russia there also existed a revolutionary socialist movement, the Populists, which looked to Russian traditions as opposed to Western European thought as a model for the future. The Populists saw the organization of the traditional Russian peasant *mir* (village) as a model for a democratic future, and the more radical Populists, out of whose ranks came the terrorists who assassinated Alexander II in 1881, explicitly counted amongst their heroes the leaders of past peasant revolts, such as Pugachev and Razin.

To rather crudely summarize, as Alexander II carried out his programme of reforms he was opposed by conservative members of the nobility and the land-owning class, who objected to the loss of their serfs as well as more subtly to the sense, so brilliantly portrayed in

Anton Chekhov's play *The Cherry Orchard* (1904), that the relatively privileged world which they knew was being irreparably changed. He was also opposed by the radical revolutionaries, who did not want to see reform of the system, but rather an entirely new system, in which there would be no role for the Tsar and the nobility. In between sat the liberals, whose aim was reform of the system in a more democratic, more representative direction.

The Soviet period, 1917–91

Russian history is for the most part dominated by a strong 'garrison' state. However, partly as a factor of the size of Russia, partly stemming from the nebulous concept of an authoritarian political culture, the Russian state has repeatedly seemed profoundly insecure about itself and so constantly sought to expand its control over society. This insecurity is not, though, ill-founded, as there are regular episodes in Russian history where the authority and power of the state collapses and 'society' rises up. Such a perspective offers one approach to the advent of rule by revolutionaries in Russia in 1917.

The Bolshevik Party – later to become the Communist Party of the Soviet Union – came to power in October 1917. There had been a 'revolution' in Russia 12 years earlier in 1905, when largely uncoordinated unrest across the Russian Empire resulted in the Tsar, Nicholas II (1894–1917), agreeing to the creation of a parliament, or Duma, whose actual influence on policy was minimal to begin with and faded thereafter. However, the hardships and social upheaval of the First World War created fertile soil for revolutionary and reformist movements to flourish, and protest became increasingly frequent.

In February 1917 unrest in Petrograd – as the Tsarist capital St Petersburg was then known – developed into a revolution which forced the abdication of Tsar Nicholas II and the creation of a Provisional Government, based on the largely liberal Duma. At the same time the revolutionary movements recreated the Petrograd Workers' Council – or 'Soviet' – which had first existed in 1905, and similar Soviets came into being in other cities. A situation of 'dual power' existed, with the Provisional Government and the Soviets both claiming legitimacy. It is only a slight oversimplification to say that the élite and the masses stood at loggerheads.

In October 1917, the Bolshevik Party staged a seizure of power in the name of the Soviets. In its implementation if not its effect, this event was more akin to a coup than a revolution. And in the immediate situation of

Petrograd in 1917 it represented simply another twist in a year of violence and upheaval which had seen a workers' uprising, the abdication of the Tsar, the creation of a Provisional Government, a failed attempt by the revolutionaries to seize power in the 'July Days', a failed counter-revolutionary reaction led by former Tsarist General Kornilov in September, and now a seizure of power by the Bolsheviks, the most radical of a number of socialist parties, in October.

Earlier in 1917 Lenin had said that he did not expect to see a revolution in his lifetime. The idea that a Bolshevik uprising in October would leave them in power for most of the century would have been greeted by many observers at the time as tenuous to say the least. However, that is precisely what happened.

The communists' first few years in power were – like the 'time of troubles' over three centuries earlier – years of civil war, foreign intervention and uncertainty. Russian novelist Boris Pilnyak captured this chaos, and what he saw as the essence of Russia's elemental spirit, in his work *The Naked Year*, originally published in 1921. He portrayed the worst year of the civil war, 1919, as a year when the civilized Western clothes of Russia were stripped away to reveal beneath the true Asiatic nature of the Russian masses. Such a force was more ready to be harnessed by the radical revolutionaries, be they urban Bolsheviks or rural Socialist Revolutionaries, than by the weak and sparse liberal élite. The tradition of peasant revolt against land-owners was replayed again under the initially supportive gaze of Lenin and his government. By a combination of propaganda, populist measures, ruthlessness and a strong minority of popular support, the Bolshevik regime survived and prospered.

By the late 1920s, with the rise to power of Josef Stalin, the state was ready once again to reassert control. Forced collectivization of agriculture, state-planned industrialization, centralization, state-induced famine, a vast labour-camp network, and political terror all combined in the 1930s to rebuild a state which was now not merely authoritarian, but totalitarian, seeking to dominate every aspect of its citizens' lives. During the Stalin years, millions of victims were incarcerated in the labour camps of the Gulag or were executed during Stalin's 'Great Terror', and all aspects of public life came under the dictatorial control of the regime.

Playing catch-up

As we have noted above, a clear pattern supports the discourse of a perennial need for Russia to 'catch-up' with Europe, and with 'the West' in general. From this point of view the motivation for reform and accompanying upheaval in Russia has regularly been realistic self-interest, a combination of economic decline and related security threats. Be it the perceived need to build a modern navy under Peter the Great, a modern army under Alexander II, or a more high-tech military-industrial complex under Mikhail Gorbachev in the 1980s, a realist motive lay behind these times of upheaval. The dictum that 'war is the locomotive of history' applies to Russia perhaps more than to anywhere.

We can add to these examples the defeat by Russia in the war with Japan, which precipitated the revolution and constitutional reform of 1905, and the defeat of the Russian forces on the eastern front during the First World War, which served as a catalyst for the collapse of the Tsarist regime and the rise of the communists in 1917. We can add, too, the industrialization of the 1930s under Josef Stalin, who explicitly stated in 1931 that Russia had to catch-up or be crushed, as war was coming within the next decade (the Stalin years will be considered in more detail below).

There are two main difficulties with the 'catch-up' approach outlined above, and an awareness of these related problems is extremely helpful for our understanding of contemporary Russia:

- First, Russia has not spent its entire history in unsuccessful pursuit of a superior European ideal. Although the periods discussed above provide examples of such a pursuit, the whole picture – both of Russia itself and even of those particular periods – is more complex. In particular, there was not always a coincidence in Russian history between modernization and westernization. Although Peter the Great, Alexander II, and others all used selective borrowing and imitation, there were other periods, such as the reigns of Alexander III (1881–94) and Nicholas II and also the Stalin years, when overcoming backwardness was attempted within more traditional approaches, such as autarky and repression. In other words there were strategies which sought to synthesize modernization and Russianness.
- The second difficulty with the 'catch-up' approach is that the idea of a backward Russia is, understandably, not one which is held dear by most Russians. This has a resonance in Russia today, in the policies of the president and the opinions of the people. A sense of injured national pride, and of being patronized by the West in the postcommunist era, has without doubt helped to shape the political discourse of contemporary Russia.

Jumping ahead of our chronology momentarily, it is worth noting that Vladimir Putin brought the duality of Russia's history into focus when he came to power, initially as Acting President, on 31 December 1999.

Although Putin called Communism 'a blind alley, far away from civilization', he was not about to junk the entire communist experience. Putin made clear early in his presidency, in an address to the Presidium of the State Council, that the wholesale rejection of what had gone before was untenable:

> Where shall we then put the achievements of Russian culture? Where shall we put Pushkin, Dostoyevsky, Tolstoy and Tchaikovsky? Where shall we put the achievements of Russian science – Mendeleyev, Lobachevsky and many, many others? Much of what all of us take pride in – what shall we do with all this? ... And do we really have nothing, except the Stalin camps and repressions, to recall for the whole Soviet period of our country's existence? Where shall we then put Dunayevsky, Sholokhov, Shostakovich and Korolev and the achievements in outer space? What shall we do with Yuri Gagarin's flight, as well as the brilliant victories of Russian arms – from the times of Rumyantsev, Suvorov and Kutuzov? And the victory in the spring of 1945? (For details of Putin's Russian Heroes see Box 1.2)

President Putin's point provides a particularly pertinent context to understanding contemporary Russia. In fact many commentators, particularly amongst national communists in Russia today, would go further than their President. For most of the twentieth century the Soviet regime represented itself as at the leading edge of global historical development. One does not have to be an apologist for the communist system to note that this case was not a wholly ridiculous one; there was a logic to it, a mix of interpretation and fact which together created a powerful discourse and a powerful state.

To make the case for Russia leading the world in the twentieth century let us go back to our discussion of political thought, and the influence of European thought in particular. Men such as the founder of the Soviet state, Vladimir Lenin, drew on Western European political thought as developed by Karl Marx and Friedrich Engels. Marxism concentrated not on the peasantry, but on the industrial working class – the proletariat – and a rejection of capitalism. Revolution would come from the proletariat, revolution would eventually be global, and the final stage of history would be communism – an end to exploitation and oppression, the emancipation of mankind and the fulfilment of humanity's potential in a technologically advanced, rationally managed society. Russian and Soviet communism, as it developed in the twentieth century, placed itself unequivocally at the head of the Marxist camp.

Box 1.2   Putin's Russian heroes

In a speech to the Russian State Council, President Putin singled out the following 14 men as indicative of the great achievers in Russian history. Putin's selection is a conservative group, in the sense that all of these would have been acknowledged in the Soviet era as great men of Russian history:

Aleksandr Pushkin (1799–1837). Known as the founder of Russian literature, and Russia's greatest ever poet.

Fyodor Dostoevsky (1821–81), was one of the great novelists of the nineteenth century. His best-known works are *Crime and Punishment* (1866) and *The Brothers Karamazov* (1879).

Isaak Dunayevsky (1900–55). Composer, particularly popular during the Stalin years and best known for his film music which fostered an upbeat view of Soviet life.

Yurii Gagarin (1934–68), in 1961 became the first person in space.

Sergei Korolev (1907–66), instrumental in the development of the inter-continental ballistic missiles which undergirded the Soviet Union's status as a nuclear superpower.

Prince Mikhail Kutuzov (1745–1813), commander of the Russian forces which repelled Napoleon's invasion of Russia in 1812.

Nikolai Lobachevsky (1792–1856). Mathematician and founder of non-Euclidean geometry.

Dmitrii Mendeleyev (1834–1907), developed the periodic table of chemical elements.

Marshal Pyotr Rumantsev (1725–96). Hero of the Seven Years War with Prussia in the mid-eighteenth century, and of later wars in Europe. Governor of Ukraine from 1764.

Mikhail Sholokhov (1905–84), the only non-dissident Soviet writer to win the Nobel Prize for Literature (1965). His best-known work is *Quiet Flows the Don*.

Dmitrii Shostakovich (1906–75), one of the twentieth century's finest composers, and arguably its greatest symphonist.

General Aleksandr Suvorov (1729–1800). Famed military commander of the latter half of the eighteenth century, Suvorov was known for his development of 'military science'.

Pyotr Tchaikovsky (1840–93), composer. His best-known works are the *1812 Overture*, the opera *Yevgenii Onegin*, and the ballet *Swan Lake*.

Lev Tolstoy (1828–1910), one of the great novelists of the nineteenth century, he wrote *War and Peace* (1865–69) and *Anna Karenina* (1873–77).

Soviet communism placed an emphasis on being at the cutting-edge of a developing global movement. Marxism provided a world view within whose framework every aspect of life could be placed. Its adherents claimed it to be scientific and rational, with the implication that it was infallible. And the Marxist view was that global workers' revolution was inevitable. This emphasis on scientific rationalism and the ongoing development of history to its end-point, communism, carried with it a contemporary edge in most areas of life. This was a creed for the newly emergent industrial working class, predominantly the younger generation:

- it embraced modern technology;
- it rejected superstition and religion in favour of mankind's ability to construct a better world itself;
- it sought common ownership of goods and planned production to meet the needs of the people, as opposed to the vagaries and oppression of the market; and
- it was a teleological ('goal-oriented') ideology, with a momentum and a purpose.

That a successful workers' revolution leading to a socialist regime occurred first in Russia, rather than in the more industrialized states of Western Europe, took a little explaining in terms of the expectations of Marx. Lenin's explanation was that the chain of capitalism broke at its weakest link – Russia – and that global revolution would follow. It did not, at least not in terms of the European powers becoming communist. However, much of the former Russian Empire became united under communist rule as the Soviet Union by the early 1920s, and thereafter – particularly in the Cold War era after the Second World War – numerous countries around the world became part of the communist bloc. In its own terms, the Soviet Union was on the cutting-edge of history's 'inevitable progress' to communism. In some sense the concept of 'the Third Rome' which would illuminate the world and never fall can be said to have been taken up by the communists.

In reality, the Soviet experiment soon soured. Whatever one's politics, for most people there can be little argument that the Stalin regime, which imprisoned in labour camps or executed around 20 million Soviet citizens between 1929 and 1953, scarcely represented the fulfilment of Marxism's emancipatory mission. Historians and politicians have disputed whether the authoritarianism, repression and dictatorship of the Stalin years in particular represent a failure of Marxism or of its Soviet implementation. Some have sought the roots of Soviet totalitarianism in the political culture of Russia. Stalin implicitly encouraged parallels between himself, Ivan the Terrible and Peter the Great, and the suggestion that Russians are somehow predisposed to rule by a 'strong hand' is fairly often cited in the literature.

Although the Stalin years represent the epitome of totalitarian dictatorship, from Lenin through to the late 1980s the Soviet Union was marked by:

- repression of opponents;
- the existence of a single party with no participation in politics by any other means;
- strict state censorship and ownership of all media;
- a preference for the rights of the state over the individual;
- a judicial system accustomed to political judgements; and
- the socialization of all citizens into the Soviet ideal.

Lenin ordered the arrest and execution of ideological opponents. Khrushchev's reformist reputation stems largely from his closure of many labour camps and his condemnation of Stalin in the Secret Speech of 1956, but nonetheless he himself instigated a brutal anti-religious campaign. In the Brezhnev years (1964–82) dissidents were subjected to compulsory psychiatric treatment; after all, the argument went, if they oppose the Soviet regime, they must be mad.

Can we then still speak of the Soviet Union in any sense leading the world? In short, yes, if only because of its development into one of two global superpowers by the middle of the century, and its consolidation of this position for over three decades. Even in the 1930s, as the Stalinist repressions swung into action and millions died in labour camps or state-induced famine, there was support for the Soviet regime on the European left. Stalin's repressions were largely hidden from the world; only in 1956 did Khrushchev begin to acknowledge them, and only after the Soviet archives opened in the late 1980s and early 1990s was their extent fully revealed.

To many observers at the time, the Soviet Union seemed to be demonstrating the superiority of the planned economy in comparison with the market. While the Great Depression devastated the economies of the United States and much of the capitalist world in the 1930s, the Soviet Union enjoyed rapid economic growth as it industrialized with unprecedented speed. As the Marxists had stated, capitalism appeared to be collapsing under the weight of its inherent contradictions, whilst the new scientific rationalism of the communist regime apparently flourished. During the Second World War, the contribution of the newly industrialized Soviet Union to the defeat of Nazi Germany can scarcely be overexaggerated.

From this perspective it is easier to gain a sense of unstoppable momentum which is central to understanding communism's place in the world in the middle decades of the twentieth century. Similarly, an elaboration of the extent and speed of the global political map's reddening in the immediate postwar decades, provides us with an insight into the influence of Soviet Communism. By merely counting the number of states which became communist between 1945 and 1975 – albeit that many were coerced into the communist camp – one might have concluded that Marx's prediction of world revolution was not completely far-fetched. With the benefit of hindsight and the knowledge of Soviet Communism's eventual failure, it is too easy to forget the enthusiasm and commitment of those in the Soviet Union and elsewhere who genuinely believed that they were pushing forward in history's vanguard. That they were wrong is another matter.

We began this section by noting two problems with the 'catch-up' approach to Russian history. The Soviet experience is by and large a demonstration of the first problem, namely, the fact that Russia has not spent its entire history in unsuccessful pursuit of a superior European ideal. For much of this period the Soviet Union travelled a path not taken by the Western nations – albeit that President Putin himself has now declared that path to have been a blind alley; albeit too that the provenance of Marxism was European, even if the 'actually existing socialism' of the communist world had Russian snow on its boots.

The second problem is that the idea of a backward Russia is not one which is held dear by most Russians. When considering the Soviet era, many Russians hold a broadly positive view, particularly of the post-Stalin years. In opinion polls in the 1990s, when Russian citizens were asked to name the best Russian leader of the twentieth century, Leonid Brezhnev repeatedly topped the list, with his time in office being voted the best period to live in Russia (Bacon and Sandle, 2002). Again, this perception cannot be dismissed as fanciful. Many Russians look back on these years as a time when living standards steadily increased, full employment and job security were the order of the day, inflation was virtually non-existent, crime levels were low, and national pride was high.

From communism to contemporary Russia

Using different but complementary approaches to Russian history, we have illuminated much of the context helpful to our understanding of contemporary Russia. It is worth emphasizing again – as will become apparent later – the resonance of history in contemporary Russian political debate. Politicians and population alike in Russia today are well-versed in their past, and given the nature of Russia's recent history it is perhaps not surprising that it plays a significant role in shaping the contemporary agenda. In the final section of this chapter we will cover the transition from communism to the present day. Much of what is covered here will be revisited in later chapters; again our emphasis is on providing the context for studying contemporary Russia.

As noted above, during the 1990s the Brezhnev years (1964–82) consistently came out on top in opinion polls of the best era in which to live from the last hundred years of Russian history. As well as the everyday factors which influence people's opinion of these years, the Brezhnev era was a time when the Soviet Union competed as an equal with the USA in the space race and the arms race; a time when Soviet musicians, dancers and composers were renowned the world over; and a time when Soviet sportsmen and women regularly competed with and beat the world's best.

In 1980 the Olympic Games were held in Moscow, in what was the first Olympics ever held in a communist state. The event was intended to crown the achievements of a great superpower, and was seen in the Soviet Union as an unqualified success despite a debilitating boycott by Western countries. Had it been suggested that within little more than a decade the Soviet Union would have weakened to the point of collapse, few would have believed it. And yet, underneath the surface, there was much wrong with the Soviet regime by the 1980s.

Mikhail Gorbachev

Mikhail Gorbachev, when he came to power in 1985, began to refer to the Brezhnev years as an 'era of stagnation'. He characterized it as a time when an ageing leadership clung to power and gave little thought to the future development of the country. After Brezhnev died in 1982 his two successors, first Yurii Andropov and then Konstantin Chernenko, both took power as sick men and died after very little time in office. The economy stopped growing, and Gorbachev inherited what he called 'a pre-crisis situation'. The later joke was that in 1985 the Soviet Union stood on the edge of the abyss, and under Mikhail Gorbachev it took a great step forward.

Gorbachev's characterization of the Brezhnev years provided the context in which he began his reform programme. It could also be argued that the military weakness of the Soviet superpower was exemplified by the inability of Soviet forces to secure victory in the Afghan War (1979–88). For a state which owed its superpower status almost entirely to its military strength, this failure in a low-tech conventional war was compounded by the Soviet Union's inability to compete with the United States in the high-tech stakes. As the arms race between the superpowers moved increasingly towards the development of smart conventional weaponry and missile defence shields (the so-called 'star-wars' programme announced by US President Reagan in the early 1980s), Gorbachev, along with many of the generals and most of the party leadership, saw that reform was inevitable in order to catch up with the West.

The Soviet economy was shrinking, and Gorbachev's solution was to radically reform socio-political relations, gradually reducing the reach of the authoritarian state and giving the people a genuine democratic vote for many key positions – though never for his own. Unfortunately for Gorbachev, a simultaneous reduction in authoritarian control and an invitation to elect political leaders led many in the national republics which made up the Soviet Union to vote for leaders who sought independence from the Soviet state. The biggest of these national republics was Russia itself, and once Russia, under its newly elected president, Boris Yeltsin, declared independence from the Soviet Union in 1991, no Soviet state remained. If Gorbachev inherited a pre-crisis situation, then by the end of his period in office it had turned into a terminal crisis for the Soviet Union.

In December 1991 the leaders of Russia, Ukraine and Belarus met and declared that their republics were forming a Commonwealth of Independent States. By the end of the month the majority of Soviet republics had signed up for this Commonwealth, and those that had not signed up insisted resolutely on complete independence. The Soviet Union no longer existed.

The Soviet collapse

When considering the short history of Russia after the Soviet collapse, the most common approach, and the most useful in terms of our scene-setting purpose, is to explain developments in terms of democratic transition. This transition approach works well for most of the 1990s, but less well by the time we come to consider the Putin era. However, as the rest of this book focuses largely on the Putin era then the contextualising intent of this historical introduction is maintained.

When Boris Yeltsin rose to power in Russia in the late 1980s and early 1990s, he did it with the support of the emergent broad democratic movement, Democratic Russia. Yeltsin, like many post-Soviet politicians, had been a member of the Communist Party of the Soviet Union for much of his adult life, and was brought into the Party's highest body – the Politburo – by Mikhail Gorbachev in 1986, having been put in charge of the Party in Moscow in December 1985. Yeltsin soon came to national and international attention as something of a maverick with a populist touch. He advocated faster and more far-reaching reform than that proposed by Gorbachev, and in 1987 Yeltsin resigned from the Politburo. Gorbachev removed him from his senior position as head of the Moscow Communist Party, but, to the surprise of many, then gave him a ministerial post in the Soviet government. In the past, this might have been the end of Yeltsin's influence, but as Gorbachev's reforms opened up the Soviet electoral system Yeltsin was able to gain election first to the new Soviet parliament – the Congress of People's Deputies – in 1989, and then, in 1990, to the parliament of the Russian republic.

In the Russian parliament, Yeltsin, with the support of the reformist deputies, was elected speaker – at that time the highest position in the Russian, as opposed to the Soviet, political hierarchy. In March 1991 Gorbachev organized a referendum across the Soviet Union on the preservation of the Soviet state. Yeltsin again saw his opportunity and, with the support of the Russian parliament, placed a second question on the referendum ballot, asking the people of the Russian republic to support the creation of a Russian presidency. Approval was duly gained, and in June 1991 Boris Yeltsin became the first-ever directly elected leader of Russia, albeit that he remained constitutionally – if not democratically – in an inferior position to Soviet President Gorbachev. It was from this position of strength that President Yeltsin moved to take Russia out of the Soviet Union.

In August 1991, Gorbachev's conservative opponents in the higher echelons of the Soviet government and party structures staged a coup attempt. Gorbachev himself was put under house arrest, a state of emergency was declared by the coup plotters, and troops were brought in to take control of Moscow. The Russian parliament and president became the focus of opposition to this coup. Thousands of supporters gathered there to hear Yeltsin – having climbed up on one of the tanks sent to enforce the coup – as he declared the state of emergency illegal and called for the immediate return of Gorbachev to Moscow and to his position as head of the Soviet Union. Although there was the real danger of an assault on Yeltsin and his parliament by special forces under the command of the coup plotters – and indeed three civilians were killed in skirmishes outside the parliament building – within a couple of days the coup had collapsed and Gorbachev came back to Moscow. He returned though to a very different political landscape. Yeltsin's moral authority and popularity had been boosted by his opposition to the coup. Furthermore, he could point to the fact that he had been elected to his position by the Russian people, whereas Gorbachev, in contrast, had never stood in a democratic election. It was from this strengthened position that Yeltsin moved rapidly through the Soviet end-game, and to the creation of the Commonwealth of Independent States noted above.

From Yeltsin to Putin

It is a commonplace of political life that to be in opposition is easier than to govern. In the last years of the Soviet Union many disparate forces had been able to unite together around a common cause, that of democratic opposition to the communist regime. Once the common goal had been achieved, these disparate forces began to fracture around the question of 'what next?'. In broad terms, the democratic opposition, Yeltsin included, wanted to establish democracy and a market economy. When it came to the specific implementation of policy, however, many differences and questions emerged:

- What about the sequencing and pace of reform? Should economic reform precede political, or vice versa? Should everything be done at once? Or would a more gradualist approach be beneficial?
- What about relations with the other former Soviet republics? A good number of those in the broad Yeltsin camp had fought for a democratic Soviet Union, but had not envisaged its total disappearance.
- And when it came to democratic transition, what form of democracy should be adopted? Parliamentary or presidential? An electoral system based on proportional representation or a majoritarian system? A single chamber or a bicameral parliament?
- And what about relations between Russia's regions and the centre?

There was clearly much to decide. Unfortunately the decision-making process was not clear. Yeltsin had risen to power in Russia with the support of the parliament, or Supreme Soviet, which, thanks to Gorbachev's democratizing moves, had at last been able to lay hold of the authority to which it had been nominally entitled throughout the Soviet period. Once elected President, though, Boris Yeltsin had a mandate direct from the people, rather than having to rely on the maintenance of a parliamentary majority. However, many of his powers as President were granted to him by the parliament, under the terms of the much amended Russian constitution. This constitution had been in force since 1978; it was a Soviet constitution in desperate need of replacing. Yeltsin wanted to replace it with a constitution setting out a presidential democracy; the parliament wanted to replace it with a constitution establishing a parliamentary democracy.

There was deadlock, and for the best part of two years, 1992–93, when the newly independent Russian state was in desperate need of fresh legislation and clear governance, President Yeltsin and his parliament were at an impasse. One solution would have been the holding of simultaneous presidential and parliamentary elections; Yeltsin was confident of re-election, many parliamentary deputies less so, and so the parliament rejected this option. Yeltsin was unable to dissolve parliament himself, as this lay outside the bounds of his constitutional powers.

Finally, after move and countermove, and an inconclusive national referendum, President Yeltsin unilaterally – and in constitutional terms, illegally – dissolved the parliament in late September 1993 and announced new elections for the following December. Parliament refused to accept its dissolution, and, with the Constitutional Court ruling in its favour, it remained in session. After a stand-off of several days fighting broke out in Moscow, as troops loyal to the parliament attacked the building of a national television station. Yeltsin responded by ordering a full-scale assault on the parliamentary building, where only two years before he had led the parliament in its opposition against the Soviet coup plotters. The parliament building was shelled, over a hundred of its defenders were killed, and Yeltsin stood as the undisputed ruler of Russia. On 12 December a national referendum passed a new and heavily presidential constitution on the same day as the people voted for the new parliament which this constitution created.

Since the elections of December 1993 there have been parliamentary elections in 1995, 1999 and 2003, and these are now settled into four-year terms, as is the presidency after its initial five-year term. Yeltsin stood again for the presidency in June 1996 and was re-elected in a second-round run-off against his communist opponent, Gennadii Zyuganov. This victory owed much to the support of a coterie of rich businessmen and media owners, who collectively became known as the oligarchs, because of their subsequent influence on the President.

For much of his second term in office, Yeltsin was in visible decline physically and mentally. He underwent a major heart operation after his re-election in 1996, and throughout his period in office was allegedly prone to bouts of heavy drinking. Ironically, having sent troops against his parliament in his pursuit of a heavily presidential constitution,

Yeltsin increasingly seemed unable to govern Russia as the century came to an end. A presidential constitution demands a strong president – Boris Yeltsin was physically weak, owed a political debt to the increasingly powerful oligarchs, relied heavily on a small group of advisers known as 'the family', and had to make a series of bilateral agreements with regional leaders in which he negotiated the division of power between the centre and the components of the Russian Federation.

It became increasingly apparent that the Russian state was weak, and this impression was emphasized by the fact that between 1998 and 2000 Russia had five prime ministers. With hindsight it was as if Boris Yeltsin were casting around for a successor, and the fact that three out of the four prime ministerial appointments which he made in this period were of men with security-service backgrounds indicates the sort of figure for which he was searching. Yeltsin wanted a technocrat rather than a politician to succeed him, someone able to strengthen the state, and someone who would both protect his legacy and guarantee him a safe and comfortable retirement.

By the end of 1999 Yeltsin believed he had found that man. Vladimir Putin had risen from relative obscurity to the post of Prime Minister in August of that year, and on 31 December Yeltsin resigned the presidency and – in accordance with the constitution – appointed Putin Acting President pending an election in March 2000. Putin duly won this election, and set about governing the Russia which the rest of this book explores. He easily won a second term as President in the election of March 2004. His immediate concerns on taking office were those issues which we have explored in this introductory chapter. As he said in his 'Turn of the Millennium' statement, the major tasks facing Russia in the twenty-first century are catching-up, adhering to the great Russian idea, and strengthening the state.

2
Land and People

The most significant physical feature of Russia is that it is vast and yet much of its territory is rendered virtually uninhabitable by harsh climatic conditions. To give a sense of Russia's expanse and centres of population, we will begin by setting out the bare facts.

Russia covers roughly 17 million square kilometres, significantly larger than its nearest competitor in terms of being the world's largest country, the United States, which covers around 10 million square kilometres. Before it collapsed in 1991, the Soviet Union was one-third bigger again, and yet Russia easily retains its lead position, even with the post-Soviet loss of the vast territories of Central Asia (Kazakhstan, Kyrgyzstan, Tajikistan, Turkmenistan and Uzbekistan), the Transcaucasian countries (Armenia, Georgia, Azerbaijan), the Eastern European lands (Belarus, Moldova, Ukraine), and the Baltic States (Estonia, Latvia and Lithuania).

In terms of population, Russia ranks seventh in the world with a population in 2002 of 145 million (the Soviet Union before its collapse had ranked third). However, Russia's population is declining and alarming demographic predictions warn of all manner of resultant difficulties in the coming decades. Russia's official government statistical agency's predictions for the population in 2050 have an optimistic variant (123 million) and a pessimistic variant (71 million).

Russia's capital city, Moscow, ranks sixth in terms of the world's most populous cities. Moscow and St Petersburg are the two cities in Russia which have the status of federal regions. Moscow is Europe's biggest city, with a population of more than 8 million (though some estimates go as high as 10.4 million if the greater Moscow area is included and allowance made for the high number of unregistered inhabitants). St Petersburg is Europe's third biggest city, with a population of over four and half million. London comes in second, between these two Russian giants, with over 7 million.

Moscow is a European city and the centre of the country's political, economic and cultural life. It is too easy to forget the vast asiatic expanse of Russia when so much in terms of contact with the West is mediated through crowded, commercial, cosmopolitan Moscow. Almost a fifth of

Russia's population live in the *millioniki* – those cities which proudly boast a population of more than a million (see Box 2.1, and Boxes 2.2 and 2.3 for Moscow and St Petersburg) – and 60 per cent of the population live in the Central, Volga, and Southern federal districts of Russia. Or, to put it the other way round, those areas officially classified as 'the North' (the Far East, Siberia, and northern European Russia) make up 70 per cent of the territory of the Russian Federation, but contain 8 per cent of the population. According to the 2002 census, over a quarter of Russia's population can still be classified as rural dwellers.

The final point to make by way of creating a true picture of Russia which moves beyond the Moscow-centric European perception is that it is a multi-ethnic federation. Over 160 different national groups were identified in Russia by the 2002 census. Although 80 per cent of the population are ethnically Russian, the diversity of the country is demonstrated in its federal structure, in its religious make-up (with around 10 per cent of the population being Muslims), and – most acutely – in the vicious conflict with separatist rebels in and around the republic of Chechnya. All of these issues are dealt with in this chapter, which outlines the physical, demographic and social bases of the Russian state.

The physical setting

Covering as it does one-seventh of the earth's land surface, Russia stretches more than 10,000 kilometres across Europe and Asia, from the port of Kaliningrad on the Baltic Sea (an enclave cut off from the rest of Russia) to Cape Dezhneva in the far north east (the easternmost point in the Eurasian land mass, named after the Cossack explorer who was the first European to sail around it). Russia extends over 11 time zones, and journeying overland

---

Box 2.1   Russian cities with over a million inhabitants (largest to smallest)

1	Moscow	>8.5 million	8	Kazan	1.1 million
2	St Petersburg	4.6 million	9	Chelyabinsk	1.1 million
3	Novosibirsk	1.4 million	10	Ufa	1.1 million
4	Nizhnyi Novgorod	1.4 million	11	Rostov on Don	1 million
5	Yekaterinberg	1.4 million	12	Volgograd	1 million
6	Samara	1.2 million	13	Perm	1 million
7	Omsk	1.2 million			

Box 2.2 Moscow

Moscow was founded in 1147 by Prince Yury Dolgoruky. With Constantinople falling to the Turks in 1453, Moscow came to be seen by the Russian Orthodox as the home of true Christianity – the 'Third Rome'. From Muscovy, Ivan the Great (1462–1505) united the Russian principalities.

In the sixteenth century Moscow grew to become one of Europe's largest cities, and by that time the Kremlin, Red Square and St Basil's Cathedral were all established. Moscow remained the seat of Russian power until Peter the Great moved the court to St Petersburg. Moscow was reestablished as the capital in 1924. May Day parades of troops and missiles on Red Square – watched by a line of Communist leaders from the mausoleum containing the preserved body of their predecessor Lenin – symbolised for many the power of the Soviet state.

A visitor to Moscow in the mid-1980s would have found a sterile city compared with today. Communist Party slogans stood in place of advertising, there were relatively few cars, shops were dull and poorly stocked, and conformity and cleanliness were abiding features. By the mid-1990s this had all changed, as Moscow became a vibrant city, full of traffic, advertising, shopping malls, restaurants, political demonstrations, noise, crime, beggars, and a chaotically hedonistic nightlife. From 1998 onwards Moscow, too, became the scene of terrorist acts such as the blowing up of random apartment blocks in 1999, and the suicide bomb on a metro train in 2004.

In recent years Moscow has seen vast capital projects, such as the rebuilding of the Cathedral of Christ the Saviour and the construction of the Manezh shopping centre next to Red Square.

Box 2.3 St Petersburg

St Petersburg was founded in 1703 as Russia's 'Window on the West', built on the orders of Peter the Great, the Westernising Tsar who saw Russia's future firmly in Europe. The city became his capital, and remained capital of Russia until the Soviet era.

In 1914, with the outbreak of the First World War, St Petersburg changed its name to Petrograd, which sounded less Germanic. Petrograd was the scene of the Russian revolution in 1917 and in 1924 was renamed again: Leningrad, after the revolutionary leader and founder of the Soviet Union, Vladimir Ilyich Lenin.

For around 900 days during the Second World War, from September 1941 until January 1944, Leningrad remained under siege by the German armed forces. Over half a million inhabitants died during this period. In 1991, with the Soviet Union on the brink of collapse, a city-wide referendum restored the name of St Petersburg.

from one end of the country to the other will take the traveller over a week. The distances involved have been a problem for successive governments seeking to make their writ run across such a vast land area.

There are a number of other points about geographic conditions in Russia which help us to understand its development and present situation. First, most of Russia is of course located very far north. Half of its land mass is above 60° latitude, that is north of a line running through Oslo, the Shetland Islands, the southernmost tip of Greenland, the middle of Canada, and southern Alaska. Sub-Arctic conditions prevail along its northern coast, and through all of Siberia bar the far south-east, since the high mountain ranges on Russia's southern and eastern borders exclude warm tropical air masses from further south in Asia. Average winter temperatures, a mild $-1°$ in the south-west, fall as low as $-45°$ in the diamond-mining centre of Yakutsk, where temperatures only rise above freezing point for four or five months a year.

Second, Russia has relatively low levels of rainfall. It is a long way from the Atlantic Ocean and protected by mountains from the Pacific. The Arctic Ocean is too cold, and the Black and Caspian Seas too small to provide much water vapour. Unfortunately peak rainfall in the better agricultural areas occurs in late summer and autumn, rather than earlier in the growing season. This growing season, particularly in the more northerly parts, lasts for a relatively short period, when intensive efforts have to be made, a fact which has tended to foster collective rather than individual forms of agricultural organization.

Just 13 per cent of the land area, virtually all located south of a line from St Petersburg in the west to Novokuznetsk in south-western Siberia, is used for agricultural purposes; 45 per cent is forested, and the remainder largely tundra, mountain and swamp which are too cold for cultivation. Even the most fertile areas in the so-called black earth (*chernozemnyi*) region along Russia's border with Ukraine often suffer from the lack of rainfall.

Russia is not then well-placed for productive agriculture. It is, however, blessed with an abundance of natural resources, with substantial coal, oil, natural gas and iron ore reserves as well as non-ferrous metals, gold and diamonds. There are very few naturally occurring minerals in which Russia is not self-sufficient. Indeed, so much of its territory is undeveloped that there may well be many resource deposits yet to be discovered. Most of the easily accessible resources in European Russia and the Urals region have been run down though, and most of the more important ones are now in more remote and inhospitable parts of the country.

Attempts to exploit these more inaccessible resources were heightened during the industrialization drive under Stalin from the 1930s

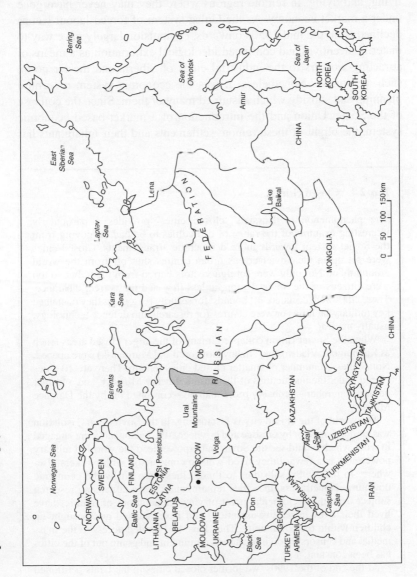

Map 2   Russia: main physical features

onwards, largely on the back of forced labourers who had no choice about where they worked. Consequently, millions of people ended up living, and dying, in remote regions where they may never have gone under a market economy. As the Gulag system of forced labour camps declined from the mid-1950s onwards, compulsion largely gave way to material incentives and continued ideological exhortation as a means of attracting workers to the industrial cities of Siberia and the far north, such as Norilsk. Nonetheless, it was the economic system of central planning and subsidy which sustained many of them. Since the collapse of the Soviet Union and the introduction of a market-based economic system, the plight of these remote settlements and their inhabitants has

---

Box 2.4   Closed cities

The phenomenon of Russia's 'closed cities' provides a particularly interesting example of the range of difficulties to be had in moving from the Soviet system towards more democratic arrangements. Closed cities were set up in the Soviet era as urban centres shut off from the world around them. Not only were foreign visitors barred from them, but so too were citizens of the Soviet Union, unless they had the correct clearance. These cities were declared 'off bounds' for security reasons, as they contained key military facilities or were centres for research into defence technology, usually nuclear.

When the Soviet Union collapsed, many of the larger closed areas (such as Kaliningrad, Vladivostok, Nizhny Novgorod and Murmansk) were opened. Nonetheless, a number of smaller closed cities remain. There are 10 cities closed under the instructions of the Atomic Energy Ministry, and a further unknown number – probably more than 30 – cordoned off by the Defence Ministry.

The world of the closed city is fascinating. In the Soviet years, isolation was compensated for by prestige and privilege – the inhabitants were engaged in work which would see the Soviet superpower lead the world in military power and as a reward they lived well in comparison with workers else-where. In the 1990s, subsidies to these cities were hit by the economic downturn. Nonetheless, the cities remain, and offer a tantalising research subject from the sociological point of view. Generations of families have lived their lives in relative isolation, and have married and brought up children within the community. They have had limited access to the mass media, and censorship on information coming in and going out of the cities has been constant.

At the end of the 1990s two former closed cities in the Urals petitioned the authorities for the return of their closed status. Most of their inhabitants – like many Russians in the 1990s – preferred the safety and predictability of their previous existence to the influx of new ideas and new people.

worsened as many are simply too big to survive economically. The closed cities created in the Soviet era provide a similar example of communities sustained by a centralized authoritarian system, but less well suited to the relative freedoms of post-Soviet Russia (see Box 2.4).

The environment

The particular difficulties of Russia's physical setting outlined above have in many cases been exacerbated by problems of pollution and environmental degradation. Although the process of industrialization produces environmental difficulties the world over, a number of factors exist which mean that contemporary Russia carries an especially negative environmental legacy.

The relative lateness of the Soviet Union's industrialization – in comparison to the rest of Europe – coupled with the desire to catch up rapidly (as noted in Chapter 1) and to prove the superiority of the communist system, meant that the middle decades of the twentieth century saw rapid and large-scale industrialization. The priority of rapid industrialization in itself left little room for serious consideration of environmental effects. What is more, the communists' ideological attitude with regard to the relationship between mankind and nature seriously exacerbated the situation. The communist view was constructivist and scientific, believing that enlightened human beings could build, on the basis of ever-increasing knowledge, a better world. Although this approach is most often thought of in terms of its application to building a new society and economy, it applied also to the natural world. Natural resources existed for people to use, exploit and improve with little attention paid to the potential consequences. So, for example, the 'virgin lands scheme' initiated by Nikita Khrushchev (Soviet leader 1953–64) saw 30 million hectares of previously uncultivated land in Kazakhstan and southern Russia put to the plough, sowed with grain, and doused with chemical fertilisers and pesticides in a grand scheme to massively increase grain supplies. Ecological issues were scarcely considered and, after initial success, soil erosion and environmental degradation set in.

There are numerous other examples of the environmental devastation wreaked during the Soviet era, most notably the Chernobyl nuclear power station disaster of 1986. Details of one other case in particular illustrate the sorts of ecological problems caused. Although the Aral Sea is no longer, since the collapse of the Soviet Union, ruled from Moscow (it straddles the border between Uzbekistan and Kazakhstan), the fate of this particular body of water is illustrative of the lack of environmental concern displayed by the Soviet authorities. The relative shortage of water in the Soviet Union led to numerous schemes being touted for the diversion of rivers. Happily many of these got no further than the planning stage. However, the irrigation of cotton and rice fields by the diversion of water from rivers feeding into the Aral Sea in Central Asia from the 1960s onwards resulted in what was the world's fourth-largest inland sea shrinking in size by three-quarters. Former fishing ports now find themselves some distance from the shore-line, increasing levels of salinity have killed virtually all of the fish and many crops, and salinity of the air has increased rates of cancer and respiratory diseases.

As if all this were not enough, from the 1930s to the 1990s the Soviet armed forces used Vozrozhdeniye island in the Aral Sea to test biological weapons, including anthrax and strains of diseases made resistant to antibiotics. With the shrinking of the sea, Vozrozhdeniye is less and less the isolated testing ground it once was; the shore is now only six miles away. The island's name means, with a sad irony, 'Regeneration' – although what is left on it is the most likely cause of the sudden deaths, in separate incidents, of a large shoal of fish in the Aral Sea in 1976, and thousands of antelopes on the nearby steppe which died together within one hour in 1988.

It is such a lack of environmental concern which is Russia's legacy. Perhaps the worst existing environmental disaster on Russian territory is the city of Norilsk, a city in remote northern Siberia which regained its closed status in 2001. The Norilsk region contains over a third of the world's nickel reserves and two-fifths of its platinum-group metals, as well as important cobalt and copper resources. Norilsk was first seriously developed by forced labour in the 1930s. Nowadays, it is claimed that the Norilsk Mining Company produces one-seventh of all industrial pollution in Russia, and the maximum allowable concentration of toxic air pollution is exceeded most days of the year. Given such conditions, it is scarcely surprising that average life expectancy for factory workers in Norilsk is 10 years below the national average. That national average at the end of the twentieth century was 59 years for men.

Geostrategic location

Straddling as it does two continents and having land borders with no less than 14 sovereign states, Russia has long found itself a player in the international affairs of a number of regions. In security terms this has

Box 2.5   The rise and fall of the Russian empire

9th century	First Slavic settlements, in present day Ukraine and western Russia. Known as the Kiev-Rus period.
1238–40	Mongol (Tatar) invasion, led by Ghengis Khan's grandson, Batu Khan. Russia under Tatar control.
1480	End of Tatar rule in Rus.
1552	Battle of Kazan signals beginning of empire-building.
16–17th centuries	Expansion through Siberia to Pacific coast.
18th century	Conquers present-day Western Ukraine, Belarus, Lithuania, Latvia and Estonia. Russians settle Alaska and parts of Northern California.
1809	Finland acquired from Sweden.
19th century	Conquers Central Asia, the Transcaucasus and Bessarabia.
1869	Sells Alaska to the United States for $7,200,000 (or 2¢ an acre).
1875	Swaps Kurile Islands with Japan for possession of the whole of Sakhalin.
1917–23	Constituent parts of Empire reconquered by Bolsheviks. Finland, Baltic states, Poland, Western Ukraine and Bessarabia lost.
1923	Country renamed Union of Soviet Socialist Republics.
1941–45	Stalin reincorporates parts of the Soviet Union lost after 1917. Yalta Conference (1945) gives USSR control over most of Eastern Europe.
1989	Collapse of communist rule throughout Eastern Europe.
1991	Soviet Union breaks up into 15 independent states.

often translated into wide-ranging threat assessments and the fear of encirclement by hostile powers. An important point to appreciate is that, situated on the Great Eurasian plain, Russia has few natural borders such as mountain ranges or oceans. Russia's international borders have shifted frequently, indeed a clear answer to the question 'Where is Russia?' remains elusive. Box 2.5 outlines the growth and contraction over the centuries of the territories ruled from Moscow.

Russia, including the Russian enclave of Kaliningrad, has land borders with:

- Azerbaijan
- Belarus
- China

- Estonia
- Finland
- Georgia
- Kazakhstan
- Latvia
- Lithuania
- Mongolia
- North Korea
- Norway
- Poland
- Ukraine

In addition, Russia has sea-borders with Japan and with the United States. The state of Alaska, which was sold by Russia to the United States for $7.2 million in 1867, lies just 56 miles across the Bering Strait.

In the aftermath of the collapse of the Soviet Union at the end of 1991, many Russians felt that parts of several former Soviet republics – in particular Northern Kazakhstan, Eastern Ukraine, Belarus, and the Narva region of Estonia – should be part of the new Russian state. Border disputes have complicated bilateral relations with a number of Russia's neighbours, such as the continuing controversy with Japan over owner- ship of the Kurile Islands, seized at the end of the Second World War. The popular post-Soviet mood was reflected in the positions of more nationalistic politicians. The Communist Party of the Russian Federation did not recognize the collapse of the Soviet Union, and the head of the Liberal Democratic Party of Russia (LDPR), extreme nationalist Vladimir Zhirinovsky, even called for the reestablishment of Russia within her 1860 borders, including Finland, Poland and Alaska. Such a call might have been treated with wry amusement by observers had the LDPR not garnered almost a quarter of the votes in the 1993 general election and scarcely less than 10 per cent of the national vote in the following three Duma elections up to 2003.

Russian politicians of all political hues continue to distinguish between the 'near abroad' of former Soviet republics, and the rest of the international community. Just as three-quarters of Russians had voted for the preservation of the USSR in the referendum held by Mikhail Gorbachev in 1991, so, as of mid-1998, a poll by the Public Opinion Foundation found two-thirds of the population agreed and only one- quarter disagreed that 'the historical mission of Russia is as a gathering of peoples in a single union, which will be a successor to the Russian empire and the USSR'.

Nonetheless, despite these regular expressions of popular opinion, there is a realism amongst the population and politicians alike. Neither the Yeltsin nor the Putin governments have sought to change the borders of Russia as constituted at the collapse of the Soviet Union in 1991. The nearest that the restoration of the Soviet Union has come is in the shaky relationship between Russia and Belarus. These two states signed the Treaty on the Formation of a Union State in December 1999. This was more a statement of intent than substance: Russia would prefer Belarus to become a component of the Russian Federation; Belarus wants a more equal relationship. Relations between the two countries have subsequently cooled, but a formal mutual commitment remains.

The peoples of Russia

Russia has always been a multi-ethnic country. The first Russian state, Kievan Rus, from its foundations around the ninth century, consisted of Slavs, Varangians (Vikings) and Finnic peoples. As Russian colonists moved southwards and eastwards across the Eurasian continent over the centuries, they found themselves coexisting with a wide variety of ethnic groups, including Caucasian, Finno-Ugric, Hunnic, Turkic and Mongol peoples, as well as a wide variety of indigenous inhabitants across the expanses of Siberia.

Russia today remains a multinational country. Results of the most recent census, carried out in 2002, counted over 160 separate ethnic groups. Of the total population of 145 million, 80 per cent are Russian. According to the 2002 census, six other ethnic groups had populations of more than one million: Tatars number over 5 million, with Ukrainians not far behind. The Bashkirs and Chuvash number just under 2 million each, and the Chechens and Armenians just over the million mark. A further 11 ethnic groups number more than 500, 000 each.

When the Soviet Union ceased to exist at the end of 1991, more than 25 million ethnic Russians suddenly found themselves living abroad, in one of the 14 non-Russian Soviet republics. The reality of this situation took some time to sink in for people and politicians alike. Many of the newly independent states had not only been part of the Soviet Union for decades, but had been part of the Russian empire before that. One of the great projects of the Communist state had been the creation of the 'new Soviet man' (or woman), to whom nationality would be far less important than solidarity with workers across the globe. On a less ideological level, there was substantial mobility within the Soviet Union; young people went into higher education or served in the armed forces, skilled workers moved to different parts of the country as the planning system established certain industries in particular areas. Naturally there was a significant amount of 'intermarriage', though it was not often thought of in those terms particularly amongst related ethnic groups. The cities in particular reflected such mobility. Across the non-Russian republics of the Soviet Union, Russians made up 16 per cent of the population as a whole, 24 per cent of the urban population, and 30 per cent of the population in capital cities.

Put yourself in the shoes of a Russian from Moscow who, say, in the late 1970s married a Ukrainian from Kiev and then lived, with their children, in Minsk (the capital of the then Soviet Republic of Belorussia). Such a family may have had little perception of themselves as anything other than a normal Soviet family unit settled in an area of their country, in a city not too far removed either geographically and culturally from their own home cities. Suddenly as 1991 turned to 1992 they woke up one morning to find themselves living in a new country, Belarus. Separate from Russia and from Ukraine. Should they stay there, in a relatively small country with an uncertain future? After all, their children were presumably Belarusians. Or should they return to their home country? And, if so, to which country, since Ukraine and Russia were now two separate states?

With 25 million ethnic Russians finding themselves abroad in the early 1990s, similar dilemmas were widespread, and the solutions settled upon were as varied as the number of complex combinations of circumstances. Many Russians returned to Russia in the 1990s, in a reversal of the trend of hundreds of years of expansion outwards from the Russian heartland. Between 1989 – the date of the last Soviet census – and 2001, there was a total immigration to Russia from the other former Soviet republics of more than five and a half million people, and a net immigration of just under four million. This flow rose to a peak in 1994 and seems, by the beginning of the twenty-first century, to have more or less come to its natural end.

As in many other countries, the immigration issue in Russia is controversial politically. The Russian situation is particularly complex since the distinction between immigrant and returnee has not always been clear. In some ways there were good reasons for allowing the relatively lax immigration policies of the 1990s. First, for ethnic Russians entering Russia there were few difficulties with cultural and linguistic assimilation – though economic integration was not so straightforward given the state of the Russian economy in the 1990s. Of course it must be remembered, too, that those returning to Russia were in many ways coming back to a different country from the one they left, to Russia, not the Soviet Union. Second, net immigration of four million went some way towards offsetting the decline in population caused by emigration, low birth rates and high death rates.

Despite these factors which would seem to undermine the arguments of the anti-immigration lobby, from the end of the 1990s onwards the Russian authorities began to tighten up the rules on immigration, bringing them more into line with those in most European states. Responsibility for overseeing migration issues was transferred in 2002 to the Ministry of the Interior, which oversees the Russian police force. This move was accompanied by much discussion amongst politicians, including government spokesmen, of the alleged higher propensity of immigrants for criminal activity. By the early years of the twenty-first century the immigration of those ethnic Russians who suddenly found themselves living abroad at the Soviet collapse had all but run itself out, and immigration debates took on more of a racial character.

Opinion polls show that the existence of xenophobic or racist attitudes is more widespread in Russia than in most developed countries, and racially motivated attacks are fairly common in Russian cities with ethnic communities. In Moscow, the situation became so bad that a delegation of ambassadors from around the world complained in 2003 to the authorities about the lack of protection against such attacks given to their citizens. Into this mix must be added the regularly reported propensity of the Moscow police to stop 'blacks' (the Russian term for anyone of a dark complexion) for questioning – this propensity heightened, and justified in the minds of the authorities, by terrorist attacks carried out by Chechen terrorists.

Russia's regions

Russia is a federation made up of 89 regions. Of these, 32 are defined by nationality and 57 by territory. Although constitutionally all of Russia's regions are equal in their relationship with the centre, there are distinctions between the different types of regions which might be seen as creating a hierarchy. Making up the regions defined by nationality, Russia has 21 republics (Box 2.6), 10 autonomous *okrugs*, and one autonomous *oblast'*. The republics are nominally the homelands of non-Russian peoples, and as such republics are the only regions of the federation which are allowed to have their own constitutions and presidents, whereas other regions have charters and governors (or, in the case of Moscow and St Petersburg, mayors).

Box 2.6   Russia's republics

Adygeya	Karelia
Altai	Khakassia
Bashkortostan	Komi
Buryatia	Marii El
Chechnya	Mordovia
Chuvashia	North Ossetia
Dagestan	Tatarstan
Ingushetia	Tyva
Kabardino-Balkaria	Udmurtia
Kalmykia	Sakha
Karachaevo-Cherkessia	

Of the non-republics, most are *oblasts* and *krais* based on territorial divisions, though there also exist within these territorial units autonomous *okrugs*, which are defined by nationality. As noted above, there are two cities in Russia which have the status of federal regions, namely Moscow and St Petersburg.

The question of the relationship between the centre and the regions is one that has not been definitively settled in the post-Soviet years. As well as the difference in status between regions which we have noted, there are of course numerous other differences. Some regions are comparatively rich, most are poor; a few regions have pushed for greater autonomy (such as Tatarstan) or even independence (Chechnya – see below), most have not; some regions are geographically peripheral, most are not; some regions are extremely large and yet sparsely populated (Sakha republic is around one-third the size of Europe and has a population of around 1 million), others are small and densely populated (Moscow's population is over 8 million). In addition, it is possible to group regions together informally and through generalization. For example, there are:

- the 'donor regions' which are sufficiently rich to be net donors to the federal budget rather than net recipients;
- the 'northern regions', which is more an economic than a geographical designation and refers broadly to remote, poor regions with harsh climatic conditions, low levels of population density, and little in the way of industrial development;
- the Islamic republics, of which there are five; and
- the 'rust belt', those industrialized regions in decline in the 1990s and therefore more likely to vote in opposition to the regime.

This list of regional classifications is by no means exhaustive, and it serves to highlight the difficulties in arriving at a coherent relationship between the centre and the regions in the post-Soviet era. Chapter 5 deals with the question of relations between the centre and the regions in some detail. For now though, let us briefly sketch their development by way of establishing a framework for understanding how contemporary Russia is organized.

When the Soviet Union broke up, many observers worried that Russia itself would soon follow suit, and regions would break away. This has not happened, but the price paid for the maintenance of Russia's territorial integrity has been war in Chechnya (see below) and a lengthy period throughout the Yeltsin presidency (1991–99) when the federal government's grip on the regions was ill-defined and weak. Only under President Putin, from 2000 onwards, has greater central control been established.

In the early years of the 1990s, Yeltsin appointed the heads of Russia's regions himself, before this arrangement was replaced by the direct election of regional heads in the mid-1990s. From 2005, President Putin reestablished presidential appointment of regional heads, though such appointments must be ratified by regional legislatures. These changes in the way regional heads are chosen show the pattern of centre – region relations in the post-Soviet period. For much of the 1990s the centre's grip on the regions was very weak, particularly in those regions which were independently-minded and had a degree of economic clout. Yeltsin's solution to the problem of holding Russia together was to allow a great deal of flexibility; the centre signed a series of 'bilateral' treaties, setting out in each case what the relationship between the Kremlin and the region in question should be. This led to a situation of 'assymetrical federalism', and the constitutional equality of all regions in their relations with the centre went by the board.

When Vladimir Putin came to power in 2000, he was determined to strengthen the centre's control over the regions, and to do this he established seven federal districts, covering all of Russia's regions and each headed up by a presidential representative. The first task of these presidential representatives was to oversee the process of bringing into conformity with federal law the estimated 70,000 regional laws which contradicted it. Gradually the Putin regime began to rein in some of the autonomy enjoyed by many regions. Nonetheless, the issue of how much the Kremlin can, or indeed should, govern Russia's regions remains far from solved. The process of appointment of regional heads by the president from 2005 may serve to further strengthen the centre's authority, but this is by no means certain. In particular, the massacre of hundreds of schoolchildren by terrorists in Beslan, North Ossetia, in September 2004 demonstrated the danger that the ethnically-based conflict in Chechnya may spread across the North Caucasus region.

The Chechen conflict

Chechnya is a republic within the Russian Federation, on its southern border with Georgia. This simple statement would of course be hotly disputed by those Chechens who believe that their republic should enjoy full independence from the Russian Federation. It is this age-old desire for independence which is at the root of the Chechen conflict.

Chechnya's geographical position makes it a far more likely candidate for secession than another occasionally independence-minded republic, Tatarstan. The latter is firmly within Russian territory and surrounded by other regions of Russia. Chechnya, on the other hand, is on the periphery of Russia.

The history of the Chechen people is one of repeated conflict with Russian invaders. Even when firmly part of the Soviet Union, Stalin felt that the Chechens were not to be trusted at the end of the Second World War, and so organized the brutal forced resettlement of the entire Chechen people to Central Asia. It was not until the 1950s that the Chechens returned to their homeland.

In November 1991, as one by one the union republics of the Soviet Union declared their independence, the Chechen leadership – under former Soviet air-force general Dzokhar Dudaev – declared their republic independent. The difficulty was, however, that Chechnya was not one of the 15 union republics, but was a republic within the Russian Soviet Federative Socialist Republic (RSFSR), as Russia was officially known in the Soviet era. The newly elected Russian president, Boris Yeltsin, whilst actively encouraging the union republics – including his own – to secede from the Soviet Union, was determined that Russia itself would not break-up. He declared a state of emergency in Chechnya and insisted that it remain within Russia.

An uneasy stand-off between Chechnya and Moscow held until December 1994, when Yeltsin sent troops into Chechnya to try and subdue the rebel republic. The Russian army was used as a blunt instrument, engaging in indiscriminate bombing and shelling of the capital Grozny, where many of the remaining inhabitants were ethnic Russians unable to flee to family in the Chechen mountains. The Chechen rebels, on the other hand, were skilled at guerilla and terrorist tactics. By the summer of 1996 the stalemate was broken by a deal which gave some autonomy to the Chechens, but no real hope of independence.

In late summer 1999, Chechen rebels encroached into the neighbouring Russian republic of Dagestan. This was followed in September by a series of devastating bomb attacks on apartment blocks in Moscow and elsewhere, which were blamed on the Chechens. Yeltsin, backed by his new Prime Minister Vladimir Putin, sent troops into Chechnya again. The result was similar to that of the first Chechen War, with the exception that reported brutality on both sides was, if anything, fiercer. Although President Putin has declared that the military hostilities are over, the conflict continues and Russian troops, as well as Chechen fighters and civilians, are regularly being killed.

Vladimir Putin, soon after becoming President in 2000, talked in terms of the Russian troops in Chechnya being the first line of defence for Europe against militant Islam. After the terrorist attacks on New York and Washington of 11 September 2001, he has repeatedly talked of the Chechen conflict within the framework of the global war on terrorism.

At the same time, the Chechen rebels have increasingly adopted the symbols of radical Islam and tactics of Islamic terrorists, as well as developing links with other Islamic terror networks. They have taken terrorism to the heart of Moscow repeatedly, using suicide bombers on the Moscow metro, outside a city centre hotel, and at a summer rock festival. In October 2002, a group of Chechens took several hundred people in a Moscow theatre audience hostage. The siege was ended by Russian special troops, who stormed the building, killing all the terrorists. Tragically, over a hundred of the hostages were also killed, not by terrorists but by the gas which the Russian troops pumped into the theatre to debilitate those inside. Within a week in August and September 2004 Chechen terrorists planted bombs which destroyed two separate passenger airlines, detonated a device outside a metro station in Moscow, and – in horrific scenes which captured global attention – killed hundreds of schoolchildren and their parents after taking them hostage in Beslan, southern Russia.

Religion in Russia

As well as being multi-ethnic, Russia today is religiously diverse. Religious activity has increased since the collapse of communism. Survey evidence suggests that around half of the adult population describe themselves as religious believers. One in three Russians attends religious services more than once a year, although only one in fifty attend weekly. Practising believers are more likely to be older, and to be women rather than men.

The dominant religion in the country is Russian Orthodoxy. There are also many other Christian confessions, a substantial Islamic minority, and established Jewish and Buddhist communities, as well as a few adherents of pre-Christian pagan religions. Of Russia's 89 regions, five are Islamic republics and one, Kalmykia, is a Buddhist republic. Table 2.1 provides data on the number of registered religious communities at the beginning of 2003, and their growth since 1991, as well as estimates of the numbers adhering to the various faiths.

The religious revival in Russia dates from 1988, the millennium of the conversion of Russia to Christianity, which, thanks to official support from previously anti-religious state authorities, became a nationwide celebration. It has a number of elements. The Orthodox Church has been resurrected as a national symbol, as indeed it was before the 1917 revolution, although it now maintains a formal independence from the state. The Orthodox Patriarch blesses the President on his inauguration, and in times of political crisis he has played a mediating role. Other politicians from across the political spectrum have been keen to associate themselves with Orthodoxy (see Box 2.7). The postcommunist period has seen the building or restoration of many churches, cathedrals, monasteries, seminaries and theological academies. Charitable and educational work by churches has become increasingly common after decades of complete prohibition. The Orthodox authorities, and those of

Table 2.1   Growth of religion in Russia, 1991–2003

Religion	Registered communities		Adherents (millions) 2003
	1991	*2003*	
Russian Orthodox (Moscow Patriarchate)	3,451	11,299	60
Russian Orthodox Free Church		18	
Islamic	870	3,467	23
Old Rite Orthodox	370	288	4
Buddhist	16	218	2
Jewish	31	270	0.3
Roman Catholic	32	268	0.3
Lutheran	88	211	0.25
Evangelical (Baptist)	602	1015	0.1
Evangelical (Pentecostal)	72	1435	0.1

Source: Ministry of Justice and estimates of adherents from the Presidential Council of Religious Associations.

other religions, continue to argue for the restitution of land and property lost in the Soviet period. While the current (1993) Russian Constitution and the 1997 Law on Freedom of Conscience and Religious Associations guarantee religious freedom, there have been concerns about an overly close relationship between the Orthodox Church and the Russian state, and about harassment of some religious minorities, a topic we examine in detail in Chapter 6.

Islam is the second largest religion in Russia, and – along with Christianity, Judaism and Buddhism – is recognized in the preamble to the 1997 Law on Freedom of Conscience and Religious Associations as one of Russia's traditional religions. As a proportion of the population of

---

Box 2.7   What is Russian Orthodoxy?

Contemporary Orthodoxy, like all religions, encompasses many different elements and interpretations. Whilst we can hardly do justice to the richness of the tradition, the following distinctive features are noteworthy:

- *The role of tradition*: the split with Catholicism in 1054 was a rejection of changes which the Western church wished to introduce. Since then, Orthodoxy has seen itself as closest of all the branches of Christianity to the traditions of the early Church. Doctrinally and in practice there have been few changes since the 8th century. Participation in an Orthodox service indeed involves an experience of changelessness and timelessness. Doctrine does not change because faith is seen as a matter of practice, not doctrine, an attitude which often causes confusion among foreign observers.
- *Greater emphasis on mysticism and spirituality*: Western religion, like Western thought, has since the Enlightenment been dominated by a tradition of rationalism, that is the belief that the human mind is capable of explaining everything, eventually. This attitude applies to theology as much as to philosophy: theological statements must be susceptible to proof and human reason. Orthodoxy does not reject truths that arise out of reason, but takes much more seriously extra-rational sources of truth: the symbolic, transcendental and spiritual. The religious icon, the form of the service, Russian religious music, and the emphasis on artistic aspects of worship, all arise out of an emphasis on experience and adoration rather than analysis.
- *Less hierarchical*: at least in the experience of worship. There are, for example, no pews in a Russian Orthodox church, and the congregation is able to come and go as it pleases, giving rise to a much more flexible and informal atmosphere than is familiar in many Western denominations. There is no equivalent in Orthodoxy of the Pope, no individual with universal jurisdiction. What holds the Church together is that its members understand it as a communion of the faithful.

the Soviet Union, Muslims made up a greater percentage than is now the case in Russia, since the break-up of the USSR brought independence to Kazakhstan, Uzbekistan, Kyrgyzstan, Tajikistan, Turkmenistan and Azerbaijan. Nonetheless, there are more than 14 million Muslims in the Russian Federation, making up 10 per cent of the population.

The size of the Jewish community is far smaller, with the 2002 census reporting that there are now only around 300,000 Jews left in Russia, down from over half a million in 1989. The emigration of Jews from Russia, mainly to Israel, has been particularly marked since the end of the 1980s when restrictions were eased. From a peak of over 180,000 emigrés in 1990, the figure fell to an average of around 60,000 in the first half of the 1990s and it has fallen still further since. Reasons behind this emigration are varied, and there is no doubt that economic factors played a major role, as they did with emigrants of all faiths or none from Russia in the immediate post-Soviet years. To some extent, though, Russia's tradition of anti-semitism was also a factor, particularly with the rise of fascist and far-right movements during this decade, marked by the significant vote for the Liberal Democratic Party in 1993.

The place of Buddhism as a legally acknowledged traditional religion in Russia owes more to its longevity and its identity with specific people groups than to any large Buddhist community. Estimates of the number of Buddhists in Russia are not easy to come by, but the country's only Buddhist republic, Kalmykia, only has around 150,000 Kalmyks, and a figure of about twice that for the number of Buddhists in Russia would not be far wide of the mark.

Who are the Russians? Culture and traditions

The culture of a group is not a fixed or given set of attitudes and ways of behaving. However, members of a society do tend to share beliefs about themselves as a collective, and about right ways of acting, and these beliefs have an important impact. They are embodied not just in social discourse, but in religious practices, art and literature, folk traditions, notions of social justice, and national symbols. Generalizing about these matters is a risky business: values are not shared by everyone, social beliefs and practices change over time. However, at the risk of stereotyping, there are cultural beliefs which, while not necessarily shared by all sections of society, are nonetheless central to understanding current reality.

The term 'Russian Idea' indicates a set of interpretations, by Russian thinkers of various political and philosophical persuasions, of what is distinctive about Russia. Not all of these formulations are identical, but they do tend to share common features. The most important of these is that Russia is different from the West. Western societies are often lumped together and stereotyped as being overly individualistic, excessively materialistic, immoral, and generally unpleasant places to live. Russia is defined, crudely, as not the West. Russians allegedly share a uniquely spiritual, communal existence, a life which concentrates not on the squalid pursuit of individual material goals, but on what is most important in existence. Values such as spirituality and communality are of course not easy to measure. However, figures for attendance at religious services or membership of those organizations which make up civil society are far lower in Russia than in the United States – casting great doubt on claims that Russians are somehow more spiritual and communal than Americans. Nonetheless, even if hard statistics do not back up the common perception, the widespread existence of that perception has influence in itself. It contributes to the construction of a national identity, and from there into the formulation of voting preferences and policies (for more details on civil society see Chapter 6, and for a more detailed discussion of 'the Russian idea' see Chapter 7).

3
Social Structure and Social Policy

As we saw in Chapters 1 and 2, the structure of Russian society was dramatically transformed in the Soviet period. As it industrialized, Russia went from being a rural country to being predominantly urban, both in terms of its demographic structure and its political priorities. The population became much more highly educated, and the number employed in administrative and professional capacities grew substantially. However, Soviet social structure took a very different shape from that found in most industrial democracies. The basis of social divisions was access to administrative power, rather than wealth. What the Yugoslav dissident Milovan Djilas had in the 1950s labelled 'the New Class', the party-state apparatus, exerted monopolistic and unaccountable control over resources and people. Unsurprisingly, this led to the development of an elaborate system of special privileges. Officials had access to goods which were unavailable to the wider population, networks of special schools for their children, private hospitals with superior facilities, luxurious dachas (country retreats), and their own holiday resorts.

The *nomenklatura* system of control over appointments – whereby political reliability was the prerequisite, and only after this might suitability for the post be a consideration – meant that this was a self-perpetuating élite. Meanwhile towards the end of the Soviet period, and particularly under Brezhnev (Soviet leader, 1964–82), income differentials among the rest of the population were not great, although rural parts of Russia tended to be more neglected. This apparently egalitarian state of affairs suited Soviet propaganda well, especially when contrasted with income differentials in the capitalist countries. However, the actual impact of monetary income on the life of a Soviet citizen was relatively minimal, with the problem for most being access to goods, rather than the ability to pay for them.

There existed what Alena Ledeneva termed 'an economy of favours' (Ledeneva, 1998), where more important than the amount of roubles in someone's pay packet was the influence of *blat* and *svyazi*. The latter word is straightforward in meaning – *svyazi* is the Russian word for

48

'connections', and knowing someone with access to goods or services was often a first step to obtaining them. *Blat* translates less easily. The Oxford Russian dictionary renders it as 'string-pulling', though a single phrase cannot adequately sum up the necessary background of mutual assistance and obligations, often mediated through a network made up of family members, close friends, work colleagues or party functionaries. To receive some good or service by means of *blat* usually meant drawing on such a network, and at some point repaying the favour.

For those whose knowledge of Russia and the Russians is firmly placed in the post-communist era, it is difficult to conceive of the rapidity and depth of the change which has taken place in the short time since the end of the 1980s. A notable indicator of that change can be found in foreign travel. During the Soviet era, the general rule was that people were not allowed to leave the Soviet bloc unless they were favoured by the Communist Party, and deemed trustworthy. Clearly certain occupations required foreign travel – diplomats, politicians, journalists, Russian language assistants to Western universities, international-standard artists and athletes – and to have been abroad, especially if returning with Western consumer goods, marked out a person as remarkably privileged. Even in those cases, travellers would be warned of the dangers of too close connections with Westerners, would expect a degree of KGB surveillance abroad, and would be required to report all contacts to the authorities on return.

A number of high-profile defections, particularly in the 1970s and 1980s, tightened up all aspects of foreign travel (for further details of connections with the West in the Soviet era, see Chapter 6). To be sufficiently trusted to enjoy a touring holiday in France – as Mikhail Gorbachev did in the 1970s – was a sure mark of belonging to the élite. Despite the Communist Party's slogan 'workers of the world unite', the concept of travel beyond the fraternal socialist countries was beyond the imagination of most Soviet citizens. Nowadays, foreign holidays are increasingly within the grasp of 'ordinary' Russians, as anyone who has visited favoured destinations such as Cyprus, Egypt or London will testify. Audio advertisements for package tours blare out over the massed Muscovites on the metro escalators, and high-quality consumer goods are readily available throughout Russia. Nowadays any restrictions come, as they do the world over, not from lack of connections and political reliability, but from lack of money.

The collapse of communism and the transformation from a planned economy to a market-based system naturally had a dramatic effect on such matters. This chapter therefore looks at changes in the structure of income, wealth and social status in postcommunist Russia. It then reviews the effects that the collapse of a planned economic system and the weakness of the state have had on various social policies. The Soviet Union was known for its 'cradle to grave' model of free social welfare provision. Although the reality of this provision was often wholly inadequate for people's needs, the post-Soviet period has seen deterioration in many respects.

Standards of living

The post-Soviet period saw a sharp decline in overall living standards in Russia. The United Nations Human Development Programme estimated that, in purchasing power parity terms (that is adjusting national incomes for relative prices), as of 2000 Russia's per capita gross national product was \$8,377. This was just under one-quarter of the \$34,142 figure in the United States, over one-third of the \$23,509 in the United Kingdom, and puts Russia, according to these data, on a par with countries such as Libya, Malaysia and Mexico. The decline had a number of identifiable causes:

- the dramatic reduction in state subsidies for basic services such as rents, public transport and energy;
- the hyperinflation of 1992 which led to rises of some 2,500 per cent in price levels and the wiping out of personal savings;
- the economic slump and rise in unemployment;
- the non-payment of wages and an inadequate welfare system; and
- the collapse of the rouble in 1998, which again wiped out the savings of many Russians.

Income inequality has also sharply increased since the end of the Soviet Union. By 1997, the ratio between the incomes of the richest and the poorest 10 per cent was around 13:1. And while in some regions, such as Moscow and the oil and gas-exporting Tyumen oblast, incomes had risen, in many others living standards had fallen by considerably more than the national average. Even adjusting for differences in price levels, average incomes in the nine richest regions were three times those in the nine poorest regions by the mid-1990s.

Just as Russian politics polarized in the early 1990s, with the concept of the 'middle ground' giving way to an almost elemental struggle between reform and reaction, so standards of living moved in opposing directions. The 'new poor' and the 'new rich' appeared. Amongst the 'new poor' were many professional people – teachers, academics, scientists – whose wages scarcely pretended to keep up with the rising costs of everyday life, even when they were being paid, which they regularly were not. A common sight in the centre of Moscow in 1992 and 1993 was the accumulation of people from all walks of life, standing outside metro stations selling their possessions in order to buy the necessities of survival. The practice ended on this large scale in the mid-1990s not because the problem went away, but because the city authorities put a stop to it.

Popular resentment of the 'new rich', more commonly known as the 'new Russians', that is the section of the population that prospered materially in the post-communist period, has been fuelled by their conspicuous consumption. There had always been a privileged class in the Soviet Union, but the luxuries enjoyed by communist élites had in general been enjoyed behind closed doors or in enclaves fenced off from the rest of the country. The expensive foreign cars, lavish lifestyles and luxurious new dachas of the post-communist period were no longer hidden away. For some of the 'new Russians' the word 'rich' seems inadequate. A very small, but highly visible, proportion of the population made serious money in the privatizations of the mid-1990s, when vast state-owned resources were sold at prices which turned out to be gross underestimates of their true market value.

For the men in control of these resources, foreign cars and lavish lifestyles were only the beginning. In 2003 one such businessman, 36-year-old Roman Abramovich, bought one of London's top football clubs, Chelsea, and proceeded to astonish the world of European football by using his wealth to pay huge transfer fees and wages for almost any player the club desired. With an estimated personal fortune of $7.4 billion, made chiefly in the oil industry, he can afford to transform the landscape in the home of the world's most popular sport. That he also gained residency in England was an added bonus, particularly given the actions taken by President Putin's regime against a number of the most powerful and richest 'oligarchs' who fell into disfavour with the Russian government. Men such as Vladimir Gusinsky and Boris Berezovsky both left Russia for 'voluntary' exile in Western Europe during Putin's first term in office (2000–04), under threat of prosecution should they ever return to Russia.

In the summer of 2003, another young and seriously rich oil tycoon, Mikhail Khodorkovsky, was imprisoned in Russia, pending prosecution for financial irregularities. Putin's stated desire, in a deliberate echo of a Stalinist phrase used to describe the 1930s campaign against the Soviet Union's 'rich peasants', is to 'destroy the oligarchs as a class'.

Many observers have noted, however, that only those oligarchs who display politically oppositionist tendencies seem to attract the negative attentions of the Russian state.

Berezovsky, Gusinsky, Abramovich and Khodorkovsky belong to the super rich of the new Russians; they are just four of the 25 dollar billionaires in Russia. Below them, however, many others have made a great deal of money in the chaotic marketization of the post-Soviet period. It is folly to use generalizations in judging any particular individual, but nonetheless there are features of the 'new Russians' as a whole which apply sufficiently to be worth identifying:

- There has been an element of élite continuity with the post-Soviet era, as those who had access to, or *de facto* control of, resources – such as factories or local networks of influence – were in a favourable position when it came to gaining ownership on privatization. Research by David Lane and Cameron Ross shows élite continuity in the older areas of economic activity, but less continuity in new areas such as retail and commerce (Lane and Ross, 1999).
- There is some truth in the assertion that no one who has made money in Russia since the collapse of the Soviet Union has done so without paying bribes, protection money, back-handers, and so on. The common view, in Russia as much as outside, is that corruption has been so rife that material success is itself a sufficient indicator of guilt. Some mitigation might be offered on two grounds. First, a market economy needs to be regulated by a complex framework of laws, none of which existed under the Soviet command system. Factors such as political upheaval and lack of expertise meant that the development of a priva-tized, proto-market environment outpaced the construction of a renewed legal framework. Inevitably old and inadequate laws were broken. Second, there are those who see the arrival of an 'incipient acquisition class' (Lane and Ross, 1999) as a necessary precursor to the creation of a regulated market economy. Once wealth has been acquired, so the argument goes, then it will be in the interests of those who hold it to support a protective legal framework.
- There is a shadowy crossover between corruption and organized crime in Russia. Turf wars between groups seeking control of profitable areas of activity – for example, banking or trade – have resulted in hundreds of contract killings of business people in the past decade.
- Success in the marketizing economy has often come more easily to the younger generation, who do not need to adjust from the old way of doing things and are far more likely to have gained business expertise

abroad or with Western companies. Of course not all Russian companies in the first decade of the twenty-first century are corrupt and have links with organized crime. As the market economy has become established, so have respectable companies, for example in manufacturing and the service industries, with high-quality products, staff and standards of customer service.

Below the level of the seriously rich, Russia has a small but growing middle class emerging out of Moscow, St Petersburg and other urban centres. According to some sources, the average wage in Russia's larger cities is now over $650 per month – as opposed to a national average of around $200. In Moscow around one-fifth of those in work take home more than $1,750 per month.

As noted in Chapter 2, Russia's major cities have changed almost beyond recognition in the past decade, with the most immediately evident innovation being the arrival of large shopping malls and out-of-town stores. Anyone arriving at Moscow's Sheremetevo airport these days will notice a vast IKEA furniture store on the outskirts of the city, along with restaurants and leisure complexes; in the centre of Moscow more and more shopping malls, replete with fashionably expensive goods, are evident; a short metro ride from the centre to the Gorbushka market will reveal a bustling indoor complex, crowded with Muscovites buying the latest electronic goods. The amount of retail space in Moscow tripled between 2002 and 2004, and such activity can only be supported by a large number of people with ready disposable income. And for the many Muscovites earning what would be a good wage almost anywhere in Europe, the growth in wages of recent years has translated readily into disposable income – since few Russians have mortgages or bank loans to contend with, and utility prices remain subsidized for now.

The emergence of a middle class has been seen by theorists of democratic transition as a key driver in establishing a liberal democratic system in Russia. However, although an identifiable middle class is apparent, there is still some way to go before it becomes the bedrock of support for deeper democracy.

- As we have repeatedly noted, Moscow is not Russia. According to a recent study by the Carnegie Foundation, only around 7 per cent of the Russian population have sufficient income to qualify as middle-class. This is some way from the idea that such a group could represent the bedrock of anything. Members of the middle class do not represent the 'average citizen' in Russia in the same way as they are often deemed to do by politicians in most Western countries.

• There is a disparity between statistical indicators of 'middle-class-ness' based on income, and what might be deemed 'middle-class attitudes'. The parliamentary elections of 2003 represented a virtual wipe-out for the liberal parties who would like to see themselves as representing the middle classes. There are of course many explanations for this, but one of these is that many educated, professional people – academics, teachers, doctors – are not middle-class in terms of income. The old Soviet intelligentsia have not by and large prospered from the reforms, and the current middle class are as likely – according to some studies, more likely – to be nationalistic and authoritarian in attitude, as to be supporters of liberal ideals.

The proportion of the population living in poverty before the collapse of the Soviet Union was usually estimated at around one in 10. Official estimates were putting the figure at around one in five of the population by 1994 and around one in three by the turn of the century, with incomes below the official subsistence minimum. Official figures released at the beginning of 2004 showed that during President Vladimir Putin's first term in office, the proportion of people living below the poverty line of $70 per month had fallen from one in three to one in five. However, individuals' own assessments of their family's economic situation do not yet reflect this apparent improvement and, in any case, 20 per cent of the population living in poverty still represents a major problem for Russia.

A survey taken across three-quarters of Russia's regions at the same time as the state statistical agency was reporting the decline in the number of people suffering poverty reveals a clear disparity between perceptions and official statistics (Figures 3.1 and 3.2).

Respondents across Russia gave practically the same answers to the question, 'what is preventing you from living better?' The top-five reasons cited were to do with poverty – low wages, unemployment, inflation, pensions, inadequate state benefits. The situation has improved since the 1990s, but nonetheless the picture presented is a bleak one: clearly large sections of the population are in significant distress, suffering from inadequate incomes and unhealthy and insufficient diets. Some sections of the population are in particular need. These groups include pensioners (both old-age pensioners and the disabled), one-parent families (increasingly common given rising divorce rates, rising numbers of extra-marital births, and the high mortality rates among middle-aged men), the unemployed, migrants, and also workers in public services such as teachers, health professionals, military personnel and employees in the state sector who during the 1990s suffered from persistent non-payment of wages.

Figure 3.1   Expectations of standard of living rises, 2004

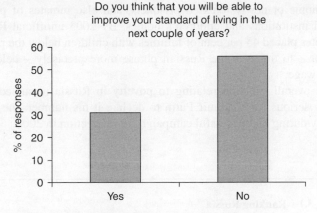

Source: Data from Rosbalt, 8 January 2004, www.rosbaltnews.com

Figure 3.2   Perceptions of regional economic situations, 2004

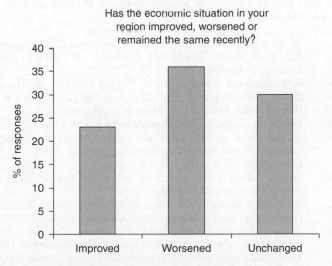

Source: Data from Rosbalt, 8 January 2004, www.rosbaltnews.com

In early 2005, tens of thousands of pensioners took to the streets across Russia in an unprecedented series of demonstrations against the monetization of benefits such as access to transport and medicines, which would see most of them in an even worse financial position.

The most vulnerable groups include the homeless, estimated at between one and two million – mostly children who have run away from home or newly released prisoners, and also inmates of prisons, mental institutions and children's homes. By 2003 unofficial Russian estimates placed 45 per cent of families with children below the poverty line, or – to translate the Russian phrase more precisely – below the living wage.

The overall situation relating to poverty in Russia remained sufficiently serious for Vladimir Putin to declare it his number one policy priority during his successful campaign for re-election in 2004.

Box 3.1   Ranking Russia

In an age seemingly obsessed by lists, it is a fascinating exercise to see where Russia comes in various 'league tables'. Although there are always arguments, particularly where the placing is based on estimates, the following examples give us a picture of Russian society in the early years of the twenty-first century.

1st	In the number of people in prison per capita (United Nations Survey of Crime Trends and Operation of Criminal Justice Systems, 1998–2000).
1st	In the incidence of abortions with 19.1 per 1,000 people. The next highest is Bulgaria with 12.9, third place Hungary is down at 7.7 (United Nations Health and Development Report).
1st	Fastest growing rate of AIDS cases in the world.
2nd	In the global suicide rates per capita, behind neighbouring Lithuania (World Health Organization figures for 2000).
3rd	In the medals table at the 2004 Olympics.
3rd	In global divorce rate per capita, behind the United States and Puerto Rico (www.divorcereform.org).
3rd	In the list of countries with the most dollar billionaires, behind the United States and Germany (*Forbes Magazine*, February 2004).
5th	In the global murder rates per capita, behind Columbia, South Africa, Jamaica and Venezuela (United Nations Survey of Crime Trends and Operation of Criminal Justice Systems, 1998–2000).
6th	In the global male smoking rates, behind South Korea, Cambodia, Namibia, China and Kenya (World Health Organization).
7th	With regard to the largest percentage gap in the world between the number of men and women in its population, with 0.88 males to each female. Of the six countries with worse ratios, five were in the former Soviet Union (*CIA World Factbook*, 2003).
130th	Out of 191 countries in the World Health Organization's ranking of health systems.

Demographics and health policy

The existence of widespread poverty stores up problems for Russia for many years to come. Children in such a situation have poor diets, are ill more often, and have lowered life expectancy. Throughout the post-Soviet period, life expectancy in Russia has been remarkably low, particularly for Russian men. By 2002, life expectancy was 72 for women and 59 for men. This represents the lowest life expectancy for males in any developed country, and the biggest gap between male and female life expectancy in the world. Why are so many Russian men dying early?

• Rising alcoholism, accompanied by the Russian pattern of drinking, has been identified in studies as a major contributory factor to the decline in male life-expectancy. An anti-alcohol campaign spearheaded by Mikhail Gorbachev (Soviet leader, 1985–91) in the second half of the 1980s led to a slight improvement in male mortality rates, but by 1994 twice as many Russian men between 15 and 64 died as had been the case in 1986.

• A particularly high rate of death by external causes (accidents or violence) afflicted Russian men in the 1990s, with such causes resulting in 80 per cent of deaths in the 15–24 age groups in certain years of the 1990s. Within this category the highest identifiable cause was suicide, followed by vehicle accidents and homicides. The male suicide rate in Russia is more than six times that for females. Alcohol poisoning *per se* came at the bottom of the list of 'external causes', but clearly alcohol abuse could have had a role under a number of the other headings. For the sake of comparison, though, it is worth noting that in 1996 in Russia over 35,000 people died from accidental alcohol poisoning, in the United States – without adjusting for the fact that the US population is getting on for double that of Russia – around 300 people a year are recorded as dying from the same cause. One further comparison emphasizes the scale of the problem: a baby boy born in Russia in 1995 would have almost a one in four chance of his eventual death being by external causes, in the UK the corresponding risk would be one in 30.

• Cardio-vascular diseases account for almost double the number of deaths amongst Russian men than external causes. Again, alcohol consumption is a contributing factor, as 'binge drinking' is associated with an increased risk of cardio-vascular disease. Throw in the fact that Russia has nearly 70 million smokers, out of a population of 144 million, and the rate of such diseases is easier to understand.

In 2002 Russia carried out its first national census since the Soviet collapse (the previous Soviet census took place in 1989), and the results reveal what can accurately be described as a demographic time-bomb. A number of commentaries noted positives such as the fact that the overall population of Russia was more than two million higher – at 145 million – than many had estimated, or the claim that the world's oldest man lives in Vladivostok (according to his passport, Afanasii Tarasov was born in 1887; his friends are reported as saying that he doesn't look a day over 80). Nonetheless, projections for Russia's future into the middle of the twenty-first century and beyond provide serious cause for concern in relation to the decline of, and the shifting age structure within, the population.

In many developed countries, the birth rate is below the replacement rate necessary to maintain the population level. Russia's birth rate, however, is well-below that in most developed countries. For a complex of reasons – largely to do with economic hardship, poor medical care and lack of confidence in the future – the number of children being born in Russia has been and will continue to be inadequate to prevent population decline. Falling levels of population in turn affect the well-being of a population in a number of ways, particularly as they are combined with a changing age-structure. In 2002, 61 per cent of the population were of working age, 18 per cent were younger and 21 per cent older. In the coming decades, however, the percentage of pensioners will continue to increase, with some estimates putting it at about 40 per cent of the Russian population by the middle of the century. This matters for a number of reasons – most obviously because it means that an ever-smaller proportion of the population is having to provide for an ever-growing pensioner sector. This is not a problem unique to Russia, but the existence of widespread poverty within Russia at the present time makes persuading working people to contribute to private pension funds extremely difficult, especially when combined with a distrust in financial institutions. Aside from issues of pension provision, the combination of population decline and the changing age-structure means fewer people to contribute to economic growth and – seen as particularly important in Russia, which is still apparently wedded to military conscription and a trained reserve – fewer people to staff the armed forces.

The demographic problems outlined above are similar to, though worse than, those experienced in a number of developed countries. However, these difficulties are compounded in Russia due to its specific features of size, ethnic mix and political culture. Where allowing an increase in immigration might be seen as an obvious solution to population decline in the abstract, in reality political pressures – including relatively widespread xenophobia and exaggerated security concerns – make such an option difficult politically. Furthermore, although a number of the demographic features outlined above may be similar in type to those experienced in many developed countries, they are greater in scale and differ in certain key details.

Taking the central issue of depopulation, Russia's fertility rate fell during the twentieth century. Nothing unusual there for an industrialized nation. However, Russia now has one of the world's lowest fertility rates. In 1992, for the first time in peacetime, Russia's population officially declined, the number of deaths exceeding the number of births plus the number of immigrants. By the end of the decade, births had fallen to 1.2 million, while deaths had increased to 2.1 million. Russia also has the highest rate of abortions in the world, with roughly two abortions for every birth. In addition, the fertility patterns of Russian women do not match those of women in other developed countries in important respects. In most of the Western world, women have been having children later as contraceptive methods have enabled, and socio-economic factors motivated, such a choice. In Russia, however, the decline in the birthrate has been accompanied by women having children earlier, with the peak age at the turn of the century being 20–24. Similarly, marriages in Russia have been occurring earlier, in contrast with later marriages in other developed countries. Between 1960 and 1995, the average age at which a Russian woman would marry fell from 26 to 22.

Fears of the depopulation of Russia on the basis of the birthrate deepen still further when turning to the health of children. According to the Russian Ministry of Health, 70 per cent of Russian teenagers suffer from chronic diseases, and the mortality rate in 2000 for 10–17 year olds was an extremely high 213 per 100,000. High levels of drug-addiction and alcohol abuse are reported for teenagers in the 15–17 age bracket, along with an increase in gynaecological ailments for girls of the same age as the phenomenon of teenage maternity becomes more prevalent. These health problems at a young age have an immediate effect in terms of the proportion of the annual call-up to the armed forces who actually get to serve. All Russian men aged 18–27 are required to serve two years in the army, but 90 per cent avoid the draft; more than half by means of the legal right to draft deferment for students, but many of the remainder on health grounds. Such immediate effects are compounded, too, by long-term effects. If the staggeringly low life-expectancy levels of Russian men in particular are to be improved, then it is important that children's health is not neglected, since illness as a child makes the adult more vulnerable.

One further major health problem in Russia which we have not yet mentioned is the especially acute threat from tuberculosis and AIDS. Tuberculosis is a disease which has for a number of years been relatively successfully treated. However, in recent years a new strain known as multi-drug resistant tuberculosis (MDR TB) has emerged. At the same time, the far more publicized spread of AIDS has constituted a growing global health threat – and of course the combination of these two threats is mutually destructive to health, as TB is one of the main infections to which AIDS sufferers become vulnerable. As can be seen from Figure 3.3, the incidence of TB has increased dramatically in the post-Soviet period, up to levels which exceed those of half a century ago.

In 2001 there were almost 30,000 TB deaths in Russia, compared with, for example, just over 750 such deaths in the United States which has almost twice the population. Russia also has – along with neighbouring Ukraine – the fastest growing rate of AIDS cases in the world. Estimates by the American demographer Murray Feshbach suggest that by 2020, if current trends continue, between 5 and 14 million Russians will have HIV, and between 250,000 and 650,000 will die from AIDS each year. For many years the Soviet and then the Russian governments appeared to live in a state of denial about HIV/AIDS, but in 2003 and 2004 signs appeared of an increasingly active awareness of the issue amongst policy-makers; President Putin even noted the dangers in his State of the Federation address. Russian health indicators for 2001 are summarized in Table 3.1.

In 2000, the World Health Organization ranked the health systems of 191 countries. Russia came in at 130, between Peru and Honduras. During the Soviet era, the state created a system of healthcare which entitled every citizen access to medical services, free at the point of

Figure 3.3   Tuberculosis incidence in Russia per 100,000 population, 1955–2010

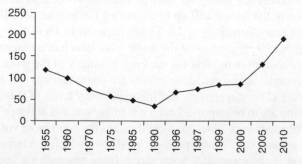

Source: Data from Olga Govor, Vladivostok State University, cited in Johnson's Russia List Research and Analytical Supplement, January 2004, www.cdi.org/russia/johnson/8019.cfm#2

Table 3.1   Russian health indicators, 2001

Life expectancy (years)	
● Total population	65.2
● Male	58.9
● Female	72.3
Child mortality, under five, per thousand	
● Male	22
● Female	17
Total health expenditure, % of GDP	5.3
Government expenditure on health as % of total government expenditure	14.5
Private expenditure on health as % of total health expenditure (2000)	27.5
Number of people hospitalized	31,000,000

Sources: Data from World Health Organization; Report of the President's Main Monitoring Directorate, www. kremlin.ru, January 2003

service. Official health indicators for decades showed improvement across a range of indicators – albeit from a low base. Healthcare of course was far from perfect; stories abound of poor treatment in unhygienic hospitals, and there were inevitable regional discrepancies across the vast territory of the Soviet Union. In general, the Soviet health system used techniques, equipment and treatments far below the level of developed nations. The health system suffered, too, from the vagaries of the centrally planned economy, with its emphasis on quantity over quality and its sometimes counterproductive use of targets. For example, targets for the number of 'bed days' led hospitals to keep patients in hospitals longer than necessary and to prioritize the number of beds rather than the quality of other resources. Furthermore, health spending in the Soviet Union was low as a percentage of GDP – typically around 3 per cent, compared with 10–12 per cent in the West. According to figures from the Russian Ministry of the Economy, around 6 per cent of all hospitals were financed and run by places of work, such as an industrial enterprise or collective farm. This figure relates to the country as a whole, and in some regions the percentage could be significantly higher.

Healthcare was not a government priority in the same way as defence spending or spending on heavy industry, and so in a shortage economy the budget and the flow of resources diminished when other demands came to the fore. Doctors' wages were relatively low – about three-quarters of those received by high priority industrial workers – and it was common for patients to give money or goods in kind to medical staff to ensure a certain level of service. With the progression of time such payments took on the character of expectations rather than gratuities. As with so much in the Soviet Union, the best-quality service came in those facilities reserved for the party élite.

As the Soviet system collapsed in the late 1980s and early 1990s, so the health system severely worsened as its funding declined dramatically in real terms. Such a situation clearly had some impact on the serious downturn in health statistics noted above. Policy responses to this took a number of forms, chief amongst these being the introduction of health insurance funds, and the decentralization of funding and delivery of services. Health-reform legislation was passed in Russia in 1991, and then in amended form in 1993. This legislation put responsibility for all but 40 of the country's hospitals in the hands of regional government and introduced a system of mandatory medical insurance to be paid by a uniform payroll tax. The health insurance fund would operate alongside central state funding. In reality such reforms, although perhaps necessary, have still fallen far short of what is needed to provide adequate, let alone high-quality, healthcare for the population.

- Health insurance paid for by a payroll tax leaves those not in employment out of the equation, and it is often such people who are more likely to need medical services. A separate insurance fund exists for non-working people, payments into which are supposed to be made from the federal and regional budgets. Payments were officially estimated to fall 75 per cent short of requirements in 2001.
- An official report for President Putin in 2003 found that Russia's health insurance fund receives only a fifth of the amount necessary to adequately sustain the health system.
- The Russian Constitution's guarantee of universal access to healthcare is undermined by the limited range of free provision available. Statistics from the World Bank suggest that over half of all healthcare in Russia is funded from the patient's own pocket.
- Russia's Ministry of Internal Affairs believes that around 7 per cent of the pharmaceutical market is made up of fake medicines.
- A lack of resources to pay for immediate needs is contributing to low levels of investment in infrastructure and equipment, leading to worse conditions and out-of-date treatment.

In keeping with his long-standing emphasis on issues relating to standards of living, President Putin has sought to address health system reform since coming to office. The main proposal, which is yet to come to full fruition, involves supplementing health insurance funds by diverting money from pension funds, which are in a relatively healthy position after several years of government surpluses.

Judicial policy

If there was one area of social policy where the Soviet Union's international reputation plumbed the depths, then it was judicial policy. In the Stalin years (1928–53) around 18 million people suffered in the Gulag forced labour camps – some of them criminals, most of them simply designated as criminals by a system with political and economic values which trumped natural justice at every turn. During the Brezhnev era (1964–82), political prisoners were 'sentenced' to terms in psychiatric hospitals, where they underwent forcible treatment via injection, electric shock and physical restraint. The working assumption seemed to be that anyone foolish enough to doubt the wisdom of the state must be genuinely mad. Throughout the Soviet period, the concept of an independent judiciary remained completely alien. Law was what the Party declared it to be, and judges took their orders from the political authorities, where necessary regardless of the niceties of evidence. Under Soviet law the presumption of 'innocent until proven guilty' was turned on its head.

When the Soviet Union collapsed, Russia inherited not only the attitudes and procedures of the Soviet era, but also many of the personnel. There was no tradition of or training in liberal democratic norms of justice. Consequently, despite reforms over the past decade, many of the old practices still continue:

- The presumption of guilt until proven otherwise is to some extent apparent in the fact that on average 99 per cent of cases in Russian courts result in the conviction of the accused (though in 2002 that average fell to 98 per cent). Anyone attending a Russian court case will be immediately struck by the fact that defendants – whether dangerous or not – give their evidence from inside a cage in the court-room, as if to emphasize the fact that they are almost certainly to be found guilty.
- Courts often depend on the good offices of the local executive for funding, and so to cross the authorities can result in difficulties for the judiciary.
- In the late 1990s the New York-based Human Rights Watch reported that torture 'now appears endemic to the Russian criminal justice system'.
- The International Helsinki Federation for Human Rights wrote a report in 2003 claiming that pre-trial detention, occasionally for long

periods of time, is used in order to break the will of prisoners 'with the intention of eliciting confessions and information'.

This list of apparent failures in the Russian judicial system should not be taken to imply that nothing at all has changed since the Soviet era. At the fundamental level, Russia's constitution, adopted by national referendum on 12 December 1993, forms the basic law of the Russian Federation and is a recognizably liberal democratic document. There is a fundamental commitment within it to the separation of powers and equality of citizens before the law (for more details of the constitution, see Chapter 4). All of Russia's recent leaders, including the last Soviet leader, Mikhail Gorbachev, have committed themselves to the rule of law. Vladimir Putin has repeatedly emphasized that the law should not be applied differentially on political grounds – though his choice of phrase left something to be desired when, in an echo of the Communist Party's commitment to a 'dictatorship of the proletariat', he called for a 'dictatorship of the law'.

Under Boris Yeltsin, Russia ceased to apply the death penalty, in line with the conditions for membership of the Council of Europe. Russian citizens are also now able to take their cases to the European Court of Human Rights. In 2002 a much-trumpeted judicial reform package was introduced by President Putin. Among its provisions was enabling legislation to introduce the constitutional provision of trial by jury on a nationwide basis, as previously it had only been available in limited locations. The reforms also sought to enhance the status and independence of the judiciary by improving judges' pay by 40 per cent, increasing the number of judges, and ending their lifetime tenure and immunity from prosecution. Measures were introduced to enhance the rights of suspects and create a level playing field for defence lawyers in relation to the previously overwhelmingly influential prosecutors. Trials in absentia have been banned; searches, arrests and detention beyond 48 hours must now be sanctioned by courts, rather than by prosecutors; plea bargaining has been introduced for offences with a prison term of less than five years; and the practice of sending criminal cases back for 'additional investigation' – that is, enabling the prosecution to patch up a poor case – has been ended.

As a package of reforms, the measures introduced in 2002 and 2003 are impressive. At the very least they indicate an awareness of continuing problems and of international norms. Nonetheless, the problems with the Russian judicial system are deep-rooted in terms of culture, and it is likely that it will take more than a list of reform measures to change them. The success, or otherwise, of judicial reform is one of the key factors to watch out for in Russia over the coming years. The establishment of a fair and independent legal system, free from political influence and staffed by well-trained lawyers, prosecutors and judges with a commitment to justice would go a long way to ensuring that Russia develops a deeper democracy. So far, under Vladimir Putin, the signs of a shift in that direction are not particularly hopeful. Legal reforms aside, the legal difficulties facing civil society (see Chapter 6) on his watch have increased rather than diminished. In early 2005, Dmitry Kozak, one of the presidential officials behind the judicial reforms, admitted that the public remains convinced that 'the system is corrupt through and through'.

If the Russian judicial system itself leaves a good deal to be desired, then this applies doubly so to the prison network. A report from the Public Centre for Judicial Reform in late 2003 illustrates a situation that is not uncommon across Russia. Prisoners smuggled a mobile phone into their cell in order to call the Centre and publicize the conditions in which they were being held – 76 inmates in a cell designed for 36, icy-cold temperatures, prisoners taking it in turns to sleep on the few cots under threadbare blankets, meals of rice for breakfast and dinner and a watered-down meat-and-potato soup for lunch. This account matches well a similar description from five years' earlier by an American who had spent nearly two years in a Russian prison for possession of a small quantity of marijuana. He, too, describes overcrowding (100 prisoners in a cell for 30, 'shoulder-to-shoulder, like riding in a bus at rush hour'), sleeping in shifts, lice-ridden mattresses, two meals of rice and one of watered-down soup. His conclusion was that 'it's hell on earth ... I'd never seen so many rats, and the cell walls were carpeted in cockroaches'.

Given conditions like those described above, it is not surprising that the Russian prison system is a breeding ground for disease, and particularly for TB. Out of around 800,000 prisoners in Russia, roughly 10 per cent have active TB, and of these a third have the multi-drug resistant strain. The high turnover of prisoners means that each year several hundred thousand prisoners leave the system and go back into the general population, taking the disease with them.

Education

As with the judicial system and the healthcare system, the story of contemporary Russia's educational provision is one of contending on two fronts: first, with the legacy of the Soviet era; second, with the economic difficulties of the post-Soviet years.

In terms of the Soviet legacy, perhaps the most interesting feature of the education system from a political point of view was its propagandistic content. The state taught what it wanted its citizens to know, from primary schoolchildren learning to read about Uncle Lenin and the fluffy cat, to final-year higher-education students desperately swotting up on their compulsory Marxism-Leninism the night before an exam in which they had little interest. Particularly contentious in terms of syllabus content was the history curriculum, with its uncritical praise for all that the Party had done, and its studious avoidance of topics such as the Stalinist terror or the ideas of 'the renegade Trotsky'. English language textbooks included accounts of poverty-stricken Londoners oppressed by the bourgeoisie. Economics and law followed narrow ideological courses, and sociology barely existed until Gorbachev embraced some of its findings to bolster his reform programme in the mid-1980s. And not only was political reliability central to curriculum content, it could also have an influence on admission to the best universities. In the Soviet period the drive to recruit working-class children to higher education gave them priority, but such priority could always be trumped by members of the new ruling class, the Communist Party leadership.

From the viewpoint of the twenty-first century it is perhaps even a little amusing to consider the effect of communist propaganda on the Soviet education system. A far more positive spin on the Soviet education system would emphasize its achievements in providing universal education, and creating a literate and highly educated population with specialists capable of rivalling the world's best. Political bias aside, there was nothing second-rate about the Soviet education system. In the post-Soviet era, however, the difficulties facing the public sector at large swept away much of the good from the old system. Whilst debates about curriculum reform occupied many specialists, schools were undermined by salary arrears, equipment shortages and a lack of teachers. The teaching profession in Russia became so unattractive in the 1990s that by the end of the decade only about half of those graduating from teacher-training institutions went on to teach in schools. The difficulties in attracting teachers were felt especially in remote regions, as the Soviet practice of requiring teachers to work in designated schools on qualification was discontinued. At the tertiary level, Russian higher education became more and more expensive and open to corruption.

Education appears to have come low down the list of priorities of the Russian government in the 1990s, faced as it was by the massive problems of economic and political reform. The major 'achievement' of the 1992 law on education, backed up later by Article 43 of the Russian Constitution, was to break the commitment to universal secondary education of which the Soviet Union had been justly proud. The law guaranteed state-funded education up to year 9, rather than year 11 as had previously been the case, thus opening the way for schools to charge fees for pupils beyond the age of 15.

It may have been that other priorities came before education and prevented serious reform of the system in the 1990s. Just as likely, though, is that barriers to reform came from the relative chaos of Russia's weak state in that decade. Reform attempts were obstructed by an exodus from the classroom by teachers, as real incomes declined or simply were not paid; regions with large ethnic minorities, or even majorities, sought to establish their own systems of education; and funding shortages were exacerbated by problems with budgetary transfers between the regional and federal levels. At the same time it was reported by the education minister in 2001 that up to two million children of school age in Russia do not in fact attend school.

When President Putin came to power in 2000, reform of the education system fitted in with his declared focus on domestic issues. In August 2001 the State Council – a body set up by Putin, with a membership made up of the heads of regions, but with only advisory status – considered the issue of education reform. In a speech to the State Council, Putin called free education 'the cornerstone' of the state system, but talked positively, too, of the contribution to be made by an ordered private system. The major reform announcement was that educational spending would become a national priority. In a reversal of decades of Soviet practice, government spending on education now outstrips spending on defence. The most obvious immediate beneficiaries of this change in policy are teachers, who saw their salaries doubled – to a figure equivalent to a meagre $80 to $100 per month. A further 50 per cent pay rise is promised for 2005.

The reforms of 2001 included a shift to a 12-year schooling system, which would allow pupils to specialize before going on to higher education. In addition, plans were announced for a standard school leaving exam, on which entry to university would be based. This latter reform is being introduced to make entry into higher education more egalitarian, and less prone to the corruption which beset it in the post-Soviet era. Further reforms in the school system include a change in teachers' terms and conditions, so that pay is closely related to hours taught, and moonlighting is diminished. Changes, too, are also being sought in the way in which pupils are taught, with the old Soviet emphasis on rote-learning of facts and figures supposedly giving way to the teaching of independent and creative thinking to pupils.

4
Politics and Government

The collapse of the communist political system in Russia in the period 1989–91 was the end of what had become widely known as the 'command-administrative system'. This was politics by central *diktat*. Power was concentrated at the centre among the senior ranks of the Communist Party, and the function of other elements of the system – parliaments, central government, republican, regional and local authorities – was to put central instructions into practice. Nor was the exercise of power restrained by legality, since laws were only arbitrarily applied, and elements of the legal code, such as the notion of 'anti-Soviet activities', were so broadly interpreted that they were frequently taken to mean any activities of which the authorities disapproved.

Command administrative politics was largely non-political politics. That is to say, what was missing in this political system were information flows, and the free interchange of ideas and alternatives for society. The atmosphere was one of instinctive secrecy and obsessive official control over information presented in the media or through the arts and literature. Russia was largely cut off from foreign influences, both benign and damaging. The use of a particular language of political discourse, the language of Marxism-Leninism, ruled out certain alternative directions of development, such as the use of market mechanisms in the economy. It also deified other practices, such as the leading role of the Communist Party, which at its worst became the belief that the Communist Party collectively was never wrong. There was no role for political opposition, let alone any possibility of opposition one day becoming government, which is the essence of democratic politics. The lack of opposition and the lack of an independent system of police and courts meant that a chronic problem for the system was accountability. In the Stalin period officials were held accountable for their actions via an all-pervasive mass terror, but after the abandonment of widespread terror during the General Secretaryship of Nikita Khrushchev, the system demonstrated inherent tendencies towards corruption and nepotism on a staggering scale.

This was broadly how Russian politics operated in the period before Mikhail Gorbachev's abortive attempts to reform and purify the system,

1985–91. It is the environment within which many of Russia's politicians today cut their political teeth. And, as the Russian cliché goes, 'You can take Ivan Ivanovich out of the Communist Party, but you can't take the Party out of Ivan Ivanovich.' Habits of command, elitism, and of seeing politics not as the comparison of alternatives and a search for compromise but as a means for the political destruction of opponents coexist with new democratic virtues of openness and honesty about the country's problems, compromise, and respect for the electoral choices of ordinary people.

Many observers looking at Russia under President Putin see a country where, after the upheavals of the 1990s, 'non-political politics' has reasserted itself:

- Russia in Putin's second term is something of a political desert, with no real alternative voices or policy proposals being heard;
- it has a constitutionally democratic presidential system but after more than a dozen years of Russian democracy there has not been a genuinely competitive transfer of power;
- President Putin has taken steps to control key media outlets and limit the opportunities available to the political opposition;
- Russia's parliament, since the elections of December 2003, is firmly in the hands of the pro-Putin party, United Russia;
- Russia's government has long been led by prime ministers who declare themselves to be managers rather than politicians. Mikhail Fradkov, appointed in 2004, is no exception; and
- public opinion in Russia has long been sympathetic to 'strong leadership', and now widely associates the term 'democracy' with the political chaos and economic decline of the Yeltsin period.

Despite all of this, however, it would be wrong to say that Russia has returned to a Soviet-type government. For all the echoes of the former regime that can be identified, there have nonetheless been revolutionary changes in Russia's governing structures since 1991.

This chapter surveys postcommunist Russian politics on a number of levels. It begins with the institutional, the formal ordering of power, the 'rules of the game'. However, institutions are clearly not the only source of power. We also need to consider such vague concepts as public feeling or 'national moods' which can impact on politicians and policy-making by a variety of means, including the media and other institutions of civil society, which we do in the next chapter. Informal aspects of politics are of particular relevance given Russia's historical tradition. Power does not often interact with institutions in quite the way that the formal structure suggests. During the Soviet period four constitutions set out the political 'rules of the game' over their respective periods. However, these constitutions masked the true picture, which was that supreme power lay with the Communist Party of the Soviet Union and was exercised by means, such as the power of appointment, that, although not unconstitutional, simply bypassed the constitution. The culture of political behaviour that exalts networks and connections above the formally constituted powers of institutions carried over into the post-Soviet era. This chapter therefore will not only lay out the formal rules of power relations in contemporary Russia, it will also deal with the relative incoherence of power relations within and beyond the formal constitutional framework.

The 1993 constitution

Our starting point is the Russian Constitution passed by national referendum on 12 December 1993. The need for a new constitution for Russia after the collapse of the Soviet Union was clear on three counts – institutional, ideological and legal.

- At the institutional level, the operative constitution in Russia in 1992–93 was the 1978 constitution of the RSFSR (Russian Soviet Federative Socialist Republic) – the old name for Russia in its communist-era existence as one of 15 republics in the Soviet Union. This 1978 constitution was therefore predicated on the existence of an institutional framework which had disappeared in 1991 along with the Soviet state. Chiefly, it implicitly assumed the existence of a one-party state. The Communist Party of the Soviet Union was the institution which had held the Soviet state together. Once this had gone then decision-making processes reverted back to the formal procedures of a constitution that had been written for another political age, and even then had never borne much relation to the way the state was really governed. In particular, the means by which the centre controlled the regions – a relationship known in Russia as the 'power vertical' – virtually disappeared along with the Party.
- At the ideological level, the old constitution adhered to communist ideology in its Marxist-Leninist form, whereas the Russian Federation after 1991 saw itself more as a Western-type liberal state. This makes a fundamental difference to the underlying concept of any constitution. In a liberal state the rights of the individual are supreme. Under Marxist-Leninist ideology, the individual and their rights come second to the rights of and obligations to society and the state.

• At the legal level the need for a new constitution was evident if one considers what constitutions are for. A constitution is supposed to be the fundamental law of a state, containing concepts that if not unchangeable are certainly meant to have a depth of durability. The constitution of the United States, for example, has only been amended some 27 times since its adoption over two centuries ago in 1787. By 1992 the old constitution of the RSFSR had been amended more than 300 times in 14 years; it could scarcely be seen as a fundamental law.

Virtually all politicians in Russia accepted the need for a new constitution after the collapse of the Soviet Union, but despite this it took two years from the end of the USSR for the new constitution to come into existence. The primary cause of this delay was the power struggle between President Yeltsin and the parliament in 1992–93 (see Chapter 1). Having abandoned Marxism-Leninism and chosen a democratic path, the Russian Federation and its political élite had to decide on their preferred form of democracy. The two key issues to be resolved were the relationship between president and parliament, and the relationship between the centre and the regions. These issues of course are central elements of the 'rules of the game' and therefore of the constitution.

President vs parliament, 1992–93

The failure to decide between presidentialism and parliamentarism held up agreement over a new constitution. Participants in this dispute between president and parliament couched their arguments largely in terms of which system better suited the nascent democracy of Russia in the immediate post-Soviet era. However, the dispute had as much to do with the past and present as with democratic guarantees for the future. It was a power struggle between parliament and the president fought in terms of not only the relative democratic legitimacy of these two institutions, but also in the end the extent to which they could command the use of force.

The Russian word 'soviet' literally means 'council' or, at the highest levels, 'parliament'. As its name suggests, the Soviet Union throughout its existence had claimed to be run by a series of workers' councils which culminated with a central Supreme Soviet where state power in theory lay. As we have seen, in practice power lay with the Communist Party, which dominated the soviets and reduced them to virtual rubber-stamping bodies throughout most of the twentieth century. Only following on from Gorbachev's reforms in the late 1980s did some real power begin to return to the soviets, and particularly to the Russian soviet, or parliament. Therefore, at the collapse of the Soviet Union the Russian parliament enjoyed more power than it had known before. Many members were understandably reluctant to see this long-denied power swiftly removed again and given to the president, particularly since the parliament had been reasonably democratically elected in 1990.

The president on the other hand could lay claim to a more recent, and arguably more democratic, mandate. Boris Yeltsin had been elected as Russia's first-ever democratically chosen leader in June 1991. Not only had he won the election, but he had won it overwhelmingly. Yeltsin had received a majority over all the other candidates combined, thereby negating the need for the second round of votes provided for in electoral rules. He believed, with some justification from opinion polls, that the people favoured a presidential system.

As if to demonstrate its inadequacy as a fundamental law, the old constitution offered no clear way out of the dispute between president and parliament. The obvious solution would have been a general election or binding referendum. However, only parliament had the constitutional right to implement such a course of action, and was unwilling to exercise this right and dissolve itself mid-term. President Yeltsin wanted to dissolve parliament but was constitutionally barred from doing so. The impasse held up policy-making and the enactment of a new constitution until September 1993, when Yeltsin unilaterally – and, strictly speaking, illegally – dissolved parliament. Some parliamentary deputies refused to accept this dissolution and remained under armed siege in the parliament until, provoked by attempts by armed parliamentary supporters to seize the central television building in Moscow, President Yeltsin ordered a military attack on the parliament building in early October which left over a hundred defenders dead.

The 1993 Russian Constitution, therefore, was drawn up against the background of the power struggle between president and parliament and near civil war on the streets of Moscow. More importantly, it was drawn up by the winning side in this dispute – the presidency. The resulting constitution consequently provides for a strong presidency and a comparatively weak parliament (see Box 4.1). Under this constitution Russia has an executive (president, presidential administration, and government) almost wholly independent of parliament. The legislature (parliament) consists of upper and lower chambers, the Federation Council and the State Duma respectively, known collectively as the Federal Assembly. The document also establishes a constitutionally independent judiciary, a Constitutional Court and a Supreme Court. Other sections of the constitution define

---

Box 4.1   The powers of the President of the Russian Federation

The president ...

- is head of state
- is supreme commander in chief of the armed forces
- issues decrees, the implementation of which is mandatory throughout Russia
- directs foreign policy
- nominates the prime minister
- appoints, dismisses and has the right to chair the government
- forms the presidential administration and the Security Council
- schedules elections to the State Duma
- dissolves the State Duma (according to constitutional procedures).

---

the Russian Federation as a democratic, law-based state where a range of human rights are observed.

This presidential constitution was put before the Russian people in a referendum on 12 December 1993, alongside a general election of deputies to the Federal Assembly. The 1993 general election therefore chose members of a parliament whose very existence would depend on the result of the constitutional referendum. To critics, then, even the very process by which Russia adopted its new democratic constitution was not entirely democratic. Referendum and election happened simultaneously, making it difficult for anyone running for election to parliament to urge a vote against the constitution which would create the very parliament in which they were seeking a seat.

In addition to a democratic deficit in terms of procedure, the actual voting on the constitution did not indicate the whole-hearted support of the Russian people for their new system of government. To be binding the referendum on the constitution had to attract a turnout of over 50 per cent of the electorate. In the event the constitution was adopted by 58 per cent of the vote with a 55 per cent turnout. That is, it was adopted on the basis of the votes of under one in three of the Russian electorate, amidst accusations from many quarters about falsification in the course of the referendum.

These difficulties surrounding the adoption of the constitution mean that the method by which constitutional amendments are introduced has considerable political significance. The procedure is quite elaborate. Two-thirds of each chamber of parliament and two-thirds of regional legislatures must approve changes. In the case of changes to chapters 1, 2 and 9, which are the sections containing the basic principles of the constitution (democracy, rule of law, the structure of the federation, as well as bans on official ideology and a state religion), individual rights and constitutional amendment, there is an additional need for the convening of a Constitutional Assembly and, if this assembly so decides, a national referendum in which at least half the electorate must participate. Given the difficulty of fulfilling the requirements for this procedure it is clearly difficult to bring about constitutional change by constitutional means.

Executive

The formal powers of the presidency in the Russian Federation enable him or her to rule with relatively little reference to the parliament. The president ultimately appoints the government and decides on the size and personnel of the influential presidential administration. This latter body (see Box 4.2) oversees all areas of policy and complements, or duplicates, the work of government ministries and parliamentary committees in much

---

Box 4.2   The presidential administration, 2004

Leadership of the administration

Head of administration, 2 deputy heads, 7 presidential aides

↓

Other key officials

Including presidential press secretary, head of presidential protocol, 9 presidential advisers, 7 presidential representatives in the regions, two presidential representatives in upper and lower houses of parliament

↓

Branches of the administration

Including the office of the Security Council, the State-Legal Directorate, and the Directorate for the Civil Service

↓

Commissions

Including Presidential Commission for Human Rights

↓

Councils

Including Council for Interaction with Religious Organizations

Source: Data from www.kremlin.ru

---

the same way as the Communist Party of the Soviet Union used to duplicate and overrule ministries and Supreme Soviet committees. It is the presidential administration which usually prepares the decrees – binding throughout the Russian Federation – issued by the president, though as we note later, the number of such decrees has decreased as the number of laws passed by parliament has increased.

Within the presidential administration, potentially the most important body is the Security Council, which is the only institution in the presidential structure to be specifically identified in the constitution. This council has sweeping powers to oversee social, political and economic threats to security, and it serves as an 'inter-agency' body bringing together key political actors and the 'power ministries' of defence, foreign affairs, the emergency ministry, security and foreign intelligence. The Security Council exercises its power under the president and so at times has been influential and at times peripheral, according to the president's wishes. There is a fluidity within the presidential administration as the president can freely set up and close down different executive bodies, for example between 1996 and 1998 a Defence Council existed to rival the Security Council. By the middle of 2002, the presidential administration employed around 2,000 civil servants and consisted of four main directorates, 14 directorates, six commissions, four councils and three other units. In 2004 the structure once again changed, with Vladimir Putin declaring that the size of the presidential administration should be reduced.

Some observers, with a knowledge of the way the Soviet system worked, draw parallels between the presidential administration and the old Party Central Committee structures of the Soviet Union. Just as in the Soviet era, although there was a parliament (Supreme Soviet) and a government, the Party had its own structures which 'shadowed' all policy areas and exercised real decision-making power, so the presidential administration operates in contemporary Russia. Furthermore, one of President Putin's first major institutional changes in 2000 was to appoint seven presidential representatives to cover the whole of Russia in federal districts – a move which many initially saw as recreating the 'power vertical' missing since the Soviet years.

The parallel between the presidential administration and Soviet-era Party structures is neat, but certainly not an exact match. The presidential administration in Russia obviously does have key influence, its primary function after all is to advise and support the president, whose powers are far-reaching. However, if a directorate under the president draws up a draft law, it still has to be passed by parliament. Up until the elections of 2003, parliament was certainly no longer the rubber-stamping institution of the

Soviet era; since those elections, however, the chances of a Putin-backed proposal being rejected by parliament are very slim. However, landslide parliamentary victories are not unknown in democratic countries the world over – it is when they become a permanent state that democracy suffers. In this regard, the next parliamentary election in December 2007 will be key.

In terms of the division of labour between the presidential administration and government, President Putin has been happy to let government govern in many key areas – particularly economic – and indeed even moved one of his closest advisers, Sergei Ivanov, from presidential administration to government in 2001, when he left his post as Secretary of the Security Council to become Defence Minister.

Legislature

Russia's parliament, or Federal Assembly, is made up of two chambers. The lower chamber, the State Duma, consists of 450 members elected, up until 2007, by an unusual combination of proportional representation and 'first-past-the-post' systems. Half of the deputies have gained their seats under a party-list system, where voters choose one party from all those standing and parties receiving over 5 per cent of the national vote take an appropriate proportion of 225 Duma seats. The remaining 225 deputies have been selected on a constituency basis, and may or may not have had a party affiliation.

However, from 2007 onwards, two significant changes are planned for parliamentary elections. First, all deputies will be elected by means of proportional representation under the party-list system; and second, the barrier which parties must overcome in order to gain seats in the parliament will rise to 7 per cent of the national vote.

The upper house, the Federation Council, represents Russia's 89 regions, each of which has two seats regardless of the size of the region. The upper house has already employed three different methods for selecting its members since its foundation in 1993. Its first convocation consisted of members elected on a regional basis at the 1993 general election, two for each region. From 1995 until the Putin era, deputies gained their seats in the upper chamber on an *ex officio* basis; these seats were taken by the heads of, respectively, the region's legislature and executive. In the latter case this would be the governor or president of a region, or, in the case of the 'city regions' of Moscow and St Petersburg, the mayor. Regional heads were, until 2005, elected on a regular basis. Now, however, they are appointed by the president, and ratified by the regional assembly.

When Vladimir Putin came to power in 2000, he put forward proposals, accepted by the Federation Council, that ended the filling of the upper house on this *ex officio* basis. Instead, as the terms of office of each region's heads came to an end they were replaced in the upper house by representatives of the regional legislature and executive, rather than by the heads of the legislatures and executives themselves. By way of compensation, the heads of Russia's 89 regions were given membership of a new body created by President Putin, namely the advisory State Council.

Power relations between president and parliament

Although not entirely toothless, the parliament's powers in relation to the president are weak, and should differences between the two institutions prove irreconcilable the last word almost always rests with the president. For example, the constitution allows parliamentary involvement in government formation on one issue only, that of the appointment of the prime minister; the president nominates a candidate whose appointment must be confirmed by parliament. However, should parliament not confirm the candidate, then the president, after three rejections of his nominee, dissolves parliament. Box 4.3 lists Russia's prime ministers since 1992.

There are three other levers of influence with which a legislature might exert its influence over an executive president. First, through its legislative power, that is by means of passing or blocking laws. Under the terms of the constitution, a law passed by parliament outranks a presidential decree, even though the latter has the force of law pending any legislative act which supersedes it. Gradually, therefore, the influence of

---

Box 4.3   Russia's prime ministers since 1992

Viktor Chernomyrdin	December 1992 – March 1998
Sergei Kirienko	March 1998 – August 1998

(Chernomyrdin unsuccessfully nominated August–September 1998)

Yevgeny Primakov	September 1998 – May 1999
Sergei Stepashin	May 1999 – August 1999
Vladimir Putin	August 1999 – March 2000

(Putin was acting president from 31 December 1999)

Mikhail Kasyanov	May 2000 – February 2004
Mikhail Fradkov	February 2004 –

parliament is increasing, as the more laws are passed, the less legislative space there is for presidential decrees. In the early period of the post-communist transition in Russia there was a legislative gap in Russia, which was filled to some extent by presidential decrees drawn up and signed in their thousands. If the parliament passes a law it is submitted to the president who either signs it, or sends it back to the parliament. If the parliament then passes the law a second time, unaltered, the president is constitutionally obliged to sign it. In this case then the last word appears to lie with the parliament.

Second, parliament might pass a vote of no confidence in the government. To force the president to take action such a vote has to be carried by a majority of the 450 members of the State Duma twice in three months. Even then the president may decide to either dismiss the government or dissolve the Duma.

Third, the final sanction which the legislature might apply against the executive is impeachment of the president. Under the Russian constitution this procedure is not easy; the only grounds allowed are those of treason or 'some other grave crime', and the process can only be completed with the agreement of the Supreme Court, the Constitutional Court and a two-thirds majority of both legislative chambers. Although half-hearted impeachment procedures were begun by the Communist Party of the Russian Federation against Boris Yeltsin over his decision to go to war against Chechnya, there was never any serious prospect that the stringent conditions for impeachment might be met.

What sort of politics?

The institutional relationship between executive and legislature has implications for the sort of politics which exists in contemporary Russia. Much of the 'politicking' which has gone on within and around the institution of the parliament in the post-Soviet years has had little impact on actual policy formation.

To illustrate this, let us consider the general elections of December 1993, December 1995 and December 1999 (Tables 4.1 and 4.2). The most popular single parties in these elections were, in 1993, the extreme-right Liberal Democratic Party of Russia and, in 1995 and 1999, the nationalist anti-reform Communist Party of the Russia Federation. These parties headed the party-list ballot with around a quarter of the national vote. Nonetheless, despite the vast effort put into electioneering and the inevitable wide coverage by domestic and foreign media, these elections

Table 4.1   Percentage of votes on the party-list ballot
for the Russian Duma, 1993 and 1995

Party	1993	1995
Agrarian Party	8.0	3.8
Communists	12.4	22.3
Liberal Democrats	22.9	11.2
Our Home Is Russia	–	10.1
Russia's Democratic Choice	15.5	3.9
Russian Unity and Accord	6.8	0.4
Yabloko	7.9	6.9

Table 4.2   Percentage of votes on the party-list ballot
for the Russian Duma, December 1999 and December
2003

Party	1999	2003
United Russia	–	37.6
Unity	23.3	
Fatherland-All Russia	13.3	
Communist Party of the Russian Federation	24.3	12.6
Liberal Democratic Party of Russia	6.0	11.5
Rodina ('Motherland')	–	9.0
Russian Democratic Party 'Yabloko'	5.9	4.3
Union of Right Forces	8.5	4.0
Agrarian Party of Russia	–	3.6

Note: United Russia was formed by an amalgamation
of, primarily, Unity and Fatherland-All Russia.

had no direct means with which to change the regime. The prime minister
remained the same, the president of course remained in office, and the
'victors' could not even successfully demand so much as a single minor
ministerial position.

This divorcing of much 'public politics' from the substance of politics
(that is, power) can serve to alienate people from the political process.
Furthermore, the parliament becomes marginalized, encouraging gesture
politics and inhibiting the direct representation of the electorate. The real
levers of power are in the hands of the president who, although popularly

elected, has little subsequent check on his powers by the people or a party organization.

Despite the number of elections which have taken place in Russia since June 1991 (four parliamentary and four presidential), Russia has not yet experienced a democratic change of regime. Parliamentary elections do not change the regime. And in terms of the presidential elections, Yeltsin won twice (1991 and 1996) before resigning early in order to provide an electoral advantage for his chosen successor, Vladimir Putin. The advantage created was two-fold. First, Putin could campaign from the position of incumbent, since as prime minister he became Acting President on Yeltsin's resignation. Second, the election had been due in June 2000; by resigning early Yeltsin forced an election in March, as the constitution stipulates that a presidential election must take place within three months of a vacancy. Yeltsin knew what he was going to do, and could prepare his team accordingly. Opposition figures, however, had to go to the polls earlier than expected.

Since President Putin came to power, the relationship between the executive and the legislature has shifted a little from that of the Yeltsin years. Under Yeltsin, as we have noted above, the influence of parliament on policy-making was minimal. Yeltsin preferred to issue presidential decrees, as he could not be certain of a parliamentary majority. President Putin has shown a clear preference for passing laws through parliament rather than issuing presidential decrees. This is largely due to the fact that the political make-up of the parliament elected in December 1999 meant that Putin was repeatedly able to secure a majority for his proposals in his first term by making use of a 'shifting majority' often made up of different factions on different issues. Since the 2003 parliamentary elections, Putin has an even clearer and more stable majority of supportive deputies in the Duma (lower house of parliament) (Figure 4.1).

Figure 4.1   Distribution of seats in the state Duma, 2004

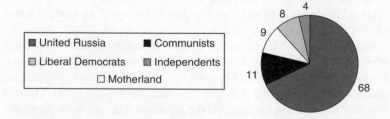

Ideas in Russian politics: political forces in Russia today

The elections for the lower house of the Russian parliament held in December 2003 provide a useful indication of the strength of the various streams of political thought in Russia today (Table 4.2).

The clear winner in the 2003 parliamentary elections was United Russia, the party which backed, and received the backing of, President Putin. In keeping with Yeltsin before him, Putin is not actually a member of his chosen party, ostensibly because as President he must be seen to represent the Russian people as a whole, though perhaps in reality this stance has more to do with an unwillingness to owe his position to a transient political party. The political position of Vladimir Putin is reflected in United Russia, whose representatives in parliament style themselves as pragmatic managers, and certainly not politicians. What then of the remaining forces in Russian politics?

The communists and the agrarians

After the collapse of the Soviet Union the previously monolithic Communist Party virtually disintegrated and was briefly banned on the territory of the Russian Federation. By the time of the 1993 Duma elections, however, a Communist Party of the Russian Federation had reemerged, and it rapidly became the largest party in terms of membership and votes received (see Table 4.1) with its leader, Gennadii Zyuganov, becoming the closest challenger to Boris Yeltsin in the presidential election of 1996 (Table 4.3).

The Communists maintained a level of around a quarter of all votes casts in the party-list ballot in the elections of 1995 and 1999, before falling to around half of that in 2003 (Tables 4.1 and 4.2). For much of this period the Agrarian Party retained relatively close links with the Communists and shared some of the votes on the statist left, before splitting

Table 4.3   Russia's presidential election, second round, July 1996

Candidate	%
Boris Yeltsin	53.8
Gennadii Zyuganov	40.3
Against both candidates	4.8

in 1999 with some gravitating towards what was to become United Russia and others remaining with the Communists.

At their revolutionary peak, in the decades before and after their seizure of power in 1917, the Communist Party represented, above all, the young industrial workers inhabiting and building the cities of the new Russia. By the 1990s the Communists could fairly accurately be characterized as the party of the elderly and the rural. They became the conservative option for those who had lost out in the upheavals of the 1990s. Increasingly their ideas – at the electoral level, if not in the detail of party programmes – moved away from Marxism-Leninism and embraced Russian/Soviet nationalism. Zyuganov wrote repeatedly about the restoration of Russian power and pride, and ideas associated with the Communists included the alleged attempts of the West to destroy Russia through poor economic advice, military encirclement and 'cultural genocide'.

There is little doubt that amongst the reasons for the Communists' relative decline in the elections of 2003 – in which they nonetheless finished second – is the sense that under Putin, as opposed to Yeltsin, the ruling regime is no longer wholly antagonistic to the Soviet era, and is itself set on restoring national pride and great power status, as well as repeatedly focusing its rhetoric on the need to raise the standard of living of the Russian people.

The nationalists

For some time in the 1990s, the more alarmist observers predicted the emergence of an extreme nationalist regime in Russia. Analysts have repeatedly raised the question of the 'Weimar syndrome' in Russia, drawing comparisons with the German state which gave way to Nazism in the early 1930s. The similarities are clear – a great power humiliated, a (Cold) war lost, and an economy in ruins. But the differences, too, are evident – in particular the lack of, indeed disdain for, ideology in the Putin regime. Nonetheless, fears of fascism did not spring from nowhere. In 1993, in post-Soviet Russia's first democratic elections, the far-right – and misleadingly named – Liberal Democratic Party, led by Vladimir Zhirinovsky, gained almost a quarter of the popular vote (Table 4.1). The Liberal Democrats' vote has fluctuated in subsequent elections (Tables 4.1 and 4.2) but remains significant, although the sense of apprehension and fear surrounding its surprise appeal in 1993 has dissipated a little as Zhirinovsky has become to some extent a licensed maverick in the political establishment – expected to give the outrageous quote, occasionally assault opponents, and yet nonetheless his party regularly votes with the government.

Votes for Zhirinovsky's Liberal Democratic Party, with its somewhat eclectic platform and personalized nature, are by no means the only measure of the strength of nationalist ideas and their varying forms of expression in Russia today.

First, opinion polls show widespread xenophobic attitudes, a fairly entrenched level of support for broadly nationalist and authoritarian stances such as the need for a strong leader, and a rejection of 'Western paths' in favour of unspecified Russian variants.

Second, throughout the past decade major contributions have been made to the literature on the Russian nation and its unique destiny in the world. Writers such as Dugin and Platonov have expressed extreme nationalist ideals in a literary and philosophical manner which feeds into deep-seated popular notions and builds on the difficulties experienced by many Russians in the post-Soviet era.

In the elections of 2003, not only did Zhirinovsky's party receive almost 12 per cent of the vote, but the big new arrival on the scene was the 'Rodina' (Motherland) block, which gained 9 per cent of the vote. Rodina's rise serves as a further indication of the strength of nationalist ideas in Russia today. Combined with votes for the Liberal Democratic Party, overtly nationalist groups received over 20 per cent of the vote in the 2003 elections. Throw in the fact that the communists are themselves strongly nationalist, and that Putin's regime has adopted the rhetoric of a strong Russia building on its own unique qualities and history, and it is hard not to see nationalism, in its various guises, as the most widespread instinct of the Russian voter.

The liberals

Having briefly explored the strength of communist and nationalist ideas in Russia, let us consider the liberals. Liberal reformers, advocating Western-style democracy and economic reforms, were supposed to be Russia's future after the collapse of the communist regime. Some would argue that they remain so, and that votes for United Russia and for Putin himself represent majority support for a democratic and economic path uniquely suited to Russia.

The argument is that the brash and ill-considered introduction of alien Western concepts to Russia in the 1990s not only did not work as well as predicted, but also received the opprobrium of the Russian people.

'Democracy' became a derogatory term, and, according to this view, a leader like Putin represents the best that supporters of market reforms and democracy can hope for in Russia at the moment. As the billionaire Mikhail Khodorkovsky wrote from his prison cell where he awaited charges brought against him by the Russian state:

> Putin is of course not a liberal nor a democrat, but nonetheless he is more liberal and more democratic than 70 per cent of the population of our country.

Such a view is backed up when considering the collapse of support for the overtly Western-oriented liberal forces in Russia in the 2003 general election. The two main liberal parties, Yabloko and the Union of Right Forces, both failed to pass the 5 per cent barrier necessary to gain seats in the lower house of parliament under the party-list side of the ballot (Table 4.2). The liberal reformers of the 1990s appear to be associated in the public eye – rightly or wrongly – with the 'get rich quick' privatizations of the 1990s and the simultaneous economic downturn for most Russians. There is no doubt that by the beginning of Putin's second term liberalism in Russia was in crisis. Vladimir Ryzhkov, one of the few liberal politicians to win a seat in the Duma in the 2003 election, reported his attempts to set up a liberal deputies group in the 450-member lower house of parliament in 2004. Ryzhkov's proud boast that 'there are already seven of us' revealed how far the liberals had fallen in political terms since their heyday in the early 1990s (Table 4.4).

It is too soon, however, to say that liberalism is dead in Russia, and opinion polls assessing political attitudes remain ambiguous. For example, although polls reveal a high level of xenophobia in Russia, other polls indicate that this stance is shifting amongst younger respondents. For a number of years two features have been apparent in Russian opinion polls. First, respondents are more hostile to the abstract concept of 'democracy' than to specific democratic values such as freedom of association or freedom of speech. Second, and to generalize, the older the respondent, the more illiberal the response.

Table 4.4   Party-list votes for liberal parties in Russia's parliamentary elections (%)

Party	1993	1995	1999	2003
Russia's Choice	15.5	3.9	–	–
Yabloko	7.9	6.9	5.9	4.3
Union of Right Forces	–	–	8.5	4.0

Away from opinion polls, there are further reasons to not announce the death of liberalism in Russia quite yet:

• First, Russia's constitution remains firmly within the liberal democratic tradition, and legal reforms at least suggest the possibility of progress towards a more law-based state, even if unfair, apparently politically-motivated trials remain a feature of Russian life (see Chapter 3).
• Second, there would be far less talk of liberalism in crisis had the liberal parties managed to avoid factional in-fighting and present a united front at the 2003 election. Although the two major liberal parties have different emphases, poor relations between their leaders also undermined cooperation. A combined liberal party would certainly, excepting electoral fraud, have passed the 5 per cent barrier necessary to gain seats in the Duma. It may well have matched the much lauded 'success' of Rodina (which polled 9 per cent).
• Third, international prestige and engagement is important to Russia, and potential membership of the World Trade Organization or continued membership of the G8 would be put at risk by a decisive turn away from liberalism towards authoritarianism.

The Supreme Court and the Constitutional Court

Constitutional government in the liberal model requires the existence of an independent judiciary. In Russia the highest judicial bodies are the Constitutional Court, the Superior Court of Arbitration, and the Supreme Court. The Supreme Court oversees the general judicial process, and the Superior Court of Arbitration is the highest judicial organ for the resolution of economic disputes. In the political sphere the Constitutional Court has most influence, interpreting the constitution and mediating in constitutional disputes between the organs of power.

The relationship of the judiciary to the politics of any country springs largely from the question of its independence or otherwise. In the Russian Federation, judges are constitutionally independent. That they are appointed on the recommendation of the president does not necessarily impinge on this independence. Appointment by the executive occurs in both the United Kingdom and the United States of America. Judicial independence is strengthened by lengthy tenure; as the length of tenure increases so the likelihood that the judge will be dealing with the politicians or even the regime that appointed him or her decreases. However, as we noted in Chapter 3, there are still serious concerns about the independence of the judiciary from the state in Russia, at both regional and national level. Although this is not universally so, some rulings in favour of the authorities seem sufficiently perverse to arouse suspicion of collusion.

In its early years following the collapse of the Soviet Union, Russia's constitutional court devoted most of its energies to highly politicized debates surrounding the issue of the separation of powers. Its chief justice, Valerii Zorkin, was given to making political statements, and as a result the court's rulings against Boris Yeltsin on a number of occasions were interpreted by many observers as being based more on political preference than on judicial procedure. After the parliamentary-presidential conflict of 1993 the court was suspended, and reintroduced, with slightly amended procedures, in early 1995. Since then its reputation has gradually improved; a leading US observer has termed Russia's Constitutional Court in the early twenty-first century 'a fair and even-handed tribunal of constitutional justice ... translating possibly contentious political disputes into manageable judicial issues and providing a forum for negotiating change through constitutional adjudication' (Sharlet, 2001).

Institutions and political behaviour: Yeltsin and Putin

Yeltsin

Many observers argue that a presidential constitution is an advantage in a country undergoing radical transition to democracy, as it enables rapid decision-making and a clear course to be set, in preference to the almost inevitable compromises and 'two steps forward, one step back' of parliamentary procedure. Although there is an apparent logic in this thinking, the flaw with presidentialism is that it places too much emphasis on the individual. This overemphasis comes in two senses:

- First, much depends on the particular character and beliefs of that individual. There is no guarantee that he will use his or her power to bring about democratic reform, as opposed to constructing an own power base.
- Second, there is the problem that the regime becomes identified with one person. Such a personalistic approach undermines institution-building.

In the case of Russia under Boris Yeltsin, both these downsides of presidentialism became apparent. In terms of his character and beliefs, Yeltsin was used to being boss. This trait had been with him since childhood, it was nurtured during his years as First Secretary of the Communist Party in the Sverdlovsk region at a time when first secretaries were given almost unlimited power in their regions. When Yeltsin came to Moscow in the mid-1980s he did not cut it as a 'team player'. He was sacked from the politburo in 1986, and when in 1991 he used his position as President of Russia to facilitate the break-up of the Soviet Union, he did so in a manner which made his personal antagonism to Gorbachev apparent to the world. As George Breslauer argues, 'the urge to rule with as few institutional constraints as possible followed Yeltsin into the Russian presidency' (Breslauer, 2001).

Breslauer characterizes Yeltsin's style of leadership as patriarchal, with the president as the benevolent tsar overseeing his court, dispensing and withdrawing patronage according to his will. Unsurprisingly Yeltsin became identified with the system which had had no existence without him. However, he did little to encourage formal institutions and procedures to fill the space between his personal position and the people. For example, whilst ostensibly presiding over the formation of a multiparty democracy, he refused to join a party, and in the 1993 constitution the post of vice-president disappeared, thereby removing another potential institutional limit on the president.

Ironically, this lack of institutional machinery around the president during the Yeltsin era served to weaken his power in important areas. Two such areas became Vladimir Putin's domestic policy priorities on taking office:

- First, under Yeltsin the federal government struggled to control the regions. The lack of an institutional 'power vertical' – such as the Communist Party of the Soviet Union had provided – coupled with Yeltsin's personalistic style of rule contributed to a series of 'bilateral' agreements, as the leaders of most regions haggled over their own unique arrangement with the centre.
- Second, the lack of strong and identifiable 'party of power' meant that in his re-election campaign of 1996 President Yeltsin relied heavily for support on a number of rich businessmen, known collectively as 'the oligarchs', who were subsequently rewarded with presidential largesse to further their ambitions in politics, finance and the media. Corruption became endemic and a parallel can be drawn between the lack of obedience to the law in society and lack of adherence to institutional norms in politics. The maintenance of the Yeltsin regime depended heavily then on perceived trade-offs between the regime and alternative power bases, such as regional leaders, big business and the media. Such trade-offs required engagement and 'give and take' not best suited to formal institutional channels.

Putin

Under President Putin there has been a significant shift away from this style. Putin moved swiftly to present a more ordered approach, in comparison to the disorder of the Yeltsin years. Under Putin the post-Soviet era has ended in the sense that Russia is no longer experiencing the transitional chaos of the Yeltsin years, when almost every policy seemed to aim at being as 'post' the Soviet Union as possible. Not of course that everything in the Russian polity, economy and society is sorted and static; but rather that under Vladimir Putin there is a more settled and familiar air about policy. The great upheavals of privatization, democratic institutionalization, and the establishment of a form of federalism have by and large passed.

Gone, too, is the iconoclastic disdain for the Soviet era *per se*. Putin's view is that although Soviet communism proved to be an historical cul-de-sac, the real achievements of the Soviet regime should not be disowned but celebrated. Instead of the 'what will happen next?' momentum of Yeltsin's transition, Putin's presidency has adopted an approach which is more 'what you see is what you get'. This is twenty-first century Russia:

- a democracy of sorts, but distinctively Russian, with a regime likely to take action if any opposition party looks like getting too near to power;
- an economic policy struggling to break free of endemic corruption and seeing a market economy with state influence at key points as the way ahead; and
- a civil society fenced on every side with new laws on religion, on political parties, on social organizations, on foreigners, on the media, and on extremists.

President Putin's popularity levels have remained remarkably high in his first years in office (see Table 4.5). Whatever the reasons behind his

Table 4.5   Result of Russia's presidential election, 2004

Candidate	%
Vladimir Putin	71.3
Nikolai Kharitonov (Communist)	13.7
Sergei Glazev (Motherland)	4.1
Irina Khakamada (Liberal)	3.8
Oleg Malyshkin ('Liberal Democratic Party of Russia')	2.0

popularity, not one of the opposition forces in Russia today appear to have any chance of gaining power in the near future. Putin has backed the formation of an avowedly non-ideological political party, United Russia, with the intention of creating a political vehicle of support for the regime. Its very name sums up much of the Putin approach to politics – the idea of politics as competing approaches and ideologies is to be replaced by the concept of management; management of democracy, of the economy, of global affairs.

It is nonetheless difficult for any politician to remain popular over a lengthy period of time. With an acquiescent parliament and strong control over Russia's regions, Putin is seen to be in a position of significant power – although the more responsibilities vested in one man, the less detailed knowledge he can have of each area of responsibility. With this power comes responsibility and – when things go wrong – blame. Such a situation has the potential to lead to a rapid fall in popularity should circumstances dictate.

The most important factor to take into account when judging the Putin presidency will be what happens at the end of his second term in 2008. If he makes way for a democratically elected successor in the constitutionally prescribed manner then his legacy will be largely positive; if he seeks some way of clinging to power, then there will be a crisis of democracy in Russia.

5
The Economy

Post-Soviet transition in Russia has meant more than political transition in the direction of a democracy, it has also meant the transformation of a state-controlled command economy towards a market-based economic system. Just as the previous chapter noted the difficulties of the ongoing process of political change, so economic reforms have seen periodic crisis and collapse accompanying progress. As with moves towards democracy, market reforms remain incomplete.

This chapter begins with an overview of the nature of the Soviet economic system and the particularly difficult legacy which it left for an independent Russia emerging in 1991. We then briefly map out the headline features of the Russian economy over two distinct periods: the initial reform moves from 1992 to the financial crisis of 1998; and the years of impressive economic growth from 1999 to 2005. Having established our main themes, the chapter deals in more depth with key features of the Russian economy, namely resource dependence, the legal environment, trade, capital flight and foreign investment.

The Soviet planning system

The economic system adopted after Stalin's forced industrialization of the 1930s (see Chapter 1) was often termed 'command planning' (Box 5.1).

The economic theorists, from Marx onwards, who had supported a planned form of political economy had hoped that it would have a number of advantages (Brus and Laski, 1989). Rational economic planning would prevent the waste caused by cyclical variations in the market economy such as mass unemployment and machines sitting idle during recessions. Resources would no longer be frittered away for useless purposes such as advertising. Elimination of private ownership would eliminate the 'exploitation of man by man' as unscrupulous capitalists appropriated surplus value to themselves. Planning would also ensure equitable distribution: 'from each according to his ability, to each according to his needs' would be the formula for distribution in a communist

---

Box 5.1   Main features of a planned economy

- State or collective ownership of almost all economic resources (some small scale agricultural production for personal use was allowed on private plots).
- Production decisions made by state planners, with economic units (factories, farms, and so on) given production targets, usually for quantity (gross output).
- Prices for all goods and services set by state planners.
- Distribution decisions also made by the planners – factories and farms instructed what to do with their output.
- A permanent bias to heavy industry, and in particular defence, and away from consumption – this was not of course a systemic requirement, but a policy decision sustained by the interests of powerful groups within the Soviet state.
- Largely monopolistic organization of industry in order to exploit economies of scale.

---

economy. Since their decisions would be able to take all factors into account, planners would be able to ensure that the full costs of economic activity, including so-called 'externalities' such as pollution, would be taken into account in making economic decisions. There would also be important motivational effects: since people were working for the good of each other, rather than for the benefit of private individuals, they would work harder. Abolition of commercial secrecy and a more rational organization of production would both lead to greater efficiency. For all these reasons, socialism would supposedly prove itself to be an economic system superior to capitalism.

The reality of the planned economy represented an enormous contrast to these hopes. To be sure there were some benefits for the country and individuals. Prices for basic goods were low and stable, and basic services were provided for free. The plan proved a successful means for rapidly industrializing the Soviet Union in the first place – albeit at great human cost – since it enabled resources to be concentrated in the areas of priority to the state. However, there were countless problems (see Box 5.2).

Economic decline

Despite problems from the start, planning had proved a successful means of creating a heavy industrial base in the Soviet Union. This industrialization was a method of generating economic growth by

---

Box 5.2   The problems of economic planning

- There was a constant problem of shortages. This was partly because if one part of the plan failed to be achieved, knock on effects followed. For much of the Soviet period consumers had to suffer empty shops and queues for the most basic necessities as a fact of everyday life.
- The plan, although ostensibly designed to foster continuing growth, was too static a conception of economic activity. A very difficult issue for planners to confront was how to manage change. For economic units to alter processes or improve products takes time and is disruptive in the short term, which threatens plan fulfilment and consequent bonuses. There was little incentive to innovate arising out of the possibility of large profits accruing to individuals who think up something new (Schumpeter, 1934) and so the economy had an inclination towards stagnation.
- Quality tended to take second place to quantity. Since it was the most measurable attribute, quantity of output tended to be the key target in plans. However, quantity is only one of a number of desirable features of production. Others include quality, range, style, and so forth. Too often plans were formally fulfilled, but the quality was so poor that end-users could not use what had been produced.
- There was a propensity to waste, as economic units had little incentive to economize on inputs of raw materials and labour. In the last instance, they were judged on achieving their targets, however many inputs they used to do so. This contributed to the fact that, in the view of some economists, much Soviet industry, far from adding value, was actually value-destroying, with the raw material inputs worth more than the final product.
- Soviet industry could also be seen as value-destroying because of irrational pricing structures. In the absence of markets, planners had no way of setting values for goods. Energy prices, for example, were very low in communist countries compared to world market prices, which meant that much industry was highly energy-inefficient.
- International trade was neglected in planned economies. This was damaging because trade allows new technologies to spread rapidly, and also because of what economists term 'gains from trade' which arise out of specialization suiting the particular strengths of individual economies.
- The gains that communist economies had hoped to make as a result of increased worker motivation never arose. The economic system was imposed by force, income distribution was never in fact egalitarian, and a low priority was put on meeting the needs of ordinary citizens. As the East European joke had it: 'Capitalism is the exploitation of man by man. Socialism is the reverse'.

---

extensive means. Rural labour surpluses were uprooted and moved to cities to work in the new factories. Collectivization of agriculture and the ruthless extraction of surpluses from the Russian peasantry provided the resources to build up heavy industry, at considerable human cost.

Subsequently economic growth remained largely extensive growth, arising out of the greater utilization of raw materials, a growing labour force, and some exploitation of previously unused land. However, by the 1970s the Russian labour force had stopped growing, and easily accessible sources of raw materials had been mostly used up. There was a need to move from extensive growth to an intensive model, where existing labour and raw materials were used more efficiently, and growth occurred as a result of technological progress. Innovation-aversion and inefficient use of resources were major areas of weakness of the planned economy. In addition, cold-war tensions meant that vast resources were being poured into military industry and expenditure on the Soviet armed forces, further weakening the civilian sector.

After the death of Stalin in 1953, his successors tried in various ways to improve the effectiveness of the planned economy. Nikita Khrushchev (Soviet leader 1953–64) sought to decentralize in order to bring planners closer to the economic units for which they were responsible; regional autarchy, however, was often the consequence, and after Khrushchev's removal in 1964 the economy was rapidly recentralized.

Khrushchev's successor, Leonid Brezhnev, and his Prime Minister Aleksei Kosygin, tried introducing some limited market reforms in the mid-1960s. They attempted to give economic units some incentive to pay attention to quality by seeking to plan in terms of amount of output sold, rather then quantity produced. However, these reforms too failed; partly because of inconsistencies in their conception, as without rational prices, sensible decisions about how to use resources cannot be made, and partly because they were never fully implemented.

The Soviet economy had achieved impressive growth rates as it industrialized in the 1930s, and in the reconstruction period after the Second World War, but such growth was from a low base and was achieved by putting resources into industrialization and reconstruction. By the 1970s, growth needed to be sought from innovation and technological advance, both of which, as we have seen, were hampered by the centralized plans of the Soviet system. According to some estimates,

> the long-run context shows that from 1928 until 1973 the Soviet economy was on a path that would catch up with the United States one day ... However, in 1973, half way through the Brezhnev period, the process of catching up came to an abrupt end. (Harrison, 2002)

The increased resources put into consumption meant that living standards for many Soviet citizens did improve a little in the late 1960s and early 1970s. However, the absence of genuine structural reform of an inefficient economic system meant that the transition to a more intensive type of economic growth never happened. Low fertility and increases in the mortality rate caused by difficulties in the Soviet health system, as well as rising alcoholism, meant that population growth was minimal. Easily accessible sources of raw materials had largely been exhausted. Collectivized agriculture frequently failed to produce enough food to feed the population, and grain had to be imported from elsewhere. Attempts to keep up with the United States militarily drained resources from civilian research and development, and diverted skilled workers into unproductive employment. By the time of Brezhnev's death in 1982, economic growth had virtually ceased.

On coming to power in 1985, Mikhail Gorbachev quite rapidly became aware that piecemeal reform of the planned economy would not be enough to solve economic difficulties, and that more radical steps had become necessary. Some measures were taken. For example, worker co-operatives and so-called individual labour activity were legalized, creating a private sector in some areas of the economy. Gorbachev's policy was also to reduce the amount of planning which went on, giving managers more autonomy to take necessary decisions. Arms-limitation agreements, it was hoped, would reduce the burden of military expenditure.

However, real structural reform and marketization of the economy did not occur in the 1985–91 period. For all their talk of restructuring the economy, and their plethora of alternative reform proposals, the Gorbachev years saw mere tinkering and talking in relation to the great economic problems facing the Soviet Union. It was these problems that were to dominate Russia's reform programme after 1991:

- The huge monopolistic industrial monoliths, which dominated the economy, continued to operate in familiar ways, and continued to be subsidized by the state.
- There were so-called 'price reforms' under Gorbachev, but prices were not freed.
- The refusal to allow unemployment meant that the labour market remained unreformed.
- No real competition was created because the government failed to address issues of bankruptcy, or to create the conditions whereby non-state economic actors could enter markets and compete with state industry and agriculture.
- Accumulated savings which Soviet citizens had been unable to spend represented so-called 'repressed inflation', and, in combination with the growing state budget deficit, meant that an inflationary surge was inevitable should real reform take place.

Overall, the Gorbachev period destroyed the effectiveness of the planned economy without replacing it with operative market mechanisms. When the Soviet Union collapsed and Boris Yeltsin came to power in an independent Russia he proved himself willing to back real reform to address the economic crisis, rather than to vacillate.

Economic reform, 1992–98

The economic team created by Yeltsin was headed by acting Prime Minister Yegor Gaidar, and contained a significant number of younger, highly pro-market ministers, such as Anatoly Chubais who was in charge of privatization. Many of them had knowledge of economics outside Russia, and were convinced that only market mechanisms could solve the deep economic problems the country faced.

Nonetheless, Yeltsin's economic team was also very aware that, however essential the policy of marketization seemed to them, it would be a far from easy path to follow (see Box 5.3). Difficulties would come in the detail of the reforms and in their social impact. A common phrase used in the early 1990s to sum up the marketization of formerly centrally planned economies was 'shock therapy'. The therapy came in the treatment of what was deemed to be a terminally failing economic system incompatible both with a globalizing world economy and with the new democratic polity being ushered in. The shock came in the inevitable hardships caused by inflation, unemployment, the closure of uncompetitive industries, the cutting of social welfare, and so on.

As the 1990s progressed, the familiar – and heartfelt – comment to be heard was that Russia's economic reforms were 'all shock and no therapy'. And indeed, culminating in the financial crash of 1998, this broad overview seems to represent a pretty sound assessment of the situation. The population experienced great socio-economic hardship, as there was a reduction in state subsidies for social goods such as housing, transport and energy; inflation wiped out personal savings; unemployment rose; and wages went unpaid for months at a time in the state sector (for details see, 'Standards of living' in Chapter 3).

Nonetheless, dealing with the substance of the economic reforms, clearly some 'therapy' was taking place alongside the 'shock'. At first sight, it is hard to discern a consistent strategy for the Russian economy between 1992 and 1998. The frequent changes of government personnel and rhetorical shifts left observers baffled as to the real intentions of policy makers. But despite the very different rhetoric of, for example, acting Prime Minister Gaidar in 1992, who was at the forefront of the push for

---

Box 5.3   What is needed to turn a planned economy into a market economy?

After the collapse of communism, the countries of Eastern Europe and the former Soviet Union were attempting something without historical precedent in seeking to move from a system of command planning to a free market economy. There was no template to work from. It was clear, however, that the following reforms would be necessary:

Ownership changes. In practice, state ownership had very often been the effective equivalent of no ownership. Managers and workers stood to gain little from committed work or forward-thinking, and knew that loss-making enterprises would be bailed out by state subsidies, a situation referred to by the eminent Hungarian economist Janos Kornai as the 'soft budget constraint' (Kornai, 1992).

Privatization of small-scale economic activity is relatively straightforward, but the privatization of whole industries is a different matter. How much are they worth? How will 'the people' participate in and benefit from the sale of what are theoretically their and the nation's assets? Should foreign ownership be allowed?

Demonopolization to create the competition which is a central dynamic feature of a market economy and an incentive for efficiency.

Bankruptcy and unemployment. Free competition means that loss-making enterprises are ultimately forced out of business. Russia's economic geography included a large number of company towns, where virtually all employment – as well as maintenance of housing stock, food supplies, holiday facilities, social services and such like – was dependent on a single employer. Close the factory and you cause serious damage to the entire community.

→

---

rapid marketization, and Prime Minister Primakov in late 1998, who took a more cautious approach, overall policy did not divert from the goal of marketization. However, because of the strength of political resistance to radical change, government strategies were increasingly couched in terms designed to mollify opposition.

Nevertheless, specific features of reform can be identified. The immediate freeing of prices, which led to initial rapid inflation, was designed to shift to a more rational price structure. In January 1992, 90 per cent of all retail prices were freed from the previous system where the state determined the price of goods. The effectiveness of all other market reforms was predicated on this. Markets cannot be efficient without a system of prices determined by the interaction of supply and demand. In addition, there was a massive amount of 'spare' money in the system – that is,

→

Price reform. The rational allocation of resources in competitive markets arises through the interaction of supply, demand and price. Free pricing is a necessary component of the free market. Economic reform would require removing subsidies and increasing prices for many basics of life, such as staple foodstuffs, domestic heating and rents.

Monetary stabilization. The rouble as currency was not one in which citizens had much confidence and it failed to act as a store of value in the way that harder currencies did.

The State Budget. Russia inherited public expenditure commitments way beyond levels that could be financed by taxation. Large budget deficits would have to be reduced by reducing state spending and increasing tax revenue.

Foreign trade and payments. Integration with world markets would enable mutually beneficial trade and facilitate foreign investment in Russia.

The infrastructure of the market economy. Developed market economies operate with sophisticated capital markets able to finance potentially profitable projects. The banking system was entirely undeveloped in Russia in 1992, and the legal basis for the operation of free markets (for example, contract enforcement and debt recovery) did not exist. A whole raft of new, and complex, legislation was required.

Federal aspects. Who owned economic assets: the central state, republics and regions, or cities and rural districts? How should resources be divided and which levels of power were responsible for what? How should budgetary revenues, mostly collected locally, be divided up among the different levels of power?

The culture of capitalism. The dominant culture of the Soviet period was to see private ownership as an evil to be eliminated. The introduction of a private sector, and of, so to speak, official permission for private individuals to become rich, might bring forth reactions of extreme resentment and hostility.

money which had been saved by citizens in a situation where its value was undermined by lack of access to goods. Freeing up prices would absorb much of this monetary overhang.

In order to combat subsequent inflationary pressures, and to create a stable currency and real money, monetary policy remained at the forefront of policy decisions. By 1995 this had been sufficiently successful for it to become possible to fix the rouble to a band of values against the dollar, in what became known as 'the rouble corridor'. Governments continued to attempt to ensure as stable a currency as possible, to control inflation, to increase domestic and international confidence in the state of the Russian economy, and to enable business to begin to make future plans with some degree of certainty.

In parallel there was a process of opening up the Russian economy to the outside world, and by 1998 Russia was significantly more integrated into the world economy than in 1992. This still did not represent free trade in key areas, with price distortions supported in some sectors by export quotas, high export duties, and import subsidies and controls.

A third strand of the reforms was the attempt to reduce the economic role of the state. Privatization took place in the mid-1990s, initially via the distribution to all Russian citizens of vouchers that could be redeemed for shares in newly-privatized companies. Subsequently it occurred via auctions, and the highly controversial 'loans for shares' policy where certain banks and industrial combines acquired shares in companies at prices far below their true market value in return for loans to the government.

The voucher privatization scheme was intended as an innovative way to solve the problem of selling-off state-owned assets. By giving vouchers to all citizens, the question of the fair distribution of property amongst the population was addressed. In addition it was hoped that voucher privatization would create at a stroke a nation of shareholders with a vested interest in the success of the economy. In addition to privatization by voucher, this stage of the process also involved giving shares in enterprises to their workers and managers.

Laudable though this approach might seem in the abstract, the results were not quite as anticipated in terms of a wide base of share ownership. Many small shareholders were persuaded to offload their shares to enterprise managers, either voluntarily or pressured by economic circumstances or managerial arm-twisting. In their turn, some such enterprises were sold on to Russia's larger business empires or, less often, to foreign investors. In thousands of cases, too, the ability of shareholders to control companies was curtailed by the government retaining a controlling interest, having declared the need to do so because of the strategic importance for national security of an enterprise.

A related aspect of the attempt to change Russia's economic structure was the creation of a legal and regulatory framework for a market economy. Some aspects of this proved much more straightforward than others. The privatization programme, for example, was conducted largely by presidential decree. Bankruptcy laws were adopted with little major resistance. However, laws on private ownership of land, foreign investment and taxation codes, to name but three, provoked major disagreements between government and parliament.

The results of these reform approaches were painful for the Russian economy and people. As Table 5.1 shows, Russia experienced dramatic and sustained economic problems in the 1992–98 period. According to official statistics, national output fell every year except 1997, and by mid-1999 gross domestic product (GDP) was little over half its 1990 level. Although we do not wish to understate the degree of economic trauma that Russia experienced in the 1990s, it is likely that these official figures overstate the true decline in GDP, and consequently social welfare, for several reasons:

- In the planned economy, output figures were inflated. Since the structure of rewards was based on plan-fulfilment and overfulfilment, economic units claimed to achieve more than they in fact had.
- Some of the economic decline was made up of an end to the production of useless value-destroying items, as well as significant falls in previously excessive defence spending.
- Official figures have difficulty in reflecting the amount of economic activity that goes on informally outside officially monitored channels; for example, households growing their own food.

In parallel with this rapid decline, the economy fundamentally changed its character in several important respects during the 1990s. Figure 5.1 shows how, in a very short period of time, Russia moved from being an economy dominated by industry to one where services predominated. Such a deindustrialization was a process experienced by many other countries perhaps two decades earlier than was the case with Russia.

This relative decline in industry and agriculture (see Box 5.4) was in part a consequence of Russia's increasing openness to the world economy, a trend visible in the sharply rising absolute volumes of exports and imports even against the background of overall economic decline. The sectors of the economy that were hardest hit by recession were in most cases subject to particularly strong foreign competition, such as clothing, agriculture and food processing, or industries such as electricity production or construction materials, demand for which directly reflects levels of output and investment. Likewise the industries that struggled least – oil and gas, basic metals and various other natural resources – are ones in which Russia is highly competitive on world markets.

The rise in the importance of service industries – both business and consumer – reflects a fundamental change in the nature of the economy. In a planned economy relatively closed off to the outside world, there was little need for accountants, management consultants, market researchers, advertisers, investment bankers and all the other job categories that help make a competitive market economy function. The relative neglect of consumers in the planned economy meant that there was an insufficient supply of, for example, plumbers, electricians, travel

Table 5.1 Russia's economic indicators, 1992–2003

	1992	1993	1994	1995	1996	1997	1998	1999	2000	2001	2002	2003
GDP, % change year on year	−14.5	−8.7	−12.6	−4.2	−3.6	1.4	−5.3	6.4	10.0	5.1	4.7	7.3
Industrial production, % change year on year	−18.2	−14.2	−20.9	−3.0	−4.5	2.0	−5.2	11.0	11.9	4.9	3.7	7.0
Fixed investments, % change year on year	−40.0	−12.0	−27.0	−13.0	−18.0	−5.0	−12.0	5.3	17.4	10.0	2.6	12.5
Unemployment, % change year on year	4.9	5.5	7.5	8.2	9.3	9.0	11.8	11.7	10.2	9.0	7.1	8.9
Inflation %	842	224	131	22	11	84	37	20	19	45	12

Source: Goskomstat.

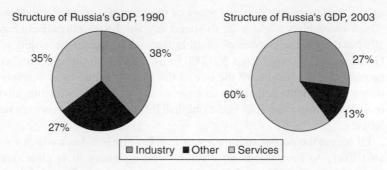

Figure 5.1   The structure of Russia's GDP, 1990 and 2003

Box 5.4   Agriculture in Russia, 1992–2004

Only about a third of Russia's land is used for agriculture. In the Soviet era, this land was owned by the state and farmed in state or collective farms, and agriculture was heavily subsidized by the state. In the years since 1991, reform efforts have concentrated on the lowering of state subsidies, the liberalization of prices, and the gradual encouragement of private farming and land ownership.

As with other areas of the economy, the 1990s was largely a decade of decline in the Russian agricultural sector, with 1998 being a particular low point. In this year, there was a record low harvest, with production of many key crops (grain, potatoes, vegetables in general, sugarbeet) being less than half that in 1992. Over a similar period meat production and livestock numbers also declined by more than a half.

Russia increasingly came to rely on imports in the 1990s, particularly imports from the United States; becoming, for example, the top foreign market for US poultry exports. The issue of 'food security' became prominent in Russia, as food prices began to rise beyond the means of the poorest sectors of society, and senior political figures fretted about Russia's dependence on imports.

Both the United States and the European Union sent substantial food aid to Russia in 1999 and 2000, and over this same period the Russian agricultural sector began to recover from its low ebb of 1998. Agricultural output grew by 27 per cent in 1991–2001, with subsequent years seeing a far slower growth rate, down to a mere 1.5 per cent in 2002–03.

Although state subsidies for agriculture have been cut in the post-Soviet era, direct and indirect subsidies still remain a drain on state resources.

The right of private citizens to own land was established in the constitution of 1993, but for years the Duma refused to pass a law enabling this right. Finally in 2001 and 2002 laws enabling the sale of, respectively, urban and agricultural land were accepted, with the latter law forbidding the sale of rural land to foreigners.

agents, automobile dealers and many of the other providers of goods on which individuals might want to spend any surplus earnings. Between 1992 and 1996 the number of small businesses in Russia, according to Goskomstat, increased from 560,000 to 840,000, with the true number probably higher because of the size of the shadow economy. It scarcely needs to be mentioned that a change in the economic structure also indicates an important shift in the political influence of various economic lobbies.

Of course the decline of industry and agriculture is a shock which was also likely to have important electoral consequences. It is clear that opposition parties of both right and left have had a base of support from workers and managers in declining parts of the economy and declining regions. The Agrarian Party of Russia reflects this in its very name (see Chapter 4).

This restructuring also has an important regional aspect. Regions that have been relatively successful tend to be either resource-rich or metropolitan centres with good international transport connections able to act as entry points for international trade. Regions whose economies declined particularly seriously are often ones especially vulnerable to competition from imported goods, or agricultural republics that were already underindustrialized.

The crash of 1998

On 17 August 1998, the Russian government devalued the rouble and announced that it would no longer be able to pay much of its domestic debt and was imposing a moratorium on payment of much of its foreign debt (see Box 5.5). Prices rose rapidly, and, not for the first time in the 1990s, citizens who had deposited money in Russian banks saw their savings wiped out. The 35-year-old Prime Minister, Sergei Kirienko, who had only been in post a few months, was dismissed by President Yeltsin. Yeltsin, although no economist, was a shrewd enough politician to realize that someone must be seen to be taking the blame and it had better not be him.

Economic progress, 1999–2004

The 1998 financial crisis seemed to act as a cleansing storm on the Russian economy, and since then the economy has seen five years of

---

Box 5.5   Explaining the 1998 crash

- According to one observer 'the 1998 crisis basically was a standard currency crisis' (*Moscow Times*, 18 June 2003). In other words, Russia's policy of achieving stability through a fixed – within certain limits – exchange rate backfired since the rouble was overvalued. Government overspending meant that a large amount of debt accrued. Coupled with significant capital flight out of the country (see later) and an economy which was not growing – along with international unease following the Asian financial crisis of 1997 – the situation proved unsustainable.
- This macroeconomic explanation is given more depth by bringing in developments – or rather the lack of them – at the micro level. According to a report by the Foreign Affairs Select Committee of the House of Commons in 2000, 'the crisis of August 1998 was above all the consequence of this contradiction: the macroeconomic stabilization achieved during 1995–98 was not underpinned by the micro level structural changes needed to make it sustainable without considerable external financial support'. Using the exchange rate as the principal means of stabilization enabled the government for too long to avoid the necessary structural reforms and budget cutbacks. According to the International Monetary Fund, between 1992 and 1998 there was no sustained downward trend in the budget deficit. In essence, the subsidization of uncompetitive enterprises which had been a feature of the Soviet system had continued – albeit hidden in a variety of procedures.

---

strong growth and the process of market-oriented reforms continued with renewed vigour as the Yeltsin regime was replaced by that of Vladimir Putin. When Putin came to power in 2000 he declared that:

> It will take us approximately 15 years and an 8 per cent annual growth of our GDP to reach the per capita GDP level of present-day Portugal and Spain, which are not among the world's industrialized leaders. If during the same 15 years we manage to annually increase our GDP by 10 percent, we will then catch up with Britain or France. (Putin, 2000: 213)

It is important to note that President Putin was talking about taking 15 years to catch up with where Portugal and Spain were at the turn of the millennium. And if things went really well, then by 2015 Russia might reach the per capita GDP levels attained by Britain or France in 2000. Putin's realism was admirable, and in setting the target in such stark terms he sought to focus the minds of his ministers. Indeed, under Putin there has developed a focus on clear targets, with a rolling 10-year programme for doubling GDP each decade being put in place.

Between 1999 and 2003, virtually all of the key economic indicators have shown positive trends (Table 5.1). Real GDP in Russia grew by an average of 6.7 per cent per year, with the strongest growth in the export-driven industries, particularly in the oil sector where high global oil prices have proved beneficial. Growth in this sector, however, is not the whole story, with the service and industrial sectors growing too, assisted by the knock-on effects of the oil price boom.

As noted by a report on the Russian economy from the Organisation for Economic Cooperation and Development, there were positive trends in many key areas by the summer of 2004:

- Real wages, and disposable incomes, were well-above levels found before the 1998 financial crisis, with the number of people living below the official poverty line having fallen by around 33 per cent between 1999 and 2004.
- Unemployment declined from 13 per cent in 1998 to 8 per cent in 2004.
- The federal budget was in surplus every year from 2000 onwards, facilitating the establishment of a stabilization fund to meet budget needs in years when external factors, particularly low oil prices, might otherwise cause a shortfall. The stabilization fund was expected to amount to around 2 per cent of GDP by the end of 2004.
- Wage and pension arrears, which had hit many of Russia's poorest citizens for several years in the late 1990s and early 2000s, were by and large no longer occurring.
- Legislation had been introduced to regulate and clarify activity in areas such as land ownership, labour, bureaucratic oversight, and customs codes. Tax reforms saw the introduction of a low level of income tax, set at 13 per cent (the lowest level in Europe) with the intention of drawing many Russians out of the shadow economy and making them taxpayers.
- During the election campaigns of 2003 and 2004 (parliamentary and presidential elections respectively) the Putin regime's campaign focused on the need to improve standards of living across Russia and to diversify the economy, so that raw materials were not so over-whelmingly important for the nation's economic health.

Nonetheless, despite the clear progress made by the Russian economy since the financial collapse of 1998, there is still plenty of room for further improvement. As one observer put it with reference to the attractiveness of Russia for foreign investors, on a scale running from 'dreadful' to 'excellent', improvement so far has been from 'very bad' to merely 'bad' (Hare *et al.*, 2004). Perhaps this should not be surprising, given the extent of the tasks necessary to transform a failing centrally planned economy into a successful market economy (see Box 5.3). On what then do concerns about the future of the Russian economy focus?

Resource-dependence

Russia's riches in terms of natural resources – particularly oil, gas and metals – have been at the root of its economic recovery since the late 1990s. It is perhaps ironic then that this should be seen as a potential problem for the Russian economy, and indeed have been termed by some observers a 'resource curse'. In what way might what seems a blessing turn out to be a curse?

The chief concern is that reliance on such natural resources makes Russia particularly vulnerable to fluctuations in the global market, particularly with regard to oil prices. According to official Russian figures, the oil and gas sector accounts for 9 per cent of GDP. According to figures from the World Bank, the true proportion is nearer 25 per cent, with official statistics distorted by hidden subsidies within the domestic energy market.

In addition, there are limits to the extent to which the export market for such resources can be expanded. Developed economies need only half as much oil per dollar of GDP now as was the case in the mid-1970s. There also exists a fear that remaining a resource-based economy will condemn Russia to somehow being a second-rate economy, supplying the resources to richer nations as they press ahead with the technological advances at the forefront of economic development. 'Brain power and computer chips are supposed to be the fuel of the modern "knowledge economy" rather than oil' (*The Economist*, 21 August 2004).

Finally, there is the question of the distortions which resource-dependence may bring into an economy, supporting a strong currency, rising imports and decreasing exports. The Russian government is well-aware of such potential difficulties, hence the implementation of the stabilization fund in 2004 (to provide some safety net in case of falling oil prices) and the proclaimed intention to create a more diverse economy. Nonetheless, there remains the danger that a sudden external shock, such as a global oil price reduction, could seriously dent Russia's hopes of getting anywhere near the doubling of GDP within a decade (in any case an ambitious target which would require annual growth of around 8 per cent).

The legal environment

As noted above, issues of land ownership, labour laws, the power of the bureaucracy and taxation matters were all addressed during the first term of the Putin administration. Nonetheless, the environment within which the Russian economy exists still remains in need of further reform. In particular, two related issues stand out, and were noted by the Organisation for Economic Cooperation and Development (OECD) in its 2004 report on the Russian economy. These issues are corruption and the arbitrary use of power.

For many years the working assumption of most observers is that no one who has made a lot of money in post-Soviet Russia has been able to do so at the same time as remaining untainted by corruption. A recent World Bank survey shows Russia ranking in the lowest 25 per cent of countries in terms of the rule of law and the control of corruption. Part of the reason for this has been that the legal framework for a market economy had to be created from scratch in the 1990s, and therefore many areas of activity were unregulated. The piecemeal introduction of laws then leads to legislative confusion, and the promotion of a culture where the law is considered neither effective nor relevant. To 'get things done' in the business world, it was often necessary to pay bribes and back-handers. State officials themselves would supplement wages by taking payment to register this or vouch for that. Such corruption has been particularly prevalent at the regional level, where the relationship between big business and regional authorities can be especially close, and so regional legislation and practice has been used to give advantages to favoured companies and to restrict the activities of others.

This arbitrary use of power by regional authorities can be the result of corruption motivated by monetary gain. However, there is also a wider issue surrounding the apparently arbitrary use of power. This relates to the ability of the state to interfere in the operation of a company, or to undermine the property rights of a private company for reasons of political control or national security. Despite movement towards market reform, there still remains a statist approach within the Russian government when it comes to control of key industries.

In 2003, one of Russia's richest men, Mikhail Khodorkovsky, the chief executive of the Yukos oil corporation, was arrested on charges of tax evasion. For many observers, the arrest of Khodorkovsky was seen to be motivated not by purely legal factors – after all, it was assumed that if he had indeed done anything wrong, it was nothing that the bosses of many major Russian companies had not done – but rather as a result of his support for the political opposition, which had allegedly displeased the Kremlin. Other suggestions are that the Putin regime simply wanted to break up a rich and powerful company in order to strengthen state control over the oil sector. The energy sector is seen by the Putin government to be a legitimate object of state control for security reasons, as well as a means of income generation and economic management. Many in Russia, however, welcomed any move which might curtail the wealth and influence which the super-rich oligarchs (see Chapter 3) had acquired in the 1990s.

Whatever the motivations of the state, and whatever Khodorkovsky is or is not guilty of, the point is that the perception was created that the state might step in and take over in the sphere of activities of private companies. Such a fear is not conducive to encouraging investment, nor to the operation of the free market as a whole. Furthermore, Yukos was at the forefront of Russian companies in terms of moving towards business transparency, a necessary feature of a market economy lacking in much Russian business activity. However, this very transparency made it easier for prosecutors to investigate the company's affairs, and subsequently served as a warning to others that copying the Yukos example may not be in their best interests.

Engagement in the global economy

According to economy minister, German Gref, Russia's share in the structure of world trade was 1.8 per cent in 2003, up from 1.65 per cent in 2001. In 2003 Russia's foreign trade amounted to $210.8 billion, which was 25 per cent more than in 2002. The Russian government aims to continue this improvement by gaining membership of the World Trade Organization (WTO).

Russia applied to join the World Trade Organization in 1993, at a time when the WTO was emerging from the Uruguay round of the General Agreement on Tariffs and Trade as the new body overseeing global trade. More than 10 years later, Russia had still to secure WTO admission, although hopes remain that it will be admitted during the first decade of the twenty-first century.

The World Trade Organization sits in judgement on international trade disputes, it sets the rules of trade and enforces them on its members. As an organization, its chief policy is one of trade liberalization, and membership for Russia would in the long term increase Russian access to global markets. Furthermore, the regulatory clarity required for WTO membership will provide a stability which should encourage foreign investment. In the short term, however, Russia's membership has been held up, amongst other things, by its reluctance to bring its trading regulations into line with WTO norms. In particular, this would require the removal of protectionist barriers in key sectors – such as banking, agriculture and metallurgy. When President Putin came to power in 2000 he brought with him a renewed vigour in terms of pursuing Russian entry into the WTO, and progress in this direction was helped by the firm support of Russia for the actions of the United States and her allies in its war on terrorism after 11 September 2001. However, in the end, WTO accession comes down to detailed negotiations on trade-related matters.

At the same time as negotiating WTO membership, Russia is also seeking to develop a closer economic arrangement with a number of the states of the former Soviet Union within the Commonwealth of Independent States. In his 'state of the nation' address in May 2004, Putin declared that, 'our priority remains working on the deepening of integration on the territory of the Commonwealth of Independent States, including within the framework of the single economic space, the Eurasian Economic Community'. It is not clear precisely what Russia hopes to gain economically from this arrangement, and it may well be that the motivation for its development comes more from Russia's commitment to having a clear geo-political sphere of influence than from the expectation of great economic gain. Putin clearly sees this Eurasian Economic Community as vital for regional and international stability.

As well as trading relations, two other indicators provide a useful assessment of confidence in the Russian economy as against the global economy as a whole:

- **Capital flight.** Since the beginning of economic reforms in the early 1990s many Russians have, understandably, thought it safer to convert their money into foreign currency and get it out of the country as quickly as possible. For much of the transition period such 'capital flight' was estimated to be around $15 billion a year, although precise figures are difficult to come by. In some years the figure was far higher, and even official government data has capital flight in 2000 as $24 billion. These government figures then show a reduction as the state of the Russian economy improves, with capital outflows estimated as $16 billion in 2001 and a little over $11 billion in 2002. Unofficial figures are consistently higher, with the Economist Intelligence Unit estimating an increase in capital flight from $16 billion in 2002 to $23 billion in 2003. Whatever the precise figure, the point is that huge amounts of money have left the Russian economy over the past decade or so – often in semi-legal ways – instead of being invested, spent, saved or taxed in the domestic economy. Russians continue to hold a large amount of their wealth in cash – probably around $60 billion, much of it in foreign currencies. Such 'mattress money' remains a further indicator of a lack of confidence in the financial sector as a whole.

• **Foreign investment.** During the post-Soviet era, foreign direct investment (FDI) into Russia has occurred at a relatively low level, with a lack of confidence in the business environment and concerns over the future development of the economy scaring off would-be investors. For much of the Putin era, FDI has been below 1 per cent of GDP. Before the 1998 crash it was around $5.3 billion per annum, and by 2002 the post-crash recovery had only brought it back up to around $4 billion. Such figures include the return of capital flight from abroad (much of it held in Cyprus). Since 2002, however, FDI has increased, with planned investments in the oil industry likely to make a significant and positive impact. Six countries account for around three-quarters of FDI in Russia. These are, in order of the largest stock of FDI to the smallest: the USA, Cyprus, the Netherlands, the United Kingdom, Germany and Japan (Hare *et al.*, 2004). Although the energy and raw materials sector is an important element in FDI, much investment into Russia has been predicated on selling goods and services to Russian consumers – the high-profile examples of Macdonalds and IKEA being illustrative of a wider phenomenon.

Conclusion

Towards the end of the Yeltsin era, when Russia's economic news was consistently bad, there was much discussion amongst analysts as to the role that Western advisers and the international financial institutions had played in Russia's transition. One view, shared by many in Russia, was that the advice given by Western specialists had been inappropriate. According to the Chief Economist of the World Bank, Joseph Stiglitz, writing shortly after the 1998 crash, standard Western advice wrongly took

> an ideological, fundamental and root-and-branch approach to reform-mongering as opposed to an incremental, remedial, piecemeal and adaptive approach ... Some economic cold warriors seem to have seen themselves on a mission to level the 'evil' institutions of Communism

and to socially engineer in their place the new, clean and pure 'textbook institutions' of a private property market. (Quoted in Lloyd, 1999)

Others argued that the trouble was not the Western advice itself, but the fact that it was not followed, and that despite this the International Monetary Fund kept granting money to shore up a Russia reluctant to undertake the necessary root-and-branch reforms. Such heated arguments are rarely heard in the early years of the twenty-first century, now that the Russian economy is performing well on many indicators. As with political reform, what we have in the Russian economy today is not exactly what the purist reformers of the immediate post-Soviet era anticipated. It remains, nonetheless, far removed from the Soviet legacy of 1992, despite – scarcely surprisingly – not having yet thrown off every last structural and behavioural vestige of that era.

6
Rights, Freedoms and Civil Society

This chapter briefly explores the Soviet legacy with regard to the application of law and the rights and freedoms enjoyed – and not enjoyed – by Soviet citizens. We then turn our attention to rights and freedoms in contemporary Russia, focusing on freedom of speech, freedom of the press, freedom of worship, and Russia's human rights record in international eyes. Such rights and freedoms are of course essential if a thriving civil society – itself seen as a prerequisite for genuine and lasting democracy – is to thrive.

Today's Russia is a signatory to the major international human rights conventions, is a member of the Council of Europe, with all the human rights requirements which that entails, and has constitutional guarantees for a whole raft of normative rights and freedoms. At the same time, though, reports of the denial of certain rights and freedoms, and at times of more serious human-rights abuses, are still heard. Is this just a matter of Western sensitivities from the Cold War era creating an extra vigilance with regard to Russia's record in this area? Or are there serious grounds for fearing that Putin's Russia will rein in the rights and freedoms expected of a democratic nation?

In March 2000, the then acting-President of the Russian Federation, Vladimir Putin, issued an 'open letter to the Russian voters', ahead of the presidential election of that month which he went on to win. In this letter he declared that 'democracy is the dictatorship of the law'. He then criticized those in positions of authority who sought to 'privatize' the law so that it served their own interests.

To those with a knowledge of how law was applied in the Soviet Union, and to a lesser extent in the post-Soviet era, this description of the 'privatization' of law rings true. The behavioural legacy of the Soviet period presents a challenge which twenty-first century Russia has to overcome if a truly law-based state is to be created.

111

The Soviet legacy

The Soviet Union had a developed legal system, backed up by a constitution outlining the rights and obligations of its citizens. (After the founding constitutions of Soviet Russia, 1918, and the Soviet Union, 1924, the USSR had two further constitutions, the Stalin constitution of 1936 and the Brezhnev constitution of 1977.) As Mark Sandle (1998) puts it, 'the basic ethos was that the rights of the individual were state based and were then delegated to the individual from the state'. In practice this meant that the authorities were above the law. Cases, particularly cases of political importance, would be decided not on judicial grounds alone, but as a result of what became known as 'telephone law'. The party and the judicial authorities would consult, and decide what the verdict and the sentence should be.

If this was the practice at the higher end of the scale, it was mirrored in the experience of many citizens in their dealings with the law, where judicial criteria might be secondary to other factors such as political reliability, favours to be granted, scores to be settled, or bribes paid. During the last years of the USSR, Soviet leader Mikhail Gorbachev (1985–91) tried to create a 'law-based state', which he described as essential to the stability of the Soviet Union. However, the ideological, institutional and constitutional confusion of the Soviet endgame did not allow for the clear development of this concept, let alone its embodiment in the behaviour of the authorities.

Gorbachev had been working towards the enactment of a new Soviet constitution. With the Soviet Union no longer existing after 1991, the task became the development of a new Russian constitution. As noted in Chapter 1, arguments over the nature of the constitution and questions of how and by whom Russia should be ruled eventually led to military action on the streets of Moscow in October 1993, and the forcible dissolution of parliament by troops loyal to President Yeltsin. It is to discussion of the 1993 Russian constitution, still not amended and still serving as the fundamental law of the Russian Federation, which we now turn.

Constitutional rights in contemporary Russia

The Russian Constitution was adopted by national referendum on 12 December 1993. A constitution can perform a variety of functions, setting out the rules of the game for political engagement, the institutional arrangement of power, the 'mission statement' of a state, the division between central and devolved powers, the limits of the state, and so on. In different chapters of this book we deal with different aspects of constitutional provision (in particular, Chapter 4 covers the institutional arrangement of power). Here, though, we are concerned with what the Russian Constitution says about individual rights and freedoms, and the supremacy of law.

Before tackling that in any detail, it is worth pointing out that, to many people, the Russian Constitution's position on the supremacy of law was compromised before the Constitution was ever adopted because of the circumstances surrounding its adoption. We have outlined in Chapters 1 and 4 the events which led to armed conflict in Moscow between supporters of the president and the parliament in 1993. The key point for our purposes here is that the dissolution of the parliament by the president in September 1993 was not allowed under the Constitution then in force. In other words, whatever the current Russian Constitution says about the supremacy of law, it was adopted on the back of a fundamentally unconstitutional act, namely the dissolution of the parliament by the president.

There is of course a counter-argument to this view; that is, that the Constitution still in force in September 1993 was void of real authority and served as a barrier to the democratic development of Russia. It was the 1978 Constitution of the Soviet-era Russian republic, and had been amended so many times that it could scarcely be called a fundamental law any more. Though this argument is correct so far as it goes, the fact remains that, from a legal-technical point of view, the dissolution of parliament in 1993 was not lawful.

Despite its provenance, the Russian Constitution provides an apparently firm foundation for the provision of human rights. We have noted that under the Soviet system individual rights were subsumed by the needs of the state. This Marxist-Leninist conceptualization of rights is replaced in the current Constitution by a liberal approach, with Article 2 declaring that 'the individual and his rights and freedoms are the supreme value'. An entire section of the Russian Constitution is then devoted to 'human and civil rights and freedoms', which are guaranteed within 'the generally recognized principles and norms of international law' (see Box 6.1).

It is clear, then, that the Russian Constitution provides a substantial legal underpinning of the rights and freedoms to be enjoyed by the citizens of the Russian Federation. The Constitution is the fundamental law of the state, and all other laws must be in accordance with it. As we shall see, though, the mere statement of something in a constitution does not in itself mean the application of that provision. After all, the constitutions

Box 6.1 Rights and freedoms in the Russian Constitution

Amongst the rights and freedoms to be guaranteed by the Russian Constitution are all of those which might be expected in a liberal democracy, including:

- equality before the law
- inviolability of the home and the person
- the presumption of innocence
- freedom of conscience
- freedom of thought and speech
- the right of association

There are also a number of rights and freedoms which carry specific echoes of the Soviet era. Some of these involve statements of rights which were often infringed during the communist years, such as the right to travel and to live where one chooses, the right to privacy of communication, and the right to own property. Others involve guarantees reminiscent of the broad social welfare provisions claimed by the Soviet state, for example, guaranteed provision of pensions, certain social security benefits, housing and education; the right to a decent environment; and the constitutional statement that 'the development of physical culture and sport ... are encouraged'.

of the Soviet era were in many ways splendid documents. It was the fact that they were not reflected in much of everyday life which was the problem. A key question to ask, then, is whether the legal guarantees of the current Constitution have resulted in a change of behaviour on the part of the state. Does the state now act in confirmation of the view that individual rights take precedence? Or does the old view that the state is more important still hold sway?

We must also bear in mind that the provisions of the Constitution are broad-ranging, and many of them require a detailed outworking in law before they can be applied. For example, the Constitution guarantees the right to buy, sell and own land. However, it is clear that the division and sale of state and cooperative-owned land presents a complex situation for which detailed law-making is required. If, though, there is a reluctance amongst law-makers to pass laws on land ownership, as was the case in Russia for the first post-Soviet decade (see Chapter 5, Box 5.4), then the application of this constitutional provision becomes problematic.

A similar example is discussed later in our consideration of freedom of worship. The Russian Constitution declares that potential conscripts into the military have the right of alternative service. Despite this, the lack of a law defining how alternative service might work meant that, until such a law was finally passed in 2002, this provision was very difficult for private citizens to enforce. The lack of such 'enabling legislation' hampered several areas of constitutional provision in the years after 1993.

Having considered the fundamental constitutional guarantees of rights and freedoms offered in Russia today, let us look more closely at their application in practice. We will look at two examples of long-standing importance in both the Soviet era and today – namely, freedom of information and freedom of worship – before considering Russia's record on the provision of rights and freedoms in the eyes of the international community.

Freedom of information

The deterioration of press freedom during the Putin presidency has been a widely discussed issue almost ever since his accession to the post in 2000. In 2003 the international 'democracy-rating' organization, Freedom House, downgraded its evaluation of the Russian media from being 'partly free' to being 'not free' in its annual Press Freedom Survey. Such a negative evaluation is, broadly speaking, the result of the closure of numerous commercially owned media outlets and the exertion of an array of pressures on the Russian media in recent years.

In the twenty-first century the concept of freedom of information has a wider application than ever before. Here we are talking of freedom of the press and broadcast media. We are also talking about state control over and surveillance of telephone conversations, e-mails and the World Wide Web. Governments across the developed world are wrestling with the questions of how and to what extent to control information flows. Russia's President, Vladimir Putin, noted this fact in his first public statement as Acting President, placing 'landslide developments in information science and telecommunications' in the front rank of issues which bring both hope and fear to the twenty-first century world. Fittingly, this first public statement was published on the presidential website.

Let us deal with the more specific question of media freedom, and build up a picture of the historical context within which today's Russia must act. The Soviet era as a whole was marked by the severest state control over newspapers, television and radio. This extended beyond the stringent editorial vigilance exerted by the Communist Party and the KGB, to an information blockade designed to prevent access to all forms of western media. Radio broadcasts from the West were habitually jammed by the authorities, and the importing of most western newspapers into the Soviet Union was illegal.

This control of information by the Soviet authorities was more effective than is sometimes believed. Of course, there were ways in which it was undermined; many families would possess short-wave radios on which, for example, the BBC Russian Service or the US-funded Radio Liberty could be heard. Furthermore, there was a wide-spread scepticism amongst the intelligentsia at least about the reliability of Soviet media, and an almost ubiquitous lack of belief in the existence of anything approaching objective media. Despite this undermining of Soviet censorship, however, the control of information was broadly suc-cessful in terms of its aims. Nearly all Soviet citizens received their daily knowledge of world affairs through the state media, and where there was intelligent scepticism it often extended to Western information sources too: 'we tell our story, they tell theirs, the truth is somewhere in the middle'. Knowledge of the West was likewise sketchy.

All this of course began to change under Mikhail Gorbachev, whose most important policy shift, amongst a number of fundamental changes, was surely that of *glasnost'*. *Glasnost'* has often been translated as 'openness', but is more accurately rendered as 'public transparency'. The introduction of this policy under Gorbachev in 1987 represented a step towards freedom of the press and free speech in general. However, *glasnost'* was not free speech *per se*, and had a clear functionalist role in the reform process. It appears to have been conceived initially as a weapon used by Gorbachev and the reformers against conservative opponents in the Communist Party. If the press was more open about, for example, corruption in the Party, then a reformist mood would be fostered and encouraged amongst other party members and the public at large against the practices of the Party conservatives.

Similar but wider possibilities presented themselves in other spheres. The more openness there was about the problems facing the Soviet Union, the more people would realize the necessity of Gorbachev's reform programme. So, instead of the 100 per cent positive view of life in the USSR which had been the staple of the Soviet media for decades, there began to appear what were at the time startling revelations about, for example, the existence of prostitution in the Soviet Union, the danger of AIDS, and so on.

At first then, *glasnost'* was as much a policy of state editorial control as what had gone before, albeit with more varied content. There were 'glasnost newspapers' such as *Argumenty i fakty* ('Arguments and

Facts'), and the glossy weekly *Ogonyek* ('Little Light'). All publications remained under state-ownership, although as the control of the state, and particularly the leadership of the Party, became more and more fragmented, distinct publications could be increasingly identified as reformist or conservative. By the end of the Soviet era, what had begun as a functionalist state policy had developed into the widespread existence of journalistic freedom. Independent newspapers began to be established, the availability of Western media became less and less controlled, and the liberation of access to previously suppressed information and to a kaleidoscope of different opinions contributed massively to the heady atmosphere surrounding the Soviet collapse of 1990–91.

In the 1990s, freedom of the press flourished relatively unchecked in Russia, as the media landscape was transformed by the rise of the super-rich oligarchs, the withdrawal of state funding for many publications, and the endeavours of journalists revelling in new-found freedoms. Of course, this statement represents a broad overview, and the decade of the 1990s was not all rosy for the journalistic profession. As in other areas (for example, freedom of worship, discussed elsewhere in this chapter), the time between the collapse of the Soviet system and the normalization of the current Russian system towards the end of the 1990s presented opportunities and freedoms which were later reined in to some extent That short period in the early 1990s when the state still funded much of the media, and yet its ability and willingness to exert editorial control had vastly diminished, is looked upon as the heyday of press freedom by some observers. Gradually as the 1990s progressed, several factors began to influence journalistic freedom.

In particular, as a few individuals gained control of a number of the main media outlets in the 1990s, editorial freedom began to diminish. Many of the newspapers which emerged out of the Soviet collapse tried to establish themselves as truly independent, but increasingly economic reality blocked their efforts as they lacked the financial resources to continue. Consequently several businessmen who had grown very rich very rapidly in the aftermath of the Soviet collapse began to acquire media assets.

The first such Russian 'media baron' was Vladimir Gusinsky, whose 'Most' group was built up to include a major national newspaper, *Segodnya*, and the national TV network NTV. He was soon followed by Boris Berezovsky, who gained effective control over a similar profile of media outlets, including the newspaper *Nezavisimaya gazeta*. Furthermore, he became known as the key figure of influence behind the major national TV station ORT, which although 51 per cent owned by the state, was largely managed by men close to Berezovsky. A number of other businessmen acquired media holdings, as did the Mayor of Moscow, Yurii Luzhkov. Clearly, with the acquisition of broadcast and print-media resources, Gusinsky, Berezovsky and others gained a measure of control over editorial policy.

The 1996 presidential election represented a key point in the development of media–political relations in Russia. At the beginning of that year incumbent President, Boris Yeltsin, languished in the opinion polls, having just seen his main rivals – the communists – emerge from the parliamentary election of 1995 as the biggest party in the Duma. On the basis of poll evidence alone, the possibility that Yeltsin might lose the presidency to his communist rival, Gennady Zyuganov, seemed very real. Nonetheless, the months preceding the presidential vote in June 1996 saw concerted support for Yeltsin across virtually all of the main print and – of particular importance – broadcast media. The big three national TV channels (ORT, NTV and the wholly state-owned RTR) all produced coverage heavily supportive of Boris Yeltsin, who of course eventually won the election.

Yeltsin's victory in 1996, and the vital role of the media in achieving it, had two particular effects of relevance to media freedom:

• First, it created an expectation amongst the media magnates that they would somehow be rewarded for supporting the regime, and thereby strengthened the links between media control and political influence.
• Second, the remarkable rise in popular support for Yeltsin in the first half of 1996 emphasized the power of the media. In doing so it increased the determination of other businessmen in the large 'financial-industrial groups' which controlled the commanding heights of the Russian economy to build up their media holdings.

Similarly, and particularly towards the end of the 1990s and into the Putin presidency, the state began to gather back control of key information media. In 1998 a state holding-company was created which controlled the national RTR TV channel, as well as nearly 70 regional TV stations and a large number of transmitters across the country. The following year, President Yeltsin created a Press, Television, Radio Broadcasting and Mass Communications Ministry, to develop a state policy on advertising and oversee the auction of broadcast licences. Many observers saw this as an attempt by the Yeltsin regime to ensure that support for his chosen successor in the 2000 presidential election would match that which he received in 1996.

The election campaign of Yeltsin's anointed successor, Vladimir Putin, in 2000 did by and large enjoy the support of the media. The situation, however, was slightly different from that in 1996. Then virtually the entire media establishment – owners and journalists alike – had felt justified in supporting Yeltsin as the only candidate capable of beating the communist Zyuganov. After all, the communists were scarcely known as defenders of media freedom. By 2000 the prospect of a Zyuganov victory seemed less likely, and the retirement of Boris Yeltsin led a number of the political and business élite to back potential successors other than Putin. By early 2000, a Putin victory, partly on the back of positive war-reporting from Chechnya, seemed assured. Nonetheless, Gusinsky's media outlets were markedly less supportive of either the Chechen conflict or of Putin than were the other main media outlets.

What then of media freedom in the Putin era? An editorial in the London *Times* in July 2000 declared that 'a healthy and vigorous press was Yeltsin's proudest legacy, the best guarantee of democratic pluralism'. Although we have expressed specific reservations about the freedom of the media in the Yeltsin era, this statement still holds. To what extent though does 'a healthy and vigorous press' continue to exist under the presidency of Vladimir Putin? The answer must be, to a much lesser extent.

As noted above, serious concerns about attacks on press freedom were raised in the summer of 1999 when President Yeltsin created a new Press Ministry under Mikhail Lesin. The aim of this ministry was to increase central state control over the media, and although the comparisons with the Soviet-era 'Main Administration for Literary and Publishing Affairs' (Glavlit) made at the time may have been over the top, events since certainly seem to indicate a new, firmer attitude toward the media in Putin's Russia.

Some of the examples of state control over the press since the summer of 1999 are familiar from earlier in the 1990s. In particular, reporters' access to Chechnya during the war there from 1999 onwards echoed similar restrictions applied during the conflict of 1994–96, and bias in coverage of the parliamentary election of December 1999 and the presidential election of March 2000 was likewise familiar from the corresponding elections of 1995 and 1996. By the elections of 2003 and 2004, such a bias in media coverage had worsened, though even then it was rarely crude and simplistic, rather manifest through shorter amounts of time and more negative coverage given to opposition candidates on the national TV channels.

What then changed almost immediately after Vladimir Putin became President to make journalists from across a range of Moscow-based newspapers publish twice in 2000 an *Obshchaya gazeta* ('Common Newspaper') aimed at defending press freedom? First, the attitude of the state markedly toughened. In February 2000 a Russian journalist, Andrei Babitsky, working behind the lines in Chechnya for the US-founded Radio Liberty was arrested by the Russian authorities and handed over to the Chechen forces in exchange for five Russian POWs. The complex tale eventually led to the release of Babitsky and his return to Moscow. Shortly after these events, the then Acting-President Putin had a book published ('First Person'), which consisted of detailed and frank interviews about his life and political views. The portrait of Putin in this book is, as would be expected, a sympathetic one. Nonetheless, the one point where Putin's responses seem the most intemperate concern the Babitsky case. Putin describes Babitsky as a traitor, working for the enemy, and justifying atrocities. He is, in Putin's eyes 'not a Russian journalist', and, most revealingly for our discussion here, Russia's president states that:

> what Babitsky did is much more dangerous than firing a gun ... We interpret freedom of expression in different ways and if you mean direct complicity in crimes, I will never agree to that.

Second, the trend towards increasing state control over the media, which we noted as gathering pace from 1998 onwards, developed into a campaign in the summer of 2000. President Putin had, to the approval of many observers in Russia and the West, declared his intention to clamp down on the influence of the mega-rich businessmen who dominated much of Russia's domestic politics in the Yeltsin era.

Within months of winning the presidential election, the state in various guises began to bring under its control the media empires of Gusinsky and Berezovsky. The cases differ slightly, in that Gusinsky's Media Most group were openly critical of Putin, whereas the Berezovsky controlled media were broadly – though certainly not uniformly – supportive. Gusinsky was briefly arrested on suspicion of fraud, but eventually charges were dropped, allegedly on condition that he facilitated the transfer of his media holdings to the huge state-controlled gas company, Gazprom, to whom Media Most was in any case in substantial debt. Berezovsky apparently voluntarily began negotiations to transfer his holdings in the ORT channel to the state, though ORT likewise was in substantial debt, in this case to a state-controlled bank. Since 2000, all of the national television channels in Russia have been under the control, either directly or indirectly, of the state – whilst Gusinsky and Berezovsky have been living in exile in Europe for fear of prosecution should they return to Russia.

Under state control, television news coverage has become more uniform and more supportive of the Putin regime, with the state demonstrably bringing the television companies back into line on occasions when they are deemed to have overstepped it. One such occasion was the Moscow theatre hostage crisis of October 2002, after which President Putin criticized coverage which he claimed undermined the anti-terrorism operation. It was clear that NTV's coverage upset the authorities – though whether the blame should be laid with them, or with those military authorities which allowed TV crews into the immediate environs of the siege is debatable – and within three months the head of NTV, who had himself been seen as a government place-man on his appointment, was removed from his post. It was notable, too, that during the key hours at the culmination of the siege, the feed of Western news coverage from, for example, CNN and BBC World, was turned off in a number of central Moscow hotels.

In June 2000, Russia's Security Council produced a draft 'information security doctrine'. It had been worked on for some time, including during Putin's tenure as Security Council chief. Although a vague document in itself, this draft backs up the conclusions we will draw here about media freedom in Russia. The Russian state, led by President Putin, sees the media as a legitimate object of state intervention and the strengthening of state control over the media as essential to national security. At the same time, though, Putin repeatedly backs press freedom. The draft information security doctrine asserts these two positions. Only in their outworking will their apparent incompatibility be tested.

Freedom of worship

According to the Russian Constitution of 1993, freedom of worship is guaranteed in the Russian Federation. To enshrine this right in the country's fundamental law marked a clear break with the past, and particularly with the Soviet era, when persecution of religious believers had been continuous and widespread. The situation for religious believers in the Soviet Union had begun to improve under Mikhail Gorbachev's leadership, and particularly from 1988 onwards. This was the year which marked the millennium of Christianity in Russia, and it was officially celebrated across the country, with the atheist communist leadership even sanctioning the production of postage stamps marking the occasion.

In 1990, the Soviet Union introduced a Law on Freedom of Conscience and Religious Associations, which was the most liberal religious law of the twentieth century in Russia. It declared the fundamental right of freedom of conscience, the equality before the law of believers and non-believers, and the right to freely choose, hold and disseminate religious or non-religious convictions. As we noted when considering media freedom, the period of the 1990s was more open and free than the situation which applies in Russia today. Old laws and practices had been swept away, and there was a sense of intoxication with new freedoms.

What did these new freedoms mean for religious believers? On the most basic level believers of all faiths could begin to attend church (or mosque, synagogue, temple, and so on) more openly and freely than before. They were able to obtain religious literature (particularly bibles) with increasing ease, religious groups were able to engage in charitable work and in the expression of their faith, and there was also a growth in contacts with fellow believers abroad. This latter point meant a growth, too, in overt evangelistic activity by different religious groups on the streets or through the media.

In short, the official recognition of religious freedom brought a surge of religious activity across a range of faiths. The Russian Orthodox Church, which still sees itself as carrier of the faith of the Russian people, was by no means excluded from such activity. Indeed it enjoyed the full range of rights, and began to enjoy financial benefits from the state, the return of property confiscated by the communist regime earlier in the twentieth century, and an increasingly prominent position alongside the state machinery. For example, the Patriarch of Russia began to participate in state ceremonies, such as the inauguration of president, and the Russian Orthodox Church once again had official links with the Russian armed forces.

As the 1990s progressed, however, there was something of a backlash against this burst of religiosity. In particular, nationalist, anti-Western elements within federal and regional government, and within the hierarchy of the Russian Orthodox Church, began to object to the activities of what they termed 'non-Russian religious sects and cults'. Several streams of thought came together in this view. There was an element of the idea increasingly found in other policy areas as the 1990s progressed that Russian should not simply accept what the West had to offer, but should build on its own traditions and civilization to find its own Russian path. There was also a fear expressed, particularly in the Orthodox Church, that the Russian people might be 'led astray'. The argument was that after decades of atheistic propaganda, the Russian people might slake their spiritual thirst on whatever was put before them, without having the depth of knowledge necessary to discern between the various faiths on offer. The existence of certain extreme cults in Russia backed up this fear, but also led to almost anything that was not Russian Orthodoxy being branded as a cult. Confessions which had existed since at least the early years of the century in Russia and persisted throughout decades of communist persecution (such as the Baptists or the Pentecostals) often found themselves referred to in this way and accused of being 'Western' faiths.

These fears surrounding the growth of religious freedom found an echo amongst a good proportion of the Russian population, and gradually regional leaders began to promulgate laws which restricted the activities of 'non-Russian' religious groups and, in doing so, often ran counter to the provisions of the Russian Constitution.

In 1997 then, after a couple of failed attempts, the Russian parliament finally passed a law on religion which the president signed. The provisions of the 1997 law 'On Freedom of Conscience and Religious Associations' were a step backwards from the 1990 Soviet-era law in terms of religious freedom, and they also appear to contradict the Russian Constitution. In its preamble, the 1997 law singles out Russian Orthodoxy as making a 'special contribution' to Russia, and then gives respect to those faiths which form 'an inseparable part of the historical heritage of Russia's peoples'. According to the Constitution of Russia, no faith is to be preferred by the secular state.

The most substantive part of the 1997 law with regard to the practice of religious freedom comes in the differentiation which it makes between different types of religious association. According to the Constitution, all religious associations are equal before the law. The 1997 religion law, however, declares that religious associations fall into two categories, they are either religious organizations, which are registered and have the full rights of a legal personage, or they are religious groups which are not registered and do not have those rights. Religious groups therefore are, amongst other restrictions, not able to own property, establish and maintain buildings, employ people, or issue invitations to foreign citizens.

The process of registration is a complex one, and those groups which have had the most difficulties are faiths with links or origins outside of Russia. In order to facilitate registration many smaller groups have had to place themselves within larger 'umbrella organizations', as belonging to a centralized religious association makes registration easier. Furthermore, the passing of the 1997 law on religion appears to have been seen, particularly by regional authorities and certain elements in the Orthodox Church, as the green light for the harassment of non-Orthodox groups. There are still fairly regular reports from Russia of church groups being evicted from buildings, of evangelistic meetings being broken up, or of foreign missionaries and priests being denied visas. In the early twenty-first century, the Roman Catholic church in particular seems to have had problems with visas for its clergy. In a number of such cases, lawyers operating on behalf of church groups have successfully appealed against the actions of officials. Nonetheless, it is clear that a group which has been denied registration will have less of a case in law than does a registered association, and that although the situation is vastly improved from the blanket persecution of the Soviet era, it is too early to talk of the firm establishment of freedom of worship in Russia.

Wider human rights and civil society issues

From our examples of media freedom and freedom of religion, we can discern a pattern in relation to rights and freedoms in Russia which is familiar from other areas of discussion in this book. The pendulum of reform swung out wide in the early to mid-1990s, and then began to swing back. For example, in the area of democratization, the situation is a dramatic improvement on that of the Soviet era, but there has not yet been a full transition to a normative Western liberal democratic system, let alone the consolidation of such a system.

Looking at human rights in general, with particular reference to Russia's place in the international sphere, we can note that Russia is a signatory to the six core UN human rights treaties. It has also accepted the human rights obligations of the Council of Europe. Nonetheless, despite these binding assertions, which take precedence over Russian law, concern has been expressed in the West about aspects of Russia's human rights record. In addition to the questions surrounding media freedom and freedom of worship, the main areas of concern are freedom of speech, individual rights within the 'closed institutions' of the military, the health service, and the Russian prison system, and the area which has had most international attention, the conduct of military action against the Chechen Republic.

We will deal with these issues in order. First, freedom of speech. There have been several cases which have gained international attention, the most noteworthy of which were the separate cases of environmental activists Nikitin and Pasko (see Box 6.2).

Allegations of human rights abuses in the Russian military, health system and prisons relate largely to the poor conditions in these institutions. Lack of resources in the military have led in recent years to poor

---

Box 6.2   The cases of Nikitin and Pasko

Both Aleksandr Nikitin and Grigory Pasko were charged during the 1990s with espionage, after revealing details of the environmental impact of Russia's nuclear naval facilities. The fact that they were investigated by the FSB (the KGB's successor), and charged in this manner, provokes comparisons with Soviet-era practice, and campaigners on their behalf made much of this. However, there was a key difference. Both men were at different times acquitted by Russian civil courts, in the Nikitin case at the very highest level of the Supreme Court, though Pasko was subsequently imprisoned under the jurisdiction of a military court and not released until January 2003. This action by the Russian judiciary provided a small hopeful sign for the rule of law in Russia, showing that officials are not always above the law.

---

standards of nutrition, substandard accommodation and frequent training accidents due to ill-maintained equipment and insufficient expertise amongst the troops. The loss, with all hands, of the nuclear submarine 'Kursk' in August 2000 appears to be the most obvious example of failings in military training and equipment. In addition to these difficulties, caused largely by lack of funding, the 'tradition' of systematic bullying of conscripts entrenched in the Russian armed forces has also led to deaths, protests and the desire to avoid conscription.

Russia has the highest prison population per capita rate in the world, at about 650 per 100,000 population. In this prison system, according to human rights group Amnesty International, over a million prisoners endure conditions which are 'cruel, inhuman and degrading'. Much of this is due to lack of resources which lead in particular to severe health problems, the most worrying of which is a new and virulent strain of tuberculosis (see Chapter 3). There are also stories of torture and ill-treatment in police custody. In terms of the health service, human rights groups have throughout the 1990s raised concerns about the treatment of the mentally ill and, to a lesser extent, the disabled, particularly children within Russia's system of state orphanages.

As noted above, the biggest single human-rights issue with which the West has been concerned in relation to Russia in recent years is the conduct of war in Chechnya in 1994–96 and again from 1999 onwards. In both of these cases, Russian armed forces have attempted to subdue separatist guerrillas by the wholesale 'invasion' of Chechnya. (Though of course, this is not an invasion in terms of international law, as Chechnya remains officially part of the Russian Federation). Critics of Russian action argue that in waging war in Chechnya, Russia has targeted civilians, mistreated prisoners, sacrificed its own conscript soldiers, harassed independent media, and denied access to international bodies such as the International Red Cross and the Organization for Security and Cooperation in Europe.

As a result of Russia's conduct of its war in Chechnya:

- the European Union limited the funds earmarked for the promotion of democracy in Russia and transferred uncommitted funds to humanitarian assistance for refugees from the conflict area;
- the Parliamentary Assembly of the Council of Europe stripped Russia of its voting rights, and declared 'totally unacceptable' the failure of the Council of Europe's Committee of Ministers to denounce Moscow's conduct of the Chechen war; and
- President Putin was widely criticized by the international community, and US President Clinton even used a speech to the State Duma in Moscow to urge a rethink of policy in Chechnya.

Despite all of these actions by the international community, support for Russian action in Chechnya remained fairly solid amongst the Russian population, albeit with some notable exceptions – such as the Committee of Soldiers' Mothers. This is partly due to the fact that media coverage of the war has largely been extremely supportive of the Russian position. It has also resulted from widespread anger and horror at terrorist attacks within Russia.

After the terrorist attacks by Al Q'aeda on New York and Washington on 11 September 2001, President Putin, and indeed the Chechen rebels, have increasingly sought to 'internationalize' the discourse around the Chechen conflict. For Putin the conflict in Chechnya is part of the global war on terrorism, and this interpretation has to some extent been accepted by some Western governments. (For more details on Chechnya, see Chapter 2. For more discussion of how the war in Chechnya fits into the larger picture of Russia's place in the international community, see Chapter 8.)

A weak state

A key to understanding rights and freedoms in contemporary Russia is a knowledge of the historical background. This applies not only to awareness of how recently authoritarianism and even totalitarianism dominated Soviet society, but also to the more recent post-Soviet history. In particular, an adequate understanding of the Putin regime's policies in these areas requires recognition of the 'weak-state hypothesis'. A consensus began to develop at the end of the Yeltsin era amongst observers of contemporary Russia that the central political issue to be dealt with was the weakness of the Russian state.

As an explanatory framework for what happened in Russia in the 1990s, stalled state-building explains much. The essence of the problem was the heavily presidential nature of the Russian state under Yeltsin and its role in hindering the development of democratic institutions and behaviour, thereby creating a weak, personalized state. Under Yeltsin the Russian state could not collect taxes, pay wages, keep order on the streets, rule its regions, provide adequate health and education services, and perform many other functions of a state.

When Putin came to power a degree of consensus existed amongst observers and the new regime alike; the state-strengthening agenda headed the list of tasks facing the Russian government at the turn of the millennium. Putin's policies in regard to state-strengthening have included bringing all regional laws into line with federal legislation, reforming the tax system with a 13 per cent rate of income tax applicable to all, and undermining the influence of 'oligarchs'. These are policies which address in a straightforward manner the problems widely acknowledged to be facing Russia at the end of the Yeltsin era. Switch the discourse a little, however, and a focus on Putin's approach can bring a different interpretation.

For some observers it is enough to put 'former KGB colonel' and 'strengthening of the state' together to conclude that Russia is becoming more authoritarian. To add more fuel to the fire, Putin's two key phrases with regard to state-strengthening echoed the communist past. In place of the Marxist 'dictatorship of the proletariat' promised by Lenin, Putin promised a 'dictatorship of the law'. And instead of Stalin's infamous declaration during his rural terror campaign of the 1930s that he would 'liquidate the Kulaks as a class', Putin said that he would get rid of 'the oligarchs as a class'.

Whether he has managed to achieve either of these in his first years in office is open to debate, but arguably progress has been made from the position which he inherited. As we have seen, with regard to the rule of law, the record in terms of high-profile cases is mixed. Increasingly courts have made decisions based on legal rather than political considerations, but this is a hit and miss affair. In cases such as the attempt to ban the Salvation Army in Moscow – on the grounds that it was a 'paramilitary organization' – or the prosecution on spying charges of environmental campaigner, Grigory Pasko, the message has been confused with courts variously striking down and restating earlier decisions. In other cases, such as that of the academic Sutyagin charged with spying, legal procedures have been far from ideal, and the suspicion that the Russian security service (the FSB) has undue influence is held by many observers.

Similarly, with regard to the liquidation of the oligarchs as a class, again the picture is mixed. The three best-known oligarchs – Vladimir Gusinsky, Boris Berezovsky and Mikhail Khodorkovsky – now either live in exile, in the first two cases, or in a Moscow prison, in the latter case. However, the motivation for their removal from influence on the part of the Putin regime has been identified by many observers as the desire to place their vast media holdings in the hands of the state, and to remove a source of funding and support for opposition groups, rather than to clean up politics. Now that this has been achieved, the liquidation of the oligarchs is a less prominent feature of Russian politics; a number of rich and influential businessmen still maintain both wealth and position, and there is talk of an amnesty for the perceived misdeeds of the 1990s.

Civil society under Putin

How then do we conceptualize contemporary Russia? Is Russia, under Putin, becoming an authoritarian regime again? The American analyst Gordon Hahn stated at the beginning of Putin's second term that Russia had a regime which could not be classified as democratic, but was rather a 'soft authoritarian' regime (Hahn, 2004). If your starting point for comparison is the Soviet era, then Russia has become markedly more liberal. If your comparison is with the somewhat anarchic liberties of the first half of the 1990s, then state-strengthening has been accompanied by an increase in authoritarianism. Making inter-state rather than temporal comparisons provides a further option, but this approach has been complicated somewhat by the 'global war on terrorism' which has shifted some perceptions of the ways in which states can justifiably act.

Broad conclusions become problematic, but in the case of Russia today the concept of 'snatch-squad control' offers a helpful framework. The analogy is straightforward. When policing a crowd, a snatch squad may identify particular individuals, move in, arrest them, and leave the vast majority of the crowd alone.

In Russia, beginning with the religion law of 1997, and progressing through laws on social organizations, political parties, extremists, migration, foreigners, the media and information security, there are sufficient regulations in most cases for the state to move with a legal basis against groups or individuals which might be considered in some sense a threat. In particular the minutiae of registration regulations and the ill-defined catch-all nature of some provisions – for example, the law on extremism's ban on 'the propaganda of exclusiveness, superiority or inferiority' – mean that for groups making up civil society transgressions of the law, witting or not, are relatively straightforward to allege or identify.

This is the situation in Russia at the moment, and a small percentage of religious organizations, political parties, and other elements of civil society have had action taken against them on the basis of these laws. The situation in civil society to some extent mirrors that in other spheres of socio-political life – great strides have been taken towards the democratization of Russia, and yet the ideological commitment to democracy of the regime remains uncertain. The Putin regime seeks first of all a manageable state. Whether once this is achieved there will be motive enough for a deeper democratic shift is doubtful.

Rights and freedoms experienced by the Russian population today are in most areas far wider than during most of the Soviet era. Although we have noted that at times the relative anarchy of the USSR's very last years produced freedoms which have perhaps been rolled back a little, overall the picture is one of greater human and civil rights in most areas. However, two negative corrections in particular need to be made to this overview:

- First, for much of the Russian population the post-Soviet era has been an economic catastrophe. Income differentials have increased dramatically, inflation has wiped out savings many times over, unemployment has increased, and the old certainties of state provision for housing, basic goods and utilities have been left behind. On a wider level, the decline in state funding across the board has led to the poverty in state-funded institutions which we have noted, and to a crumbling physical infrastructure in many sectors of the economy. Against this background, the constitutional rights to work, to receive social security, housing and medical care, and to benefit from a decent environment are all undermined.
- Second, there is fear amongst a number of observers that the Putin era will increasingly see the strengthening of the rights of the state over those of individuals. We have noted somewhat negative trends in relation to media freedom, religious freedom and the conduct of war in Chechnya. Against this, though, we have also noted the occasional willingness of the Russian judiciary to make judgements against what

are perceived as the wishes of the powers that be. The strengthening of an independent judiciary coupled with continued interaction with the international community in this sphere – for example, Russian citizens now have the right to take their cases to the European Court of Human Rights – has an important role to play in ensuring that the rights and freedoms of Russian citizens are protected even whilst Putin's political project of state-strengthening continues.

7
Ideas and Culture

There are few countries in the world where the concept of a 'national idea' is quite as strong as it is in Russia. Nor perhaps are there many countries where arguments are so fierce over precisely what makes up this idea and how important it is. In this chapter we explore the question of the Russian idea, as a precursor to a discussion of the importance of ideology and identity in Russian life. In order to understand a little about how Russians live, it is essential to know something of the shared national experiences which shape national consciousness.

We investigate, too, the place of culture in Russia today, looking at the role played by literature, music and other art forms in illuminating our understanding of the Russian nation and its people. The nation which gave the world great writers such as Pushkin, Tolstoy and Dostoevsky, and great composers such as Tchaikovsky and Shostakovich, has an impressive heritage on which to draw. Although the post Soviet era has not been an easy time for the identification of contemporary literary and musical stars, the twenty-first century is beginning to throw up names known in Russia and beyond. We consider briefly, too, the place of sport in the life of Russia, and Russians, today.

The Russian idea

A glance at the titles of a number of academic books written about Russia in recent years reveals that there are elements of commonly acknowledged Russian-ness which go beyond political and socio-economic explanations to touch something deeper. *Russia and Soul* (Pesmen, 2000), *The Agony of the Russian Idea* (McDaniel, 1996), *Russian Messianism* (Duncan, 2000), *Night of Stone: Death and Memory in Twentieth Century Russia* (Merridale, 2000), *Russia in Search of Itself* (Billington, 2004) – all of these are academic books published in the past few years from a range of disciplines which have in common an awareness of distinctive elements of the Russian identity.

The Russian idea is, at its broadest, the sense that there is a destiny and identity inherent within Russian-ness which is not Western, which has different cultural roots and different core values. It is the idea – or perhaps more accurately, the myth – that Russians are less materialistic, less individualistic, and less shallow than their Western counterparts, and instead have a greater commitment to spiritual values, egalitarianism, community, and the deeper mysteries of faith and eschatology. As discussed in Chapter 2, the empirical evidence for such claims is weak, but the strength of these claims comes in their widespread acceptance. Russians go to places of worship and get involved in the collective institutions of civil society far less than do – in this order – Americans, West Europeans and even, as Marc Morjé Howard found out in a recent study, the inhabitants of other post-communist states. Nonetheless, such hard data as church attendance figures and engagement in civil society do not measure a more elusive inner sense and self-perception. Indeed, an authentically Russian response might be to deem as typically Western and materialist any attempt to measure the inchoate depth of such concepts as community, togetherness, spirituality and national identity.

It is perhaps difficult to talk about a vague 'Russian idea' without falling into clichés and generalizations. As Dale Pesmen points out in her book *Russia and Soul*:

> Some Russians and others dismiss Russian soul as a hackneyed notion irrelevant to tough millennial post-Soviets. Some mourn it, implying that whatever it was died. Some figure good riddance. In all these cases, Russian soul's vitality is assumed to have disappeared. Russian soul was certainly a myth, notion, image, consoling fiction, trope of romantic national self-definition, and what romantic foreigners came to Russia for. (Pesmen, 2002)

Pesmen's research notes that many Russians themselves are aware of the myth-like elements of the Russian idea, and talk of it in self-mocking, satirical terms. And yet, as noted in many places in this book, there is a reality to the generalizations which finds outlet in political debate, policy formation, international relations, and so on.

James Billington (2004) identifies three forces which give Russian culture its distinctiveness:

- **A traditional religious base**. During the 1990s – with the loss of the certainties of communism – the Russian state, and arguably its people, sought to define a national idea (indeed a state-sponsored competition was held, with a prize awarded to the essayist who best summed up what it means to be Russian). Almost without fail, writers and politicians – atheists and believers alike – settled on Russian Orthodoxy as a key locus of Russian identity. Russian Orthodoxy celebrates the mystery of faith, ahead of the intellectual explanations of Western protestants. It promotes a community of believers ahead of the hierarchies of Roman Catholicism. Politicians of the left, right and centre frequently seek to portray themselves as supporters of Orthodoxy, since nothing else better serves to identify them with Russia, its uniqueness, its history, its people.

Religion in Russia, however, is not just about nationalism and Orthodoxy, or even about nationalism and Islam. There is a tradition of an openness amongst the Russian people to spirituality, as opposed to organized and doctrinally precise religion. Russian peasant faith often drew from diverse sources, including asiatic shamanism and paganism. Within such a setting, superstitions, premonitions, curses, blessings and ecstatic experiences all had a place. As, too, did the figure of the 'Holy Man' or 'Holy Fool', archetypally a bearded, somewhat wild, mystical figure who might live apart from society and be called upon as adviser and healer. Grigory Rasputin, the womanizing Siberian monk who wielded significant influence in the court of the last tsar, is a version of this figure. Such spiritual and mystical elements of life do not by any means belong solely to Russia's past; they remain part of the experience of many Russian citizens today (Lewis, 2000).

- **Periodic borrowing from the West**. As noted in Chapter 1, the question of 'catching up' with the West is a recurrent feature in Russian history. Such borrowing entails an ambiguity, with a desire to take the best that the West can offer whilst retaining Russian identity and resisting the overrunning of Russian culture. Russia in the past decade or so has demonstrated this ambiguity in many areas, with a broad opening up to the West resulting in the cautious embrace of many of the facets of 'globalization' combined with a determined resistance against what the more extreme opponents of Westernization have called 'cultural genocide' (see below, 'Culture and Contemporary Reality').
- **A special feeling for land and nature**. Russia was urbanized more recently than most other European nations, and in most families it is only a matter of a generation or two at most before rural, predominantly peasant, roots can be found. Furthermore, the vast expanse of Russia's territory means that it contains some of the most sparsely populated areas on earth. Nature and the land continue to play a part in many lives, even for urban inhabitants. The celebrated *dacha* (summer

house) beyond the boundaries of the cities is the destination for millions of Russians in the summer months.

Trips to the countryside to pick berries and mushrooms in season are regular motifs in Russian literature, and continue to be regular occurrences for many Russians. At the dachas, and even within the environs of the cities, private plots where vegetables and fruit can be grown are common – indeed there is strong evidence to suggest that such private agriculture kept the Soviet Union going when the official state-administered agricultural industry failed.

This feeling for the land has more recently made particularly controversial those post-Soviet reforms seeking to open up the market for buying and selling land (see Chapter 5, Box 5.4). At some deep level the sale of land taps at the root of the cry of peasant revolts across Russia's centuries – 'the land belongs to the people'.

Alongside the elusive questions of the Russian soul and the Russian idea, it is also possible to point to identifiable experiences in history and repeated features of everyday life which help to explain contemporary Russia's cultural identity.

Death and martial culture

The experience of violent death and social chaos marked the Russian people as a whole in the twentieth century. From the First World War of 1914–18, revolution in 1917 and the civil war of 1918–20, with its attendant shortages and famines, through the largely self-inflicted famine of 1932–33, and the mass arrests and executions of the Stalinist terror – over 30 million Russians died prematurely even before the Second World War. Between 1941 and 1945 the war claimed a further 28 million victims, far more than any of the other combatant nations. Soviet military losses alone were over 8 million, US military losses were under 350,000 and British losses nearer to 300,000.

Such experiences cannot but help leave an impact on the Russian people. No family remained untouched by the devastation of war. In comparison, the second half of the twentieth century was relatively less traumatic, with the war in Afghanistan (1979–88) being the major conflict of note. Nonetheless, some observers have portrayed the upheavals of the 1990s as of significant magnitude, with the British historian Christopher Read writing tentatively of the difficulties involved comparing the political mass murder of the Stalin years with the 'economic mass murder' of the 1990s (Read, 2001).

The impact of the Second World War on the Russian nation is difficult to overstate. If the veneration of veterans is noteworthy in, say, Great Britain or the United States, then it is doubly so in Russia, which has of course a particularly Russo-centric view of the Second World War. The Great Patriotic War, as it terms the Second World War, started for Russia in June 1941 and ended with the German surrender on 9 May 1945. Little mention is made of the pact between Germany and the Soviet Union in 1939, which led directly to the occupation of a divided Poland by invading Nazi and Soviet forces and left Great Britain standing alone against Hitler's forces in Europe for almost two years. Nor is much made of the continuation of the Second World War outside of Europe until victory over Japan in September 1945. For Russians, 'Victory Day' is 9 May, which remains a universally celebrated public holiday in Russia.

During the atheistic rule of the Soviet Communist Party elements of reverence for the military provided key unifying features where perhaps religion might previously have played a role. For example, the tradition developed that on their wedding days couples would follow a civil ceremony with a visit to the local war memorial, where photographs would be taken. This practice continues today.

Of course the martial culture of Soviet society was enhanced by the facts that:

- the Soviet Union's superpower status depended above all else on its military strength, especially its nuclear arsenal;
- military training formed a compulsory element of the school curriculum; and
- conscription into the armed forces was also compulsory.

In contemporary Russia, conscription remains in place, but the majority of potential conscripts manage to avoid it by taking advantage of the variety of exemptions and loopholes available. Military training as part of the school curriculum was dropped in the immediate post-Soviet era, but by the end of 2003 a new education bill which would reintroduce it was given its first reading in the Russian parliament. Broad support for this move reflects the widespread respect for the armed forces which still exists in Russia, where post-Soviet opinion polls have long shown the army to be the second most trusted public organization, after the Russian Orthodox Church.

Physical expression of respect for these pillars of Russian identity can be seen in the new developments in Moscow under Mayor Luzhkov from the mid-1990s onwards. In 1995, in time for the 50th anniversary of the end of the Second World War, a vast new memorial, 'Victory Park', was opened – although its accompanying metro line was not completed until some seven years later. In 1996 a statue of the most famous Russian commander of the Second World War, Marshal Zhukov, was erected near the entrance to Red Square. Perhaps the most noticeable new addition to the Moscow cityscape in recent years has been the Cathedral of Christ the Saviour, built between 1995 and 1997 in time to mark the somewhat contrived celebratory anniversary of 850 years since the foundation of the city.

'Byt': the concept of everyday life

The Russian word 'byt' expresses the concept of life as it is lived, those features of everyday life which are common and recognizable to most as elements of daily existence. The very prevalence of such an idea as 'byt' demonstrates an awareness amongst many Russians of elements in national life which are sufficiently common to count as communal experience. 'Byt' stands in opposition to the soul, in that it tends towards the negative side of life, those things that drag people down. This sense of an everyday life which burdened all was perhaps particularly marked in the Soviet years, when the ubiquity of the Party's rule and its fetish for conformity, order and controlling the lives of its citizens meant that the inhabitants of Minsk would readily recognize the lives lived by the inhabitants of Vladivostok, thousands of miles to the east.

In the first decade of the twenty-first century it is difficult to identify precisely those elements in Russia's identity and everyday life which owe their existence simply to the Soviet experience and those which are part of some deeper Russian-ness. For example, the root communist ideal that the workers of the world would unite was sown in fertile ground in Russia, where the concept of *sobornost'* – a mystical unity – was central to national Orthodox identity. Similarly, the workers' councils, or *soviets*, of the Soviet era could build on the tradition of the peasant village council, or *mir*.

And what about the ubiquitous influence of bureaucracy in Russia? Anybody doing business in Russia today will complain about the difficulties imposed by often contradictory regulations, unknown to the many, but zealously applied by the few. It is easy to see the roots of bureaucratic power in the deadening hand of the Soviet centrally planned economy, with its oversight of the most miniscule details across the length and breadth of its vast empire. Nonetheless, a cursory glance at some of the classics of pre-Soviet nineteenth-century Russian literature reveal that the overweening bureaucrat did not spring newly formed from the flames of the communist revolution. Nikolai Gogol's comedy, *The Government Inspector* (1836), is based on the premise that such people wielded inordinate influence in Russia, and was written almost a century before the centrally planned economy was established.

Ideology

We have dealt so far with the realm of ideas and the cultural currency of contemporary Russia. In any country there exists a storehouse of assumptions, commonplace attitudes, clichés, humour and shared experiences. A lack of awareness of these will swiftly identify an outsider, and it is part of our task so far in this chapter to touch upon some of the central elements of this common existence. We will conclude the chapter with an overview of key elements in Russian culture and popular life (literature, film, music and sport). Before that, however, let us consider the more formal and political side of ideas and issues, concentrating on the role of ideology in shaping contemporary Russia.

There has been no state in history to which ideology has been more important than it was to the Soviet Union. As noted in our discussion of 'byt' above, the Soviet state demanded conformity, and this conformity extended to the opinions expressed by state and people. The very legitimacy of the state depended on acceptance of its central idea, and the resources of the state were applied to propagandising this idea throughout everyday life. Undergirding all other legitimating factors, as set out in Box 7.1, was the supreme legitimation of ideology. Put starkly, the only justification which the Soviet regime could put forward for its seizure and retention of power in 1917–18, particularly after the forcible dissolution of the national assembly in 1918, was belief in the correctness of Marxist ideology. As outlined in Chapter 1, Lenin's regime saw the Marxist framework as a scientific explanation which offered the correct interpretation of history and the only way to understand the world. To be carriers of 'truth' was sufficient legitimation for the seizure and retention of power.

Not until the very end-game of the Soviet Union in the late 1980s, when 'almost democratic' elections were held, did the Soviet leader seek to shift this legitimation. Were the question to be asked of the regime at any point in the Soviet Union's history, 'why are you in power?', the only answer which could be given was that Marxist ideology correctly interpreted the world, that the building of communism was the goal of

Box 7.1   Legitimation in Russia

Political science theory on the legitimacy of regimes suggests a range of
different means by which rulers become legitimate. The Soviet regime
based its legitimacy on the ideology of Marxism-Leninism. Of course, as
with all regimes, other legitimating factors came into play. Such factors
included:

- **Meeting the people's needs.** The survival of the regime may have been
  at stake had Lenin not sought to meet the people's basic needs by the tac-
  tical retreat of the New Economic Policy in the 1920s, when he allowed
  the pragmatic approach of freeing up trade in order to provide food,
  rather than insisting on the Marxist line against free trade.
- **Gaining the support of the élite.** The desires of the Soviet élite were
  pandered to shamelessly in the Brezhnev era (1964–1982), when those at
  the top of the Soviet tree enjoyed material privilege and, for the most
  part, security of tenure in post.
- **A charismatic leader.** During the cataclysmic turmoil of the Stalin
  years, the regime benefited from an almost ubiquitous acceptance –
  fostered by the propaganda of the 'cult of personality' – that its 'Great
  Leader' was a man of extraordinary gifts, prescience and charisma.
- **Popular support.** Throughout the Soviet Union's existence, a framework
  of elections, councils and a parliament (Supreme Soviet) provided a means
  by which the one party supposedly demonstrated, in its own peculiar definition of democracy, that it had the almost unanimous support of its people.

history, and that the Communist Party of the Soviet Union was at the
vanguard of history. Little wonder, then, that the Soviet authorities set
such store throughout the USSR's existence, in propagandising its ideology throughout society.

Soviet schoolchildren were taught the ideology of Marxism-Leninism,
political officers in the armed forces and party representatives in the
workplace or district made sure that regular political meetings were held
and attended, and, in a country without private ownership and capitalist
competition, 'advertising' hoardings and slogans on high-rise buildings
exhorted the people to implement the decisions of the latest Party congress. At first glance the Soviet Union appeared to be an ideological
monolith, where dissenters from the official line were few and persecuted.

Before looking at the impact of the USSR's ideological emphasis on
contemporary Russia, let us briefly take a top-down view of Soviet society:

- At the very highest level of politburo and regional first secretaries little room existed for straying beyond the ideological norms of the
  regime, though disputes over the detail of these norms were common.

- Below the highest level of leadership there were many working within the Soviet apparatus for whom the relative ideological openness of the Khrushchev years (1953–64), and the ideals of the reformist Czech communists in the 'Prague Spring' of 1968 – ideals which were crushed by Soviet tanks – represented their preferred way forward. Such 'men of the sixties' as they were known were eventually to come to power and influence with Mikhail Gorbachev in the mid-1980s.

- More broadly in society as a whole, but particularly in urban society, there existed for many people a gap between what they professed to believe – for reasons of career progression, or the need for new accommodation, or simply a peaceable existence – and what they might say to trusted friends around the kitchen table. The extent of this dissonance between real and professed belief is impossible to measure, and the degree of difference between the two varied from person to person. True believers in the cause existed alongside closet dissidents. Again, though, when Mikhail Gorbachev provided the opportunity for openness it became clear that despite the massive state ideological apparatus, belief in Marxism-Leninism was held very lightly by many people.

The legacy of ideology in today's Russia

What then does this brief survey of ideological belief in the Soviet era have to tell us about contemporary Russia? Most importantly, it provides a context against which to better understand the role of ideas in contemporary Russian affairs. Two important consequences resulted, which had some bearing on the collapse of the Soviet system and its aftermath:

- First, the Soviet people as a whole were heavily politicized. They were denied the freedoms available in the West to explore a range of ideas, but they were also denied the freedom to opt out of political discourse. Marxism-Leninism formed a compulsory element of the university curriculum, as well as being proclaimed in workplaces across the land. Consequently, as the Soviet Union collapsed and the Russian state was reestablished, democratic institutions were not planted on virgin political land, but in one of the world's most politicized countries.

- Second, the nature of the politicization of the Soviet people tended towards duality and polarization. The propaganda of Marxism-Leninism revolved around the clash of two systems, capitalism and communism, engaged in a zero-sum game. In this black and white conceptualization, little room existed for shades of grey, for compromise, for the borrowing of ideas, or for cooperating with ideological opponents.

The consequences of both these factors – politicization and polarization – can be discerned in Russia today. Once the Soviet state and ideological apparatus were no longer in place, a noticeable 'anti-politics' faction grew up not only in Russian society but, somewhat ironically, within the political system itself. Having for all of their lives been obliged to participate in some form or other in political life, many now wanted the freedom to not be involved in politics. The popular conceptualization of a people coming out from under the authoritarian yoke of the Communist regime and at last grasping the opportunity to freely pursue new ideas of course held true to some extent, but not universally. As a survey of elections in 1990s Russia pointed out:

> The unvarying insistence on supporting the party-state in the Soviet Union had the … perverse effect of demobilizing the voters … Many Russians reacted to such pressures by becoming 'negatively integrated' in the political system, and this legacy remains in postcommunist Russia … the great majority of Russians see major gains in freedom from the communist effort to mobilize and control their everyday lives. It is particularly significant that one of the major gains in freedom is the right to decide for oneself whether or not to take an interest in politics. (White *et al.*, 1997)

This 'anti-politics' attitude was built on a distrust of political parties in general, and, particularly as the corruption and policy failures of the Yeltsin years became increasingly apparent, on a distrust of politicians and of political ideologies. The culmination of such an attitude is apparent in the Putin government of 2000 onwards. President Putin, following the approach taken by Viktor Chernomyrdin (Russian Prime Minister, 1992–98), makes a virtue out of rejecting 'politics' and ideology. On taking power, Putin criticized ideological policy-making, declaring that:

> merely experimenting with abstract models and schemes taken from foreign textbooks cannot assure that our country will achieve genuine renewal … the mechanical copying of other nations' experience will not guarantee success (Putin, 2000).

Similarly Putin's 'party of power', United Russia, boasts of its lack of an ideology, and proclaims itself to be a party of managers rather than politicians. The calculation is clear. To a sufficiently large proportion of people in Russia, 'politics' and 'ideology' have become dirty words, whose rejection is an electoral virtue. In early twenty-first century Russia, the anti-politicians have come to power.

Culture and contemporary reality

The importance of literature and art in the lived experience of educated Russians was heightened by the strict censorship which the Soviet authorities exercised in these areas during much of the twentieth century. State control of literature, music and art in order to force it into the strait-jacket of service to what was a fundamentally utilitarian, anti-spiritual, some might say philistine, regime acted on the intellectual psyche of the Russian people.

To love art forms for their own sake was to defend a small area of personal independence from the authorities. Literature and music were used to express subtle – and not so subtle – dissatisfaction with the dominant ruling party, and to interpret these messages required a high-level of artistic literacy. Intellectual debates still rage, for example, over the precise meaning of passages in Shostakovich's symphonies. In the Soviet era the heavy literary journals would regularly sell out on publication, and people would pass round carefully copied typescripts of banned works. The word *samizdat* (literally 'self-published') became – like *glasnost'* several years later – a term sufficiently well-used to be understood by many in the West, referring as it did to illegal literature of all forms, from heavyweight novels, through political statements against the regime, to religious tracts.

Although strong state censorship was in place for most of the Soviet era, the state education system nonetheless helped to produce this highly literate population which knew not only the Russian classics of Pushkin, Tolstoy and Dostoevsky, but also a range of foreign classics too. Russian knowledge of, and respect for, the works of Shakespeare, for example, can often seem to exceed that in England. In the early 1990s, as the Soviet Union dissolved itself and censorship disappeared, many Russians avidly snapped up those works which had previously not been available. Multi-volume sets of the works of dissident Soviet authors such as Solzhenitsyn, Pasternak and Bulgakov appeared on the bookstalls swiftly set up around the Moscow metro system, alongside complete works of other literary giants, copies of the Bible, and the ubiquitous 'Teach Yourself English' courses which were increasingly *de rigueur* for Russians seeking to make a life for themselves in the uncertain new world of the market economy.

If at first in the post-Soviet era the bookstalls and kiosks of Moscow reflected the relatively highbrow tastes of the intelligentsia and focused on Russian works, they swiftly branched out as the almost anarchic freedoms of the early 1990s took hold. Western pornography (Russian pornography had yet to break into the market) began to be sold openly on the streets of Moscow, attracting such crowds of browsers that stall-holders began to charge for leafing through the merchandise at the stall as well as for actually purchasing it. Kiosks selling pirate video copies of the latest Hollywood blockbusters appeared, often able to pro-vide purchasers with films within days of release. Similarly, pirate CDs of previously unobtainable Western and Russian musicians became eas-ily available. Back on the bookstalls things were also changing, with classic literature giving way to detective stories, thrillers, science fiction and fantasy. Russian translations of Western bestsellers such as Agatha Christie and Tom Clancy elbowed the more highbrow literature out of the way.

As the 1990s progressed, however, the somewhat naïve excitement of the first flushes of cultural liberty began to give way to a more sophisti-cated and unique popular culture. The clichés of the late Soviet period revolved around the supposed desire amongst young Russians for any-thing Western – scarcely a Western traveller to the Soviet Union in the 1980s was sent off without being advised to pack an extra pair of Levis for selling on arrival – and the apparent preoccupation of Russians with outdated Western music, notably the Beatles and 1970s heavy rock bands.

Whatever truth existed in these clichés was swiftly blown away in the 1990s. Russian youth movements emerged with a distinctly indigenous edge; literary genres and musical styles alike drew on Western examples and swiftly added Russian ingredients. Russian detective writers found plenty of material in the crime-ridden business culture of the new Russia, and other genres too (notably fantasy and science fiction) soon identified their own authors instead of merely accepting translations of Western bestsellers. A similar process of adoption and adaptation occurred across musical genres, culminating in the unprecedented dominance of the UK and European pop and dance charts for several weeks in 2003 by Russian artists, the teenage faux-lesbian duo Tatu.

In the world of advertising, the successful companies were those who quickly noted the obvious – that simply dubbing Russian language onto Western advertisements was culturally inappropriate and commercially ineffective. Some took the 'non-Western' nature of their products and turned it from a perceived handicap into an aggressive selling point. In the 1990s one particular advert for a brand of Russian cigarettes, strug-gling against its ubiquitous Western competitors, pictured their product as a spaceship hovering above New York, drawing on the imagery of the hit sci-fi film 'Independence Day' and carrying the strapline 'retaliatory strike'. Like all good advertising, this encapsulated a whole complex of ideas in a simple phrase – smoking these cigarettes was, it implied, patriotic, independent, and a blow against the multinationals and cultural imperialism.

Literature

As with any country, the literature of Russia reflects the state of the nation. The great novels of Tolstoy and Dostoevsky in the second half of the nineteenth century addressed the 'accursed questions' of the human soul, alongside the questions of Russia's place in the world and the social divisions within Russian society. We have already mentioned in Chapter 1 the prescience of Anton Chekhov's play, *The Cherry Orchard* (1904), closing with the sound of an axe striking a tree, symbolizing the blows being struck to the old social order as the revolutionary twentieth century dawned.

During the Soviet era, as noted above, the communist regime sought to subjugate literature to its own demands and ideas. The genre of 'socialist realism' told stirring tales of devotion to work and building the new industrialized Soviet state, for example, in works such as Nikolai Ostrovsky's *How the Steel was Tempered* (1934). The official policy was that literature should be positive and optimistic. The counterpart of socialist realist literature in painting and sculpture was the healthy, well-proportioned, muscle-bound worker, sleeves rolled-up, a smile on the face, and a hammer or sickle (sometimes both) raised aloft. Such images fitted the self-conceptualization of the communist élite, which incidentally happened to control all publishers, exhibition halls, concert venues, and so on.

Of course the best artists and writers almost by their nature are most unlikely to shape their output in line with such crass strictures. Boris Pasternak and Aleksandr Solzhenitsyn were both awarded the Nobel prize for literature, though the Soviet regime persuaded Pasternak to decline his award. Both smuggled their greatest works, respectively *Dr Zhivago* and *The Gulag Archipelago*, to the West for publication and were vilified by the authorities at home. Pasternak remained in the Soviet Union until his death in 1960, Solzhenitsyn was exiled until finally returning to Russia in 1994 where he still lives. Other writers, such as Yury Trifonov, somehow managed to remain within the pale of official Soviet literature and yet touch on topics which, so far as their readers were concerned, were much more 'realistic' than socialist realism's tales of building communism. Trifonov wrote, earlier than most but relatively obliquely, about the difficulties of the Stalin years.

From the 1960s onwards fiction dealing with the more risqué topics – such as the purges, the drudgery of modern urban life, and the double domestic/professional burden carried by Soviet women – became increasingly common. Although the state sought to control and guide the content of literature throughout the Soviet era, the degree of artistic licence allowed did ebb and flow at different times. There was something of a cultural thaw in the Khrushchev years (1953–64), and in the late 1960s and early 1970s more controversial works, such as Solzhenitsyn's devastating labour camp critique *One Day in the Life of Ivan Denisovich*, were published in the Soviet Union, before later being banned.

As the Soviet era came to an end and censorship disappeared, it was something of an irony that the state of Russian literature can be said to have declined somewhat. There were two main reasons for this:

- The new freedoms meant that many readers turned to what had previously been unavailable – the banned works of Soviet dissidents, Western literature, and the less highbrow genres of fantasy, crime and thrillers.
- The removal of the dead hand of the state from its monopoly control of publishing meant an end to the focus on more literary works – albeit of varying quality – which the Soviet system encouraged.

For most of the 1990s then, pulp fiction became the dominant force in Russian literature, with a number of authors selling books in their millions, producing novels at a great rate, and being paid royalties far below what would be paid to authors in the West. The stories of Aleksandra Marinina, Viktor Dotsenko and many others are set in the world of the mafia and criminal gangs. Liberally sprinkled with the jargon of that milieu, such works do not shy away from the sex and violence associated with the lives they portray. Set all of this within a fast-paced and tightly plotted story, and the sales follow. The very best-selling authors are set apart from their competitors by the creation of strong hero figures who become the centre of their novels, such as Marinina's female detective, Anastasia Kamenskaya.

The literary purists may bemoan such a state of affairs, as Russia has become far more like the rest of the world in its dealings with literature. No longer are writers quite so venerated and so much a part of public and political discourse as they previously were, in many ways the Russian people's special relationship with literature has gone – or at the very least, been put on hold. Nonetheless, there is no doubt that the realities of post-Soviet Russia are reflected in the crime stories of writers such as Marinina and Dotsenko. Indeed it is this world which, in different ways, is reflected, too, in the writings of those more literary authors who have begun to emerge in the late twentieth and early twenty-first centuries. Foremost amongst these is Viktor Pelevin, whose prose reflects the chaotic Russia which he portrays. Pelevin's writing shows a nihilistic world infused with materialism, Buddhist philosophy, drug-taking, computer games, advertising slogans and violence; he writes in a style which is cinematic, episodic and impressionistic. In this approach Pelevin certainly taps into and reflects a particular strand in Russian literature, his writing in places being reminiscent of Dostoevsky's psychological portraits, such as *Notes from the Underground*, or Pilnyak's portrayal of post-revolutionary Russia in 1919, *The Naked Year*.

Although Pelevin has to some extent become known outside of Russia, such fame has been amongst those who follow Russian literature rather than amongst the Western-reading public in general. Boris Akunin, however, has made the breakthrough that Pelevin has not, and is a Russian author who publishes and sells in Europe and the United States. Akunin writes detective thrillers, but of a slightly more genteel type than the blockbuster mafia novels discussed above. Instead, Akunin's stories are set in the nineteenth century, with his hero, Erast Fandorin, owing more to Sherlock Holmes than to contemporary movie heroes.

Film

As with so much in contemporary Russia, the world of film follows a pattern from the late 1980s to today of liberalization, Western influence, and then a rebirth of a more distinctly Russian approach. In the last years of the Soviet era the most noteworthy films were those which began to break the taboos imposed by state censorship. *The Cold Summer of '53* (1988) dealt with the labour camps and Khrushchev's decision in 1953 to release large numbers of criminal – as opposed to political – inmates, and *Little Vera* (1988) tackled the social problems of the late Soviet period, becoming renowned both for this and for breaking taboos by its inclusion of a nude scene.

When the Soviet Union collapsed, so too did its state-controlled and therefore state-funded studio system, known as Goskino. This meant that funding for Russian films became increasingly scarce. At the same time, Russia opened up to Hollywood blockbusters. Many of the new glossy magazines which began to appear carried the sort of gossip and tittle-tattle surrounding the lives of American film stars which is familiar in the West, and the cinemas showed American films on global release, dubbed into Russian. This state of affairs continues today, but at the same time indigenous film-making has recovered to some extent.

In the 1990s, Nikita Mikhalkov's *Burnt by the Sun* – an account of the brutalities and betrayals of Stalin's terror – and Sergei Bodrov's *Prisoner of the Caucasus* (*Prisoner of the Mountains* in its Western release) were both critically acclaimed and funded by private investors, but made next to no box-office impact in the West. *Burnt by the Sun* won an Oscar for best foreign film, and *Prisoner of the Caucasus* was nominated in the same category. In a similar vein in the early years of the twenty-first century, Aleksandr Sokurov's *Russian Ark* (2002) received rave reviews for its cinematographic brilliance. Lavishly costumed and filmed in the Hermitage museum in St Petersburg, this sweep through 200 years of Russian history is the first full-length feature film ever to be composed of a single unedited shot running uninterrupted from beginning to end. Once again, though, artistic acclaim did not lead to box-office success.

Music

Most of the big names in Russian popular music are little known abroad, with the exception, as noted above, of the duo Tatu who briefly shot to the top of the European charts in 2003. It is fair to say, however, that an essential part of understanding the cultural make-up of Russians whose formative years were the 1960s and 1970s is an awareness of the icons of Soviet popular music. Two names in particular stand out, Vladimir Vysotsky and Alla Pugacheva:

- Vysotsky was a gravelly voiced, hard-living, maverick actor turned singer-songwriter, in some ways a Soviet Bob Dylan in that he played guitar, had a highly distinctive voice and – most significantly – wrote lyrics which were a literary and poetic comment on the world around him. Vysotsky died young, aged 42, in 1980. In his lifetime his politically 'unreliable' lyrics meant that none of his songs were officially released, and his following was built on unofficial cassettes of his music, and *samizdat* publications of lyrics.
- Pugacheva, on the other hand, was a more traditional figure. She enjoyed official approval in the Soviet era, becoming the Soviet Union's first and greatest pop star. During her career she has sold over 200 million albums, and has successfully made the transition to the

post-Soviet era, enjoying a legendary status amongst Russian citizens and emigrés alike – of a certain age.

In the sphere of classical music, Russia's ability to produce some of the world's finest performers continues unabated. In the Soviet era the likes of the dissident cellist Rostropovich or the pianist Sviatoslav Richter achieved global fame for their virtuosity. Today Russia can continue to boast some of the greatest of contemporary musicians, such as the conductor Valerii Gergiev, who has a famed commitment to Russian music, the young pianist Boris Berezovsky, and the violinist judged by many to be the world's best, Maksim Vengerov.

Sport

The Soviet Union devoted impressive resources to the development of leading sportsmen and women, seeing international success as a sign of the supremacy of the socialist system. This socialist supremacy was apparent in some sports more than others, notably gymnastics and athletics. The tradition created in these sports continues today, and in addition new areas of excellence are springing up.

In the 2004 Olympic Games in Athens, the Russian team came second or third in the medals table, depending on which method of counting is used (in terms of total medals Russia came second to the United States; if weighting is given for gold, silver and bronze, then Russia came third behind the United States and China). Russia's women, as they have traditionally done, excelled in the field events, winning discus, hammer, high jump and pole vault golds. Performances which stand out include the remarkable gold and silver achieved by Yelena Isinbayeva and Svetlana Feofanova, respectively, in the pole vault, the 800 metres gold won by Yurii Borzakovsky, and the near-miss overall performances of veteran gymnasts Aleksei Nemov and Svetlana Khorkina.

Since the collapse of the Soviet Union there is one sport where Russia has become increasingly dominant, namely tennis, and women's tennis in particular. Of the top ten women's seeds at the US Open in 2004, five of them were Russian. Within one year, over 2004 and 2005, all four of the major tennis tournaments had a Russian winner in the singles. Anastasia Myskina won the French Open final, beating fellow Russian Elena Dementieva. Dementieva was beaten again in the US Open final by Svetlana Kuznetsova, and Wimbledon was won by Maria Sharapova. In early 2005 Russia's top male tennis player, Marat Safin, won the Australian Open.

In terms of spectator sports, football remains the most popular in Russia, although Russian teams have rarely enjoyed huge success either internationally or in European club competitions over the years. Moscow dominates Russian football, as it dominates so much in the country, with the major teams (Lokomotiv, CSKA, Spartak and Dynamo) all based in the capital.

A final area of traditional Russian excellence is chess, where the world game has been dominated by Russian players and administrators for decades. Only the American Bobby Fischer in the early 1970s briefly interrupted a continuous list of Soviet and Russian world chess champions in the postwar era. The world chess federation, FIDE, is headed by the President of the Russian republic of Kalmykia, Kirsan Ilyumzhinov. In the 1990s, however, the chess world was split, as world champion Garry Kasparov refused to recognize FIDE's authority and created his own world championship, which was won in 2000 by Vladimir Kramnik.

8
Russia and the World

Our penultimate chapter turns from domestic issues to the question of Russia's place in the international arena. Chapter 1 used as an organizing theme the duality present in Russian history with regard to relations with the West, and the influence of this on Russian domestic affairs has been apparent throughout this book. Let us now return in a sense to where we started – where does Russia fit into the twenty-first century world? Starting from a discussion of what made the Soviet Union a superpower we quickly proceed to considering the post-Soviet situation. We analyse relations between the former Soviet republics which became 15 independent states in 1991, as well as considering Russia's place in the wider world, its relations with Europe, the United States and China, and its role in the 'war on terror'.

The death of a superpower

The Soviet Union's superpower status was based on a number of factors, not the least of which was military strength. From the end of the Second World War in 1945 to the end of the 1980s, global international relations were dominated by the existence of two great opposing power blocs – East and West, communist and capitalist, led by the Soviet Union and the United States, and projecting their military strength through two alliances, the Warsaw Pact and NATO. The military preeminence of these blocs came from their capability to fight an all-out nuclear war, the consequence of which would be global annihilation.

Clearly, such a war was never fought. Nonetheless the 'Cold War' between the two blocs was founded on the possibility that an actual conflict might occur. It is perhaps difficult for someone who has grown up since the mid-1980s to grasp the proximity to nuclear conflict that was perceived in West and East alike, amongst both the populace at large and the politico-military professionals. At key times, notably the early 1960s and the early 1980s, a superpower confrontation seemed to be edging closer, and certainly the presumption of military planners had to be that nuclear war should be prepared for.

The arms race that existed throughout the cold-war years saw priority given to defence production in the economic plans of the Soviet Union. By the end of the 1980s, there was a rough parity of some 10,000-plus 'active' nuclear weapons on each side of the US/Soviet divide, though the Soviet Union had more nuclear weapons than the Americans – almost as many again – in its non-strategic reserve. Nuclear weapons, however, although essential for superpower status, were not the sole focus of the arms race. In the 1970s and 1980s, in particular, the Soviet Union refocused attention on the development and production of conventional weapons.

There were two main reasons for this. First, the achievement of rough nuclear parity with the West resulted in a slightly increased confidence that the USSR's missiles would serve to deter nuclear superpower confrontation. Second, the technological advances which were eventually to lead to the 'smart weapons' of the 1990s and beyond were gathering pace in the West. Soviet conventional strength had traditionally been built on quantity. Now the quality of weapons systems – particularly in relation to computers and electronic technology – became increasingly important.

As well as the vital military component, a number of other factors had contributed to the superpower status of the Soviet Union:

- **Imperial** – the Soviet bloc, those countries whose political systems were installed and maintained by the USSR, reached into the heart of Europe and, after 1979, the Soviet empire had begun to extend southwards by means of the eventually doomed invasion of Afghanistan. Furthermore, as the leader of one pole of a bipolar world, the Soviet Union had significant influence with allies across the globe, notably in Southeast Asia, the Middle East, Africa and Central America.
- **Ideological** – the USSR was an ideological state. Its self-legitimation came from a belief in Marxism-Leninism, and the presumption that the Communist Party of the Soviet Union led the world on the path to communism and workers' power. Although easy to dismiss today, such an ideological underpinning strengthened and guided the international policies of the Soviet leadership. It provided a sense of mission and influenced the decision of some client states to ally themselves with the USSR.
- **Economic** – although the Soviet economy was rapidly failing by the early 1980s (see Chapter 5), trade relations played a key role in giving substance to the ideology of international relations. Towards the end of the Soviet period some two-thirds of the country's foreign trade was with other socialist countries. Furthermore, the Soviet Union strengthened ties with key countries by subsidizing arms exports. In the

Gorbachev years (1985–91) only a third of arms exports were paid for directly, the rest were sold under advantageous credit conditions, subsidized massively, or given away for free.

The bipolar world of the cold-war era finally collapsed in 1989–91. Anti-communist revolutions in Eastern Europe broke up the Warsaw Pact, the nations that had made up the Soviet Union became independent, and the USA led a coalition of forces from across the developed world to victory in the short war with Iraq in early 1991, leading to talk of a 'new world order' and a unipolar system. It was into this world, and with the legacy of the superpower status outlined above, that Russian foreign policy emerged.

The legacy of superpower status in post-Soviet Russian foreign relations

There are a number of key ways in which Russia's international relations since 1991 have been shaped by aspects of the Soviet Union's standing in the world. On the break-up of the Soviet Union, Russia became the official successor state to the USSR, and therefore took over one of the five permanent seats on the United Nations Security Council, as well as accepting primary responsibility for fulfilling treaty obligations and taking over the institutional structures necessary for the conduct of foreign policy (for example, the Ministry of Foreign Affairs (MFA), embassies, and the Foreign Intelligence Agency).

Immediately then, Russia identified itself as one of the 'great powers', and at the time of the Soviet Union's break-up there was little international surprise at or argument with this assumption of succession on the part of Russia. In the West it alleviated concern that the disintegration of a superpower to be replaced by 15 independent states would lead to massive instability, particularly with regard to the proliferation of nuclear weapons. Amongst the clear majority of the 'successor states' themselves there was a recognition that only Russia had the capabilities and standing to take over the USSR's role on the international stage.

Identification as one of the UN 'permanent five' fitted the continuing insistence in Russian foreign policy that Russia is indeed a great power and should be treated as such. Discerning the rationale for and appropriateness of this insistence reveals some of the key features underlying foreign-policy formation in Russia. On the one hand, in terms of geopolitics, the Russian Federation is the largest country in the world and occupies an area contiguous with Europe north and south, the volatile north Caucasus region, Central Asia, China and, across short stretches of water, Japan and the United States. Furthermore, one legacy of Soviet superpower status is the vast nuclear arsenal under the Russian Federation's control. On these criteria then, great power status seems deserved.

On the other hand, the Russian economy does not even make the top 70 of global economies measured by gross domestic product per head at the turn of the century, a fact which led a number of commentators to ridicule Russia's admission to the élite G8 group of leading industrial nations in the 1990s (although Russia is not included in all of the economic discussions of the original G7). Furthermore, the Russian military, as will be discussed below, has existed for most of the post-Soviet era in a state of demoralized disarray and poverty. It scarcely has the capabilities to subdue separatist Chechens within the borders of the Federation, let alone to project into the international arena. Were 'great power status' to be conferred on the basis of economic or military strength, then Russia would hardly be able to lay such a claim, except with regard to its possession of a vast nuclear arsenal.

On taking office President Putin declared, in 'Russia at the Turn of the Millennium', his belief in the greatness of Russia:

Russia was and will remain a great power. It is preconditioned by the inseparable characteristics of its geopolitical, economic and cultural existence. They determined the mentality of Russians and the policy of the government throughout the history of Russia.

Two further legacies of superpower status need enumerating before we go on to consider in more detail the military, diplomatic and economic aspects of contemporary Russia's place in the international arena. The first of these is the existence of the 14 other 'successor states' to the Soviet Union. The second is the need to review military and security policy in the light of changing international allegiances.

The Commonwealth of Independent States

With regard to the other 'successor states' to the Soviet Union, 11 of these, along with the Russian Federation, make up the Commonwealth of Independent States (CIS). The three Baltic republics of Estonia, Latvia and Lithuania declined to join the CIS, and consistently pursued membership of NATO and the European Union, gaining both in 2004.

In the short term immediately after the collapse of the USSR, Russia and the other post-Soviet states were faced with concrete issues of disentanglement and the reorganization of relations which inevitably result from the fracture of what was one country into 15.

- Russian troops had to be withdrawn from a number of the newly independent states, notably in response to demands for immediate withdrawal from the Baltic republics.
- Property had to be shared appropriately, leading, for example, to disputes over the Black Sea Fleet in Ukraine and the Baikonur space-launching facility in Kazakhstan.
- Economic linkages faced disruption and renegotiation, with independent currencies being established, and the rouble zone abolished in 1993.
- Even such apparently minor matters as representation at the 1992 Olympic games and the establishment of national football teams involved careful negotiation, resolved by the creation of interim Commonwealth of Independent States teams.

With the exception of Belarus, which has since 1996 been negotiating an ever-closer union with Russia, there has never been any serious suggestion that the other former Soviet states would re-unify.

The Commonwealth of Independent States (CIS) was formed in December 1991 out of most of the states emerging from the Soviet Union (the Baltic states of Estonia, Latvia and Lithuania have never been members). From its very inception some members – Russia in particular – saw it as a means of holding on to some aspects of the Soviet Union, others saw is as a means for achieving a 'civilized divorce', a dividing up of what once belonged to the Soviet Union, before the newly independent states went their own ways.

The CIS is not a state itself. It has no flag, no constitution and no capital. It rests on a mix of formal multilateral treaties and a growing network of more substantial bilateral agreements between Russia and individual states. Historically, Russia has dominated its 'near abroad', but it cannot take organizational leadership of the CIS for granted, and is trying to build influence through security arrangements and economic links.

The non-Russian CIS is no monolith. Each member state has interests which deviate to different degrees and at different times from those of Russia. There are complicated dynamics in a series of relationships, and any attempt by Moscow to make the CIS a tighter organization would risk its disintegration through centrifugal forces. For simplicity's sake, the CIS countries can be represented as an inner core of countries which want closer ties, and an outer ring joined primarily by the desire for greater freedom from Russian influence, and indeed from the CIS itself (Box 8.1).

Box 8.1   The Commonwealth of Independent States

• The closest formal relationship is between Russia and Belarus, who are committed to a treaty on the formation of a Union State, though with little sign of anything of real substance coming of this in the near future.
• The inner core consists of Belarus, Kazakhstan, Kyrgyzstan, Russia and Tajikistan, making up the Eurasian Economic Community founded in October 2000.
• Armenia joins this group in the Collective Security Treaty Organization (CSTO), founded in September 2003 on the basis of the six remaining signatories to the Tashkent treaty of 1992. However, Armenia is more Westward-looking and seeks integration into European structures.
• Turkmenistan is a largely passive member of the CIS, doing its best to avoid commitments to regional cooperation.
• The outer ring is made up of a loose, semi-official grouping of states, known by the acronym GUUAM (Georgia, Ukraine, Uzbekistan, Azerbaijan and Moldova), and founded in 1998. Its aim has been to avoid Russian dominance of the regional agenda, but it seems to have declined in activity and influence in recent years.

This conceptualization of the CIS as an inner core and outer ring is useful, but does not convey the complexity of relations between the 12 independent states:

• The Shanghai Cooperation Organization, founded in June 2001, consists of China, Kazakhstan, Kyrgyzstan, Russia, Tajikistan and Uzbekistan. It has become increasingly active, developing cooperation on a range of security issues.
• Members of the GUUAM grouping vary in their desire or ability to distance themselves from Russia – leadership changes in Azerbaijan, Georgia and Ukraine in 2003–04 means that the situation remains fluid.

If the short-term difficulties of imperial break-up are complex and fraught with tension, they are at least readily identifiable. The longer-term legacy has been a forced drawing-in of the Russian sphere of influence. What were republics within the Soviet Union are now independent countries and therefore subjects of international law and objects of international relations. Were the Russian Federation to engage in expansionist policies – and it has shown virtually no inclination in this direction – then these are now front-line countries to be expanded into, rather than launching pads for further aggrandisement. The post-Soviet equivalent of the Soviet Union's war with Afghanistan (1979–88), in terms of the attempt to secure Russia's southern flank, has been two wars with the Chechen Republic, which is not even one of the post-Soviet states but rather legally a member of the Russian Federation. When Russia has wanted to base troops in surrounding republics, it has had to do so by means of careful negotiation, combined with activities such as peace-keeping and border-guarding. Furthermore, it is not only Russia which has stationed troops in the former Soviet republics. During its invasion of Afghanistan in 2001, the United States established a military presence in Kyrgyzstan, Uzbekistan, Tajikistan and Georgia.

Clearly, therefore, Russian foreign policy has become more closely focused on a reduced sphere of influence than was that of its Soviet predecessor. This has again provided something of a post-imperial psychological shock for Russia's policy-makers. The very concept that, for example, Ukraine is a foreign country, has been a difficult conceptual leap for élite and masses alike to make, as was made dangerously clear when Russia allegedly attempted to interfere in Ukraine's presidential election in 2004. The term 'near abroad' is still widely used in Russia to refer to the former Soviet republics, as if to reinforce the fallacy that these countries are somehow not quite abroad.

This difficulty with post-Soviet identity has been apparent, too, in the institutional arena. Although immediately after the break-up of the Soviet Union the first Russian foreign minister, Andrei Kozyrev, assumed responsibility for relations with the former Soviet states, in practice so many of the problems of disentanglement related to military and security matters that it was the Ministry of Defence and the Security Council which led in these areas. Later President Yeltsin established a separate ministry for relations with the CIS, as if to emphasize again some 'not quite foreign' status, and it was not until 1998 that relations with these countries once more came under the purview of the MFA.

Security policy

Let us now turn to the final element of the superpower legacy to be con-sidered, namely Russia's need to review military and security policy in the light of changing international allegiances in the post-Soviet era. As outlined above, the superpower status of the Soviet Union was based largely on its military strength. The security of the USSR was seen to stem from nuclear parity, and from the existence of a 'buffer zone' of Soviet bloc states in Central and Eastern Europe, which allowed for the forward deployment of Warsaw Pact forces. The collapse of the Soviet bloc, and thereafter the Soviet Union, clearly meant a change in military and security policy. Such a change though is complex. International treaties agreed under the old situation were no longer so appropriate, as was the case with the Conventional Forces in Europe arms-control agreement of 1990 which was drawn up assuming the existence of the Warsaw Pact and NATO. With the collapse of the Warsaw Pact, the Russian Federation began to seek a new 'security architecture' – or system of alliances – and became increasingly frustrated that, far from following suit and dissolving itself, NATO in the post-Soviet era has steadily expanded towards Russian territory (see Box 8.3).

Beyond the need to renegotiate international agreements, the old security policy of the Soviet Union was of course reflected in the size, equipment, location, doctrine and training of the armed forces. To adapt to changed circumstances meant reform in all of these areas. Again these are complex tasks with knock-on social effects touching millions of conscripts and employees, not only in uniform, but also in the vast military industrial complex which traditionally dominated the Russian economy.

In 1993 a new military doctrine was approved which, taking account of the drawing in of Russian forces' international position and the existence of 14 other newly independent states, focused on the need to be able to engage in small-scale local conflicts. This line was reinforced at the end of 1997 with the publication of Russia's 'Concept of National Security', which declared the threat of large-scale aggression against Russia to be largely absent in the foreseeable future, and once again emphasized local warfare close to the state borders. By 2000, however, a new 'Concept of National Security' was published, which reflected Russian concerns of the time that NATO, and the USA, having just waged a brief but successful war against Russia's traditional ally Serbia, once more posed a threat to national security.

A new Foreign Policy Concept, also published in 2000, expressed similar concerns regarding US hegemony, and a new military doctrine in the same year took a slightly more aggressive stance with regard to Russia's rights to defend itself with all weapons necessary, including nuclear. As well as each of these foreign policy, security and military blueprints having changed within a few years of their first publication, there are also important differences of emphasis between them; reading all three points up continuing problems in Russia's coordination of foreign and security policy.

Russian foreign policy in the 1990s

The preceding two sections have concentrated on the shift from the USSR's role in the international arena to the role of the Russian Federation.

The legacy of the Soviet era has not, however, simply been discussed for background; it still exerts a great deal of influence on Russia's place in the world today. We now turn to look in more detail at the development of Russia's foreign policy in the 1990s and into the twenty-first century.

Since the collapse of the Soviet Union and the implementation of a truly independent Russian foreign policy, the dividing line between Russian politicians has been the extent to which the Russian Federation should conduct a pro-Western policy. In the initial flush of post-Soviet euphoria, the first Russian foreign minister, Andrei Kozyrev, took an openly Westernizing stance. He spoke of Russia becoming a 'normal' country, by which was implied a Western-type country, economically prosperous, democratic in the Western liberal sense, and unencumbered by prescriptive ideology. In practical terms this would mean:

- cooperative participation in the major international organizations, such as the United Nations;
- an end to the divisive competition of the Cold War, for example the arms race, and competition for influence in the developing world; and
- the opening-up of Russia economically and culturally to Western involvement.

The West, and in particular the United States, would be an ally not an adversary, and eventually Russia might join NATO and the European Union. In opposition to this Westernizing stance, however, came the views of those, often termed 'Eurasianist', who see Russia's destiny as separate from that of the West.

This Westernizer versus Eurasianist division became apparent in Russian foreign policy almost immediately after the collapse of the Soviet Union. In 1992 the control of foreign policy became a matter of contention between the Ministry of Foreign Affairs (MFA) under Kozyrev, and the Security Council under Yurii Skokov. The main area of debate came over the formulation of an official foreign policy concept, and it was the Security Council which eventually took the lead in drawing this up. The resultant document took a more Eurasianist stance than that taken by the Ministry. It asserted Russia's 'great power' status and made particular reference to its sphere of influence in the Commonwealth of Independent States, which, it argued, should retain an integrated military infrastructure. As with similar documents, its broad-brush analysis did not fully reflect reality, and a continuing unified military command for the CIS was a non-starter. Russia swiftly made tacit recognition of this with the creation of a separate Ministry of Defence in May 1992.

Box 8.2   Russia's foreign ministers

Andrei Kozyrev	November 1991 – January 1996
Yevgeny Primakov	January 1996 – September 1998
Igor Ivanov	September 1998 – March 2004
Sergei Lavrov	March 2004 –

The rise and fall of eurasianism and multipolarity

So, from the viewpoint of the early twenty-first century, who has won out in the debate over Russian foreign policy? The short answer is, to some extent, both the Westernizers and the Eurasianists.

In the second half of the 1990s, particularly whilst Yevgeny Primakov was Foreign Minister (1996–98; see Box 8.2), the Eurasianist stance came to the fore. There are several overlapping explanations which we shall explore for the rise of a less pro-Western foreign policy in the second half of the 1990s in Russia. Such a policy shift can be given a number of badges – 'Eurasianism', 'multi-polarity', 'Russia-first-ism' – but whatever it is called it was based on several factors, notably: public opinion, disappointment with the results of pro-Westernism, the perception that Russia was being treated as a 'junior partner' in international affairs, the desire for a multi-polar world, and Russia's role as a regional leader.

Public opinion

The general election of December 1993 in Russia produced a result that surprised all observers, when the far-right 'Liberal Democratic Party of Russia' (LDPR), led by Vladimir Zhirinovsky, received 23 per cent of the national vote on the party-list side of the ballot. Much of Zhirinovsky's campaign rhetoric had been concerned with the 'humiliation' of Russia for which he blamed the West. As he told *The Times* shortly after the 1993 election:

> We must ask ourselves, with whom are we interested in good relations? What does the West do for us? Westerners come here to buy cheap resources, to conquer our markets, to pay us slave wages. The West takes everything from us: the material products of Russia and the brains of our people. (*The Times*, London, 21 December 1993)

If not taken seriously, Zhirinovsky's reported statements on international affairs seemed comical: Russia should extend its sphere of influence to the Indian Ocean, re-take Alaska, share a common border with Germany, and settle its territorial dispute with the Japanese by nuking them. The difficulty for Russia's apparently pro-Western leadership was that almost a quarter of Russian voters in 1993 took Zhirinovsky seriously enough to support his party above all others.

In the sphere of Russian foreign policy there were arguably two results of Zhirinovsky's success:

- First, following the election of 1993, the tone of Russian foreign policy became sharper. The MFA attempted to reassure Western interlocutors that too much attention should not be paid to this change in the rhetoric of foreign policy, as it was the substance that mattered; the rhetorical change was there simply to appease domestic opposition. The difficulty with this argument, though, is that in foreign policy, rhetoric is an integral part of the package. To separate rhetoric from substance is by no means straightforward.

- Second, and related, the MFA used the growth of nationalist opinion in Russia as a negotiating tool with the West. Effectively the argument went that for the West, the Yeltsin–Kozyrev team was far preferable to the alternative hardline opposition in Russia. The West, therefore, should bolster domestic support for Yeltsin and his foreign policy by showing it to be effective and beneficial for Russia.

One of the major concrete issues around which this increasingly nationalist foreign policy line developed was the war in Bosnia-Herzegovina. In December 1992, Foreign Minister Kozyrev made a speech at the Conference on Security and Cooperation in Europe meeting in Stockholm. This speech shocked listeners as it appeared to represent a radical toughening of Russia's stance on a number of issues, particularly the Bosnian conflict. In a somewhat bizarre piece of diplomacy, Kozyrev, after a short interval, soon explained that in effect he was only joking, and that his speech was a dramatic representation of the policy which would be followed should hardliners come to power in Russia.

The irony is that within a couple of years Kozyrev was making similar speeches, this time for real. Increasingly, instead of cooperating with Western policy, the Russian Federation took a pro-Serbian line, and by the middle of 1995 the MFA was asserting that NATO action against the Bosnian Serbs exceeded the United Nations mandate and could lead to 'genocide'.

This pro-Serbian stance led to an ever-widening gap between the West and Russia, as NATO geared up for and fought a war against Serbia in 1999. The beginning of NATO's bombing campaign against Serbia provided an illustration of the poverty of relations between Russia and the West by the end of the 1990s. Yevgeny Primakov, who was by that time Russia's Prime Minister, was informed of the bombing whilst halfway across the Atlantic en route to a meeting with US Vice-President Al Gore. He immediately ordered his plane to turn around and return to Russia.

To be in Moscow at this time was to be aware of strong anti-Westernism, and deep anger, expressed in the media by many otherwise pro-Western politicians as well as by the more nationalist-minded. This anger sprang from a variety of sources: a feeling of kinship with Russia's Slavic and Orthodox brethren in Serbia; a fear that, in the same way as action was being taken to protect the Muslims in Kosovo from Serbian armed forces, NATO might take action to protect the Muslims in Chechnya against Russian forces; and most of all, a feeling of impotence, that Russia no longer mattered and that NATO could wage war in Europe irrespective of Russia's feelings. However unrealistic these views may seem from the point of view of the West, they were widely held.

At the end of the Kosovo conflict, the tensions between Russia and NATO came to the fore, when Russian peacekeeping forces in the area preempted NATO troops by seizing Pristina airport. Later reports say that the NATO Supreme Commander, General Wesley Clark, ordered British General Mike Jackson to stop the Russians getting to Pristina airport first, to which order Jackson reportedly replied 'I am not going to start the Third World War for you'. Although insignificant in the great scheme of the war, this action was greeted with some satisfaction in Moscow; a small but important reminder that Russia should not be ignored.

Disappointment with the West

As noted earlier, the broad aim of pro-Westernism in the early 1990s was that Russia become part of the Western community, fully involved in international organizations and, more abstractly, in the building of the new post-Cold War world order. At the popular level, closer links with the West would surely bring economic benefits and a rise in living standards towards Western levels.

As time went on it became apparent that the perceived benefits of a pro-Western policy were not appearing as rapidly as had been anticipated.

The economic situation is discussed in Chapter 5. In the international arena the apparent lack of interest in Russian sensitivities over Serbia on the part of NATO represented just one of several disappointments. Membership of the Council of Europe was delayed until early 1996 due to concerns over Russia's commitment to human rights, and Russia's voting rights in the same body were removed during the second Chechen War (from 1999 onwards). Even the Partnership and Cooperation Agreement signed between the European Union (EU) and the Russian Federation in June 1994 was not fully implemented as a sign of the EU's displeasure at the first Chechen war, 1994–96. The real impact of these measures was not great, however, and did little to either curb Russian actions in Chechnya or indeed to harm longer-term relations with the EU.

Perhaps the most significant issue to foster Russian disappointment with the West was the question of NATO expansion. The decision by NATO countries to expand the alliance eastwards disappointed Russia's Westernizers, who saw it as a betrayal of their avowedly friendly stance, and confirmed the suspicions of Eurasianists, who believed that the West was determined to gain maximum advantage from its post-Cold War strength, and Russia's post-Cold War weakness.

Russia's initial post-Soviet hopes were that an entirely new European security architecture could be built. If Russia itself could not join NATO, then such a new system could perhaps be based on the Organisation for Security and Cooperation in Europe (OSCE), with NATO's role declining. However, this was not to be, and instead of diminishing in importance NATO began to talk of expansion eastwards. As the leading Russian observer of international affairs and former deputy chair of the Duma International Affairs Committee, Aleksei Arbatov, by no means a hardline nationalist, put it:

> While Moscow was agreeing to the reunification of Germany and to having that country stay in NATO, to disbanding the Warsaw Pact and then the very Soviet Union, to deeper reductions of nuclear and conventional forces than in the West, to the hasty withdrawal of half a million troops from comfortable barracks in Central Europe to tent camps in Russian fields – while Moscow was agreeing to all of these things, nobody took the trouble to warn Russians that NATO, the most powerful military alliance in the world, would start moving toward Russian borders. (Alexei Arbatov, 'As NATO Grows, Start 2 Shudders', *New York Times*, 26 August 1997)

Of course this is a one-sided view, nonetheless it is representative of views widely held in Russia particularly after the 1997 NATO Madrid summit, at which the Czech Republic, Hungary and Poland – the latter of which borders the Russian territory of Kaliningrad – were invited to join NATO.

Proponents of expansion, however, saw things differently. NATO declares itself to be a purely defensive alliance. The key right and obligation of member states is that of collective defence, and therefore any state can be invited to join so long as it is willing and able to meet the obligation of collective defence and other member states are willing to accept its right to the same. Under these terms, the Russian Federation has nothing to fear from NATO, and – more pointedly – why should Russia have any say in whether independent states in East-Central Europe are able to join a military alliance or not? Russia in turn recognizes the validity of these arguments, but argues that NATO enlargement does not reflect the new security realities of the contemporary world. Nonetheless, the Putin regime has been content merely to disagree with NATO expansion, and not to try to actively stop the second wave of 2004, which included countries formerly part of the Soviet Union, namely Estonia, Latvia and Lithuania (see Box 8.3).

Throughout the process of NATO enlargement, the Russian Federation took up a stance based on the belief that Russia is a 'great power' and should be treated as such. This can at least be seen to have produced some benefits, in the form of the Russian – NATO Founding Act of May 1997. If taken at face value, then the declarations in this agreement give the lie to the existence of what President Yeltsin called a 'cold peace' between Russia and the West. The Founding Act claimed to mark 'the beginning of a fundamentally new relationship between Russia and NATO' based on common interests in stability, consultation, cooperation and joint decision-making. Furthermore, the Founding Act also set up a Permanent Joint Council (PJC) to provide a forum for engagement with these common interests.

Box 8.3   NATO expansion

1999	**2004**
Czech Republic	Bulgaria
Hungary	Estonia
Poland	Latvia
	Lithuania
	Romania
	Slovakia
	Slovenia

The war on terror

The optimism of the 1997 Founding Act was soon blown away by tensions over the Kosovo conflict (see above), and Russia withdrew from regular PJC meetings. However, it was another international crisis and conflict – the terrorist attacks on New York and Washington on 11 September 2001 and the subsequent NATO-backed war in Afghanistan – which for a short time put Russian–NATO relations on a stronger footing than they had ever been. Russian support for the US-led, NATO-backed war against terrorism led to Western efforts, headed up by the United Kingdom in the form of Prime Minister Blair and NATO Secretary General Lord Robertson, to reward Russia with greater integration into NATO by the creation of a Russia–NATO Council in 2002. This Council, in the jargon of the official NATO webpage, 'brings together the 19 Allies and Russia to identify and pursue opportunities for joint action at 20'. The difference between the PJC and 'NATO at 20' lies in the latter's intention to provide genuine joint decision-making across a range of security issues, rather than NATO simply reaching agreement at 19 and using the PJC to present Russia with a *fait accompli*.

The role of 'junior partner'?

The Russian Federation is one of the permanent five members of the United Nations Security Council and, after 1997, sat on a Permanent Joint Council with NATO chiefs, the aim of which was to ensure consultation and cooperation. Nonetheless, these apparent signifiers that we are dealing here with a 'great power' were not, certainly in the eyes of Russia's leaders, always matched in the world of events and decision-making.

The events of the second half of 1998 provided a clear example of this aspect of Russian foreign policy thinking. In August 1998 the United States launched missile strikes against suspected terrorist bases in Afghanistan and Sudan. It had long been Russian policy to stand shoulder to shoulder with the USA and other world powers engaged in the fight against terrorism. On this occasion, however, President Yeltsin issued an unexpectedly firm denunciation of American action. By the end of the year such firm denunciations of American, and British, air strikes were to become commonplace, as the short Anglo-American bombing campaign against Iraq got underway in December 1998.

The reaction of virtually all senior Russian officials to these raids seemed to presage a major split with the United States in particular. President

Yeltsin charged that the USA had 'crudely violated the UN Charter and the generally accepted principles of international law'. Defence Minister Sergeyev expressed widely felt anger at Russia's perceived role of junior partner when he questioned Moscow's continuing cooperation with NATO: 'How can we talk about cooperation and partnership with the alliance now, when Russia's opinion is openly ignored?'

Moscow temporarily withdrew its ambassadors from Washington and London. However, without substance such gestures remained mere gestures, and as such indicated the extent to which the superpower status of the USSR has faded. In terms of concrete actions, the ratification of the START II arms control treaty by the Russian Duma was again delayed, but the Duma had long been delaying this treaty, usually as much to the annoyance of the Russian executive as to that of the United States. Beyond this, what could Russia do?

Multipolarity

What Russia did in the period 1999–2001 was to increasingly concentrate its diplomatic efforts on attempting to create a multipolar world, in contrast to what was widely perceived as a unipolar world dominated by the United States. Russia effectively adopted, in the late Yeltsin and early Putin years which spanned the turn of the century, a policy of 'counter-hegemony' in foreign affairs. Although such a policy need not by definition be an anti-US policy, its aim was nonetheless to build up other poles of influence and power in order to rein in US hegemony. Foreign Minister Primakov's Eurasianism led to his favouring the building up of a tripartite alliance in Asia, and so Russia's relations with China and India increased in significance both in diplomatic terms and practically, for example in the increased arms trade between these powers.

When President Putin came to power in 2000 he proved himself to be far more of a foreign policy activist than his predecessor. Within a year of succeeding Boris Yeltsin, he had visited the United Kingdom, Germany, France, Italy, Spain, China, Japan, Mongolia, the two remaining Marxist-Leninist countries of Cuba and North Korea, and the CIS states of Belarus, Ukraine, Azerbaijan, Uzbekistan, Turkmenistan and Kazakhstan. There was concern in some quarters in the West, the United States in particular, that Putin was creating a pole of influence out of those states which had long-standing quarrels with the USA. Russia's closer relations with North Korea, Cuba, Iran and Iraq led to talk of an 'alliance of the aggrieved'.

Putin, on the other hand, declared his foreign policy to be 'Euro-centric', again raising the possibility that a wider Europe might increasingly represent a separate pole of influence in a multi-polar world.

After the terrorist attacks on New York and Washington in September 2001, President Putin decisively sided with the USA in its 'war on terrorism' – a stance which appeared somewhat unpopular amongst the more anti-American members of the Russian élite. However, this broad support for US action against al-Qa'eda and the Taleban regime in Afghanistan did not signal a total abandonment of multipolarity, but rather a shift in its character. Russia's policy was to engage with the West on a case by case basis, with Russian interests to the fore.

In 2002 and 2003, Russia – along with China and France – played a restraining and blocking role on the UN Security Council in the face of the United States' and the United Kingdom's more aggressive policy against Iraq. Russia, in alliance with France and Germany, staunchly opposed the Iraq war of 2003, arguing instead that more UN-backed weapons inspections were the way forward.

Russia as 'regional leader'

As noted earlier, the legacy of the Soviet Union remains pertinent to Russia's place in the international arena today. The emergence of a prag-matic 'Russia-first' foreign policy in the 1990s repeatedly included the assertion that the Russian Federation has its own sphere of influence in Eurasia. Russia is the 'regional leader'. This is not wholly a view based on grand perceptions of geopolitics and great power status. It also has a basis in the objective realities of economic and military infrastructures remaining from the Soviet era, and in the moral claim to influence given by the existence of a Russia diaspora up to 25 million strong in the former Soviet states in 1989. Such realities, however, diminish over time, and most of the Russians who wanted to have returned home (see Chapter 2).

It seems clear that the future of the CIS, so far as its European members are concerned, is tied in with the success of their attempts to become more closely integrated in pan-European structures. By the end of 2004 the determination of Russia to hold onto, or indeed recreate, its influence in Europe's second largest country, Ukraine, became evident in its initially staunch support for the more pro-Russian candidate, Viktor Yanukovych, in Ukraine's disputed presidential election. Yanukovych's eventual defeat to Yushchenko, amidst charges of electoral fraud and dirty tricks, represented a serious error of judgement on the part of President Putin and Russia, serving to emphasize Russian impotency in its supposed sphere of influence.

Russian defence and security doctrines have consistently taken the line that the Russian Federation has key security interests in the CIS. Involvement for example in the civil war in Tajikistan in the 1990s was justified partly by the assessment that the Federation could be destabilized by Islamic extremists. Moscow has deployed peacekeeping troops in Georgia, Moldova and Tajikistan, and has a military presence of some sort (peacekeeping, border guards, bases, and so on) in many of the former Soviet states.

Once again, therefore, there is the perception created of a potentially neo-imperialist Russian state asserting its strength in the region over which it claims influence. However, the cold fact remains that the Russian Federation has not sought at any time in the post-Soviet era to recreate an empire over the former Soviet space. Asserting influence does not quite equate to imperial expansion, and three factors need emphasizing to provide a balanced picture:

- First, Russia has consistently maintained recognition of post-Soviet borders.
- Second, the financial cost of expansion is prohibitive. Even the voluntarily agreed union with Belarus, first signed in 1996, has been repeatedly downgraded to the level of rhetoric rather than substance due to the potential costs involved in supporting the Belarusian economy.
- And third, the Chechen wars have indicated that *even if* Russia wanted to expand militarily, the state of the armed forces is such as to preclude any such adventure.

Beyond multipolarity? Russia in the new world order

Let us return to the question which prefaced the last section of this chapter: who has won out in the debate over Russian foreign policy? We noted above that the shift away from a foreign policy emphasis on the West held sway, broadly speaking, from the mid-1990s until 2001 when once again Russian policy became more 'Western-centric'. This is an oversimplification, but broadly true. It is possible in the same way to pinpoint the turning point in Russia's relations with the West as 11 September 2001, when New York and Washington were attacked by al-Qa'eda terrorists. In the immediate aftermath of this terrorist attack, President Putin was the first world leader to offer his sympathy and support to President Bush. The strength of this support, then and subsequently, took many observers by surprise, and brought Putin some criticism at home, especially from within the military. The Russian response to 11 September usefully illustrates the key features of foreign policy in contemporary Russia. Why did Putin respond so favourably to the US 'war on terrorism' in the aftermath of 11 September 2001?

First, it is important to note that although 11 September provides a useful point from which to date a shift in policy, there were already signs of such a shift before then. That the Islamic terrorism of Osama Bin Laden was a mutual threat to Russia, the United States and Europe had certainly not escaped the attention of policy-makers across these areas, and there had reportedly already been discussions about possible joint action against al-Qa'eda before 11 September 2001.

Second, it is clear that Russian foreign policy has been to pursue a deeper rapprochement with the West since 2001. However, the move ment has not been in only one direction. After 11 September, harder attitudes in the West regarding Islamic terrorism could be seen as moving closer to the position which Russia already held. In his letter to President Bush immediately after the attacks on New York and Washington, Vladimir Putin stated that the Russian people, perhaps above others, could empathize with the United States, having experienced similar attacks on their capital city. It was exactly two years earlier that terrorists – allegedly Chechens supported in at least some indirect way by Osama Bin Laden – had blown up two apartment blocks in Moscow, killing hundreds. Russia had been engaged in a second brutal war in Chechnya since then, in the face of much Western criticism. Throughout that time the line taken by Putin had been that Russia was defending Europe against Islamic terrorism. After 11 September, Putin's line was listened to more in the West rather than dismissed out of hand, and Western criticism of Russian action in Chechnya decreased.

Third, under President Putin, foreign policy – indeed all policy – is much less prone to emotionalism and 'knee-jerk' reactions than under President Yeltsin. Putin is an avowed realist who puts the national interest squarely at the top of his policy-making priorities, rather than blustering about things over which he is relatively powerless. A good example of this came with the stationing of US troops in a number of countries on Russia's borders, as part of the war against the Afghan Taleban in 2001. Although these countries are often touted in Moscow as being in Russia's area of interest, they are independent countries and if they wanted to allow American troops to be stationed there, then there was little Russia could do. Putin realized that even if he was uneasy about US troops in the former Soviet Union, it was far better to welcome a *fait accompli* and gain US gratitude than to posture in vain against their actions. The bigger picture of Russian integration in the wider global community outweighed any sense of being taken for granted.

Conclusion

We set up the duality of the 1990s as 'pro-Western idealism' versus 'Russia-first realism', whereby the Westernizers naïvely believed in an easy transition to a democracy and market economy and a Russia in partnership with the international community, and the Eurasianists more realistically noted the reluctance of the West to embrace a hesitantly reformist Russia, and pointed to such events as NATO expansion in defence of their case. After the cooling of relations between Russia and the West in the second half of the 1990s, and a shift by Russia to an emphasis on multipolarity, Vladimir Putin has adopted a synthesis of these two extremes:

- As a realist he reluctantly recognizes the dominance of the United States as the single superpower, but has nonetheless not rejected multipolarity outright. He is in favour of Russia's integration into the global community, but would reject the aim of post-Soviet Russia's first Foreign Minister, Andrei Kozyrev, that Russia should be a 'normal' country in the arena of international affairs.
- Militarily the Russian armed forces in the early twenty-first century are in a poor state. Nonetheless, the major military factor in Soviet superpower status, the nuclear arsenal, still remains, and Russia's decisions of 1998 and 2004 to develop new generations of nuclear missiles indicate a clear perception of their importance to the country's military strength.
- The imperial nature of the Soviet Union has almost disappeared in the contemporary Russian Federation. Even if Russia might lay claim to influence over the former Soviet space, for example in relation to Ukraine's election in 2004, influence is not empire. The nearest Russia has come to threatening military action in its neighbouring states have been statements reserving the right to strike at terrorist targets beyond its borders – with Georgia being the most likely target.

In Vladimir Putin's world view, Russia is not a 'normal' country but a regional leader of global significance. Putin believes in Russia's 'great power' status. He aims to retain what is left of it, and build on that.

Conclusion

The major theme of this book has been Russia's reemergence as an independent country, after 74 years of Soviet rule. In each chapter we have considered the impact of the Soviet legacy on different areas of activity. It has been clear too, however, that disentangling Soviet influence from more long-standing features of Russia's existence is far from easy. With or without the Soviet Union, Russia has long stood on the edge of 'the West'. Russia's European territory alone makes it the continent's largest country, it contains two of Europe's three largest cities, and yet the majority of its vast land mass lies in Asia. From this separateness stems the idea of a distinct Russian way, be it the 'third Rome' concept, the place of Russia at the forefront of global communism in the twentieth century, or the popular view in twenty-first-century Russia that a distinctly Russian form of democracy is to be favoured.

For centuries intellectual life in Russia has seen a marked tension between those who want a society and political system unique to Russia, and those who are less convinced about Russian 'specialness' and want to adapt practices used elsewhere to Russian circumstances. The tensions between these two positions have been an important driving force in Russian politics. In opinion polls shortly after President Putin's easy re-election in March 2004, three-quarters of those polled stated a preference for a uniquely Russian path of development, rather than a Western one.

In Russian, and Soviet, history we tend to find a distinctive view of the role of the state and the nature of political leadership. One way to understand this is to compare Russian political ideas to those of the founding fathers of the American Constitution. The American political system is one which manifests a suspicion of power. There has been a tendency in Russia, on the other hand, to see power as a solution in itself; governments do not need to be politically restrained, hence the lack of countervailing political institutions compared to some other parts of the world. If you know the answer, you are building the 'new Jerusalem', so political opposition serves little purpose, and hence the concept and the practice remains underdeveloped in Russia.

One important consequence of this conception is that it tends ultimately to undermine government when rulers turn out after all not to be perfect. When their actions begin, as is inevitable, to favour some groups over others, and fail to realize their utopian promises, disillusionment sets in. This disillusionment has periodically in Russian history, including the end of the periods of rule of Mikhail Gorbachev and, to a lesser extent, his successor Boris Yeltsin, led to legitimacy crises and a breakdown of state power.

The belief system has some important consequences. The glorification of the notion of equality between people can lead to a tendency to be suspicious of individual success. The vision of a society in which fundamental values are basically shared leaves little space for difference of any kind, whether racial difference or difference in lifestyles. President Putin's vision of a 'unified multi-ethnic state' is a neat phrase, but it covers up a problem which is yet to be resolved. Putin is attempting to bring the regions of Russia into line, under the clear authority of the federal government; this will be no easy task. To achieve his aim, the legitimacy of the centre must be strengthened and maintained. Democracy, economic success, élite satisfaction and effective leadership are all potential tools for such legitimization, but for some areas of the country – certainly Chechnya, and possibly the northern Causcasus more widely – lasting legitimacy remains a long way off, and has been usurped by the use of force to hold the federation together.

The prioritization of the supposed common-sense values of the community over abstract laws from outside makes it more difficult to operate, for example, a contract-based free-market economy, or a fair and just system of law and order. Russia's first two post-Soviet Presidents, Boris Yeltsin and Vladimir Putin, as well as the last Soviet leader, Mikhail Gorbachev, have all proclaimed their belief in the rule of abstract law. Nonetheless, Russia remains a country where connections, influence and political expedience regularly appear to undermine the equitable application of the law. Not for nothing was the team around Boris Yeltsin at the end of the 1990s known as 'the family'. In anointing Putin his successor, Yeltsin made sure that the first act of the new president would be to grant him immunity from prosecution.

There are clear tensions in assessing contemporary Russia in relation to its immediate past. On the one hand, Russia has come a long way relatively quickly. Within a few short years after 1991 Russia had adopted the basic features of democratic government, a market economy, peaceful engagement with international bodies such as NATO and the G8, a free press, freedom of movement for its citizens, and so on. In other words, the central elements of the largely dictatorial Soviet regime had been removed under the leadership of Boris Yeltsin, following on from the reformist initiatives of the last Soviet leader, Mikhail Gorbachev.

At the same time, however, there is another story to tell. When the Soviet state collapsed, so did many of the mechanisms by which Russia was ruled. Between 1991 and 1993 governance remained unclear, as president and parliament quarrelled over the division of power. From 1993, as we have seen, power in theory lay with the president. However, the Russian state continued to be markedly weak. This was partly thanks to Yeltsin's own physical weakness – bouts of activity followed by long periods of illness and convalescence – which did little to portray him as a resolute leader. It was partly, also, to do with the rise of the oligarchs, who gained immense wealth and political influence through the imperfect privatization and marketization policies of the 1990s. The oligarchs demonstrated that money could buy political influence in Moscow and in the regions; talented young Russians could make far more money working in business than working for the state; and much tax went unpaid because of deliberate non-payment, corruption and the confusing state of the tax code.

Alongside this weak state, there came great economic hardship – low and unpaid wages, savings wiped out, and high levels of inflation. On the international scene, many saw Russia as belittled following 'defeat' in the Cold War. The 'empire' was lost, Russia's territory was the smallest it had been for centuries, NATO expanded to Russia's borders and attacked Russia's long-standing ally, Serbia. Whatever the rights and wrongs of these events and others, once framed in terms of Western hegemony over a weakened Russia, the negative assessment of them by most Russians is understandable.

The mood in Russia in the 1990s – and indeed to some extent today – seems a far cry from the sense of national pride and achievement which was felt for example about the Soviet Union's successes in the space race with the launch of the first man-made satellite (Sputnik) in 1957, and again four years later when Yuri Gagarin became the first man in space. The sense of optimism at the time was memorably captured in the boast contained in the 1961 programme of the Communist Party of the Soviet Union that the country would catch up with and overtake the United States in economic terms by 1970, and that by 1980 Soviet citizens would be living under true communism.

In the 1990s, against a background of economic decline, mass poverty, lawlessness and environmental devastation, these promises, and the optimistic era from which they came, became a distant memory.

Commentators who are more critical of the communist experience stress the negative influences on morality of the 'double life' Russian citizens were compelled to lead under communist rule, paying lip-service to an ideology of public service and striving to build a communist utopia, while in practice not being able to discuss social problems which every-one knew to exist and being party to a culture of irresponsibility at work and in public life. Those who dislike the economic policies of the recent period stress how these policies have directly led to a rise in undesirable qualities such as greed, nepotism, corruption and organized criminal behaviour. Whatever the case, the first post-Soviet decade created a mood in Russian society of pessimism, powerlessness, hopelessness about future possibilities, moral decay, cynicism and general despair.

Under Vladimir Putin's leadership, although virtually all of the prob-lems outlined above continue to exist, the national mood has changed a little. Putin himself has retained exceptionally high levels of personal popularity (see Table 9.1) since becoming President, scarcely falling below 70 per cent approval ratings in the opinion polls up to 2004, and then dipping to a 'low' of over 60 per cent during the benefit reform protests of early 2005. His popularity can partly be put down to impres-sive economic growth which has accompanied his first four years in office, though how much of this is because of high oil prices and how much because of economic policy is debatable.

Beyond economic good news, however, Putin was initially popular because he is not Yeltsin. For much of his time in office, Yeltsin was an erratic and impulsive leader, prone to public and private drunkenness and

Table 9.1   Who do you consider the most successful leader of the country since 1917?

Leader	%
Putin (2000–)	37
Stalin (1928–53)	18
Brezhnev (1964–82)	11
Lenin (1917–24)	9
Andropov (1982–84)	8
Khrushchev (1953–64)	4
Gorbachev (1985–91)	2
Yeltsin (1991–99)	1

Source: Data from ROMIR, February 2004, www.romir

suffering from a variety of illnesses. He oversaw a period of national decline in terms of living standards, the strength of the state and international prestige. Although his time in office may well go down – with sufficient passage of time – as the most democratic years in Russia's long history, Yeltsin regularly comes last in polls seeking the best leader of Russia's recent history (Table 9.1). Putin, in contrast, is an energetic, intelligent leader, whose behaviour on the international stage seems almost exemplary. He is widely seen to have restored the authority of his office and the state, both at home and abroad.

During Putin's first five years in power, however, there is no doubt that democracy has been rolled back. The state has taken a firm grip on the national broadcast stations; the oligarchs have been reined in, with legal action being reserved for those who do not want to cooperate with the regime; and free elections have been undermined by state-sponsored media bias. The presence of the security services is far more apparent in many areas of life, particularly where groups or individuals engage in activities which, though legal, meet with the disapproval of the authorities. The right of federal subjects to elect their own leaders (governors, mayors, presidents) which had been established by Yeltsin in the mid-1990s was withdrawn by Putin from 2005 onwards. Increasingly concerns are being expressed in the West, and in Russia, about growing authoritarianism under Vladimir Putin.

The picture, then, is mixed. If we oversimplify the account set out above, then under Yeltsin democracy grew, the economy floundered, and the people were miserable, whilst under Putin democracy has declined, the economy has grown, and the people are a little happier. President Putin himself puts this apparent conflict between democracy and the well-being of Russia and the Russians in terms of a tension between democracy and the state. There is no doubt that when he came to power in 2000, the Russian state was dangerously weak. In February 2005 Putin made his position on democracy explicit at a meeting with US President Bush in Bratislava. Declaring, rightly, that 'any return to totalitarianism would be impossible' in Russia, he nonetheless gave only a guarded commitment to democracy, saying that it 'should not be accompanied by the collapse of the state and the impoverishment of its people'. In other words, Putin's priorities are economic prosperity and the strengthening of the Russian state.

* * *

As we move into the second half of the twenty-first-century's first decade, Russia continues to undergo fundamental change in the way it is ruled, whilst at the same time the root issues of identity, the relationship between state and society, and relations with the rest of the world remain as apparently permanent factors in the life of the Russian nation. President Putin, who has enjoyed the support of the majority of the Russian people ever since coming to power, has opted for policies of a strong state, an independent 'great power' line in international politics, the limiting – but not renunciation – of democracy, and a focus on economic growth and improving standards of living.

Significant challenges lie ahead for Russia. In the economic sphere, reliance for economic growth on the export of natural resources (oil and gas) is risky in that global price fluctuations can have a big impact on the Russian economy. There is also the danger that a concentration on the production of these resources will mean insufficient attention being paid to the development of other more future-oriented industries, with their accompanying technology and infrastructure. Furthermore, state control of the key natural-resource industries, for reasons of security and economic management, may lead to inefficiency, decisions made for political not economic reasons, and the reluctance of foreign investors to get too deeply involved.

In the political sphere, the key questions revolve around the Putin regime. How deep is Vladimir Putin's support amongst the Russian people? He has been remarkably popular since becoming President, but a failure to deliver in terms of economic growth and increased standards of living, coupled with unexpected crises – of the sort brought about by international events, major disasters or terrorist activity – would provide a clear test of the depth of public support for him personally and for his party, United Russia. The parliamentary election of 2007 and the presidential election of 2008 will provide a good guide to Russia's political future. Putin's constitutional allowance of two terms ends in 2008. If he leaves office on time and there is a democratic succession, then this will strengthen democracy in Russia. President Putin has long denied speculation that he might try to extend his term in office. Another suggested scenario, involving an amended constitution which would create a parliamentary system headed by Putin as prime minister, is fraught with potential institutional pitfalls. Under current arrangements, the president can operate relatively independently of the parliament, and future presidents are likely to want to retain this situation.

Further challenges for Russia include the seemingly intractable question of Chechnya and, perhaps the most significant medium-term problem, Russia's impending demographic crisis. On current projections, the world's biggest country will find its population spread ever more thinly, causing difficulties in terms of personnel shortages for all key sectors. One solution is to lower barriers to immigration, though with a strong nationalist lobby in Russia there is little political will for this.

As we noted in Chapter 1, Russia is a country which has grown used, particularly in the last century, to massive social and political change, periodically accompanied by great suffering. It is also a country with a strong sense of national pride, identity and even destiny. In the early years of the twenty-first-century Russia has enjoyed a welcome degree of stability and economic growth, following on from the upheavals of the 1990s. Nonetheless, its economy still remains at a level far below that to which it aspires. At the same time, its movement towards liberal democracy has slowed down, or even been thrown into reverse. The challenge for Russia now is to continue to combine economic growth and stability with a deepening of democratic processes, including the protection of individual rights and freedoms.

Recommended Reading

There is a wide range of literature on Russia, though in comparative terms the pool of academics working on Russia-related topics is relatively small and so the constant need for updated material is not always met in every field of study covered in this book. Aside from academic writers, Russia is one of those countries which is sufficiently distinctive for it to make a keen impression on Western journalists and travellers, leading to a steady stream of memoirs, travel books, and so on. In this brief guide, we set out a few key texts which will enable you to widen your knowledge of the themes covered in each chapter of this book.

1 The Historical Context

A good and recent overview of Russian history is provided by Hosking (2001), and an accessible overview of the past two centuries is available in Westwood (2002). There is a vast amount to choose from in terms of histories of the Soviet era, from books covering the entire period, such as Service (2003) or Volkogonov (1998) to those devoted to particular leaders. For Lenin and Stalin recent comprehensive biographies are those written by Service (2000 and 2004 respectively). A definitive account of Khrushchev and his time in power is that by Taubman (2003). Brezhnev still awaits such treatment, but recent books by Bacon and Sandle (2002) and Tompson (2003) give useful introductions. The Gorbachev years are well-served by authors such as Brown (1996) and McCauley (1998), and Yeltsin, aside from the three volumes of his own memoirs, is the subject of a useful biography by Aron (2000). There are many accounts by participants and observers of the years around the collapse of the Soviet Union, and perhaps particularly engaging for Western readers are those by the British and US ambassadors of that time, respectively Braithwaite (2002) and Matlock (1995).

2 Land and People

A geographical overview of post-Soviet Russia is available in Shaw (1999). Environmental matters are dealt with by Oldfield (2005) and by Feshbach (1992); Feshbach deals also with the demographic problem facing Russia. The story of the development of Moscow is provided by Colton (1996); Ross (2004) gives an assessment of the regional policy pursued by Vladimir Putin; and a useful account of the Chechen conflict, at least so far as the first Chechen war goes, is Lieven (1998). The second Chechen conflict is covered in Bowker (2004). An up-to-date assessment of religious matters can be found in Knox (2005).

3 Social Structure and Social Policy

Compared with overviews of Russian politics, the number of book-length accounts of Russian society is relatively small. Health issues are covered well in Cockerham (1999) and an account of developments in the judicial sphere is available in Jordan (2000) and Sharlet (2001). For an assessment of reforms in the education system in the post-Soviet era, these are comprehensively and accessibly outlined in Webber (1999).

4 Politics and Government

A vast amount has been written about the politics and government of contemporary Russia, with the most comprehensive being Sakwa (2004), Brown (2001) and White *et al.* (2005). Remington (2001) provides a fine assessment of how Russia's parliament operates, and Fish (2000) likewise the presidency. Accounts of the Putin era are as yet inconclusive, with many observers seeing Putin's first and second terms as markedly different. Nonetheless, Putin as leader is the topic of Shevtsova (2003). March (2002) focuses on the fortunes of the Communist Party, and the development of oligarchic politics is the theme of Hoffman's (2002) account. The nationalist right is dealt with by Vujačič (2001).

5 The Economy

A fine guide to the workings of the Soviet economy is to be found in Hanson (2003). There are a number of assessments of the reform attempts in the 1990s, largely focused on a 'where did it all go wrong?' theme; for coverage of this period see Freeland (2000). An insight into the criminality and corruption of the early post-Soviet years is available in Brzezinski (2002). The economic developments of the Putin era are not so widely covered, but, nonetheless, an excellent and concise overview is given by Tompson (2004), and the OECD (2004) provides an authoritative and statistically detailed assessment of the state of the Russian economy in 2004.

6 Rights, Freedoms and Civil Society

The situation in the Soviet Union in relation to rights, freedoms and civil society is dealt with well in an account of the life of Sergei Kovalev, Boris Yeltsin's human-rights commissioner in the 1990s, see Gilligan (2004). Howard (2003) sets out the legacy of communism in relation to civil society, though this book does not focus solely on Russia. Belin (2002 and 2004) provides useful accounts of the development of the media under Yeltsin and into the Putin era. For an assessment of freedom of worship over the same period see Anderson (2003) and Bacon (2002). Rights and freedoms in the Putin era are the subject of a journalistic and episodic account by Politkovskaya (2004).

7   Ideas and Culture

Concepts of the Russian idea and the Russian approach to life are the subject of McDaniel (1996) and of Pesmen (2000). An excellent literary account of Russian perceptions of life on the threshold between the Soviet and post-Soviet eras is to be read in Hobson (2001). Russian identity in the post-Soviet era is surveyed in Billington (2004) and the place of death and memory in Russia is splendidly evoked in Merridale (2000). Literature in contemporary Russia forms the subject of Laird (1999).

8   Russia and the World

The legacy of the Soviet Union in foreign relations is dealt with well in Nogee and Donaldson (1992), and the development of relations in the Commonwealth of Independent States forms the subject of Webber (1997). A good account of US–Russian relations for most of the Yeltsin era can be found in Talbott (2002). Broader perceptions on foreign policy in the Yeltsin years are available in Webber (1996), and the best account of Russia's foreign relations under Putin is Lo (2003).

Russia online in English

A small selection of useful websites covering various aspects of Russian affairs is listed below.

General

State Statistical Agency http://www.gks.ru/eng/

Government and politics

President http://www.president.kremlin.ru/
Parliament (upper house) http://council.gov.ru/index_e.htm

News

The Moscow Times http://www.moscowtimes.ru/
The Russia Journal http://www.russiajournal.com
Red News (Communist newspaper) http://www.rednews.ru/
Radio Free Europe http://www.rferl.org/
CDI's *Russia Weekly* http://www.cdi.org/russia/

Academic articles

Program on New Approaches to Russian Security http://www.csis.org/ruseura/
ponars/
Carnegie Moscow Centre http://www.carnegie.ru/
Royal Institute of International Affairs – Russia programme http://www.riia.org/
index.php?id=68

Economics

http://www.bof.fi/bofit/fin/4ruec/index.stm

Miscellaneous

The Moscow Metro www.metro.ru
Russian religious news http://www.stetson.edu/~psteeves/relncws/
Forum 18 http://www.forum18.org/index.php

Bibliography

Ahdieh, R. B. (1997) *Russia's Constitutional Revolution: Legal Consciousness and the Transition to Democracy 1985–1996* (Pennsylvania: Pennsylvania State University Press).

Alexander, J. (2000) *Political Culture in Post-Communist Russia:Formlessness and Recreation in a Traumatic Transition* (Basingstoke: Palgrave Macmillan).

Anderson, J. (2003) *Religious Liberty in Transitional Societies: The Politics of Religion* (Cambridge: Cambridge University Press).

Antonenko, O. and Pinnick, K. (eds) (2005) *Russia and the European Union* (London: Routledge).

Aron, L. (2000) *Boris Yeltsin: A Revolutionary Life* (London: HarperCollins).

Bacon, E. (1998) 'Party Formation in Russia', in P. Davies and J. White (eds), *Political Parties and the Collapse of Old Orders* (New York: State University of New York Press).

Bacon, E. (2002) 'Church and State in Contemporary Russia: Conflicting Discourses', in R. Fawn and S. White (eds), *Russian after Communism* (London: Frank Cass).

Bacon, E. (2004) 'Russia's Law on Political Parties: Democracy by Decree?', in C. Ross (ed.), *Russian Politics under Putin* (Manchester: Manchester University Press).

Bacon, E. and Sandle, M. (eds) (2002) *Brezhnev Reconsidered* (Basingstoke: Palgrave).

Belin, L. (2002) 'The Russian Media in the 1990s', in R. Fawn and S. White (eds), *Russian after Communism* (London: Frank Cass).

Belin, L. (2004) 'Politics and the Mass Media under Putin', in C. Ross (ed.) *Russian Politics under Putin* (Manchester: Manchester University Press).

Berliner, J. (1988) *Soviet Industry from Stalin to Gorbachev: Essays on Management and Innovation* (Aldershot: Elgar).

Billington, J. H. (2004) *Russia: In Search of Itself* (Baltimore, MD: Johns Hopkins University Press).

Bowker, M. (2004) 'Conflict in Chechnya', in C. Ross (ed.) *Russian Politics under Putin* (Manchester: Manchester University Press).

Bowker, M. and Ross, C. (eds) (2000) *Russia after the Cold War* (Harlow: Longman).

Braithwaite, R. (2002) *Across the Moscow River: The World Turned Upside Down* (Newhaven, CT: Yale University Press).

Breslauer, G. (2001) 'Personalism versus Proceduralism: Boris Yeltsin and the Institutional Fragility of the Russian System', in V. E. Bonnell and G. W. Breslauer, *Russia in the New Century: Stability or Disorder?* (Boulder, CO: Westview Press).

Brown, A. (1996) *The Gorbachev Factor* (Oxford: Oxford University Press).

Brown, A. (ed.) (2001) *Contemporary Russian Politics: A Reader* (Oxford: Oxford University Press).

Brus, W. and Laski, K. (1989) *From Marx to the Market: Socialism in Search of an Economic System* (Oxford: Clarendon Press).

Brzezinski, M. (2002) *Casino Moscow: A Tale of Greed and Adventure on Capitalism's Wildest Frontier* (New York: Free Press).

Cockerham, W. (1999) *Health and Social Change in Russia and Eastern Europe* (London: Routledge).

Colton, T. (1996) *Moscow: Governing the Socialist Metropolis* (Cambridge, MA: Harvard University Press).

Danks, C. (2001) *Russian Politics and Society: An Introduction* (Harlow: Longman).

Duncan, P. (2000) *Russian Messianism: Third Rome, Revolution, Communism and After* (London: Routledge).

Feshbach, M. (1992) *Ecocide in the USSR: Health and Nature under Siege* (London: Aurum Press).

Fish, M. S. (2000) 'The Executive Deception: Superpresidentialism and the Degradation of Russian Politics', in V. Sperling (ed.), *Building the Russian State: Institutional Crisis and the Quest for Democratic Governance* (Boulder, CO: Westview Press).

Freeland, C. (2000) *Sale of the Century: Russia's Wild Ride from Communism to Capitalism* (New York: Random House).

Gill, G. and Markwick, R. D. (2000) *Russia's Stillborn Democracy?: From Gorbachev to Yeltsin* (Oxford: Oxford University Press).

Gilligan, E. (2004) *Defending Human Rights in Russia: Sergei Kovalyov, Dissident and Human Rights Commissioner, 1969–1996* (London: RoutledgeCurzon).

Goldman, M. I. (2003) *The Piratization of Russia: Russian Reform Goes Awry* (London: Routledge).

Hahn, G. M. (2004) 'Managed Democracy? Building Stealth Authoritarianism in St. Petersburg', *Demokratizatsiya: The Journal of Post-Soviet Democratisation*, 12(2).

Hanson, P. (2003) *The Rise and Fall of the Soviet Economy* (Harlow: Longman).

Hare, P., Schaffer, M. and Shabunina, A. (2004) 'The Great Transformation: Russia's Return to the World Economy' (Edinburgh: Centre for Economic Reform and Transformation, Herriot-Watt University) (www.sml.hw.ac.uk/cert/wpa/2004/dp0401.htm).

Harrison, M. (2002) 'Economic Growth and Slowdown', in E. Bacon and M. Sandle (eds), *Brezhnev Reconsidered* (Basingstoke: Palgrave).

Herspring, Dale (ed.) (2002) *Putin's Russia: Past Imperfect, Future Uncertain* (Lanham, MD: Rowman & Littlefield).

Hobson, C. (2001) *Black Earth City: A Year in the Heart of Russia* (London: Granta).

Hoffman, D. (2002) *The Oligarchs: Wealth and Power in the New Russia* (New York: PublicAffairs).

Hosking, G. (1998) *Russia: People and Empire, 1552–1917* (London: Fontana Press).

Hosking, G. (2001) *Russia and the Russians: A History* (London: Allen Lane).

Howard, M. M. (2003) *The Weakness of Civil Society in Post-Communist Europe* (Cambridge: Cambridge University Press).

Jordan, P. (2000) 'Russian Courts: Enforcing the Rule of Law?', in V. Sperling (ed.), *Building the Russian State: Institutional Crisis and the Quest for Democratic Governance* (Boulder, CO: Westview Press).

Kahn, J. (2002) *Federalism, Democratization, and the Rule of Law in Russia* (Oxford: Oxford University Press).

Knox, Z. (2005) *Russian Society and the Russian Orthodox Church: Religion in Russia after Communism* (London: RoutledgeCurzon).

Kornai, J. (1992) *The Socialist System: The Political Economy of Communism* (Princeton, NJ: Princeton University Press).

Laird, S. (1999) *Voices of Russian Literature: Interviews with Ten Contemporary Writers* (Oxford: Clarendon Press).

Lane, D. and Ross, C. (1999) *The Transition from Communism to Capitalism: Ruling Elites from Gorbachev to Yeltsin* (Basingstoke: Palgrave Macmillan).

Ledeneva, A. V. (1998) *Russia's Economy of Favours: Blat, Networking and Informal Exchanges* (Cambridge: Cambridge University Press).

Lewis, D. (2000) *After Atheism: Religion and Ethnicity in Russia and Central Asia* (London: Curzon).

Lieven, D. (1998) *Chechnya: Tombstone of Russian Power* (Newhaven, CT: Yale University Press).

Lloyd, J. (1999) 'The Russian Devolution', *The New York Times Magazine*, 15 August.

Lo, B. (2003) *Vladimir Putin and the Evolution of Russian Foreign Policy* (Oxford: Blackwell/Royal Institute of International Affairs).

McCauley, M. (1998) *Gorbachev* (Harlow: Longman).

McDaniel, T. (1996) *The Agony of the Russian Idea* (Princeton, NJ: Princeton University Press).

Maes, F. (2002) *A History of Russian Music: From Kamarinskaya to Babi Yar* (Berkeley, CA: University of California Press).

March, L. (2002) *The Communist Party in Post-Soviet Russia* (Manchester: Manchester University Press).

Matlock, J. (1995) *Autopsy on an Empire: The American Ambassador's Account of the Collapse of the Soviet Union* (New York: Random House).

Meier, A. (2004) *Black Earth: Russia after the Fall* (London: HarperCollins).

Merridale, C. (2000) *Night of Stone: Death and Memory in Russia* (London: Granta Books).

Midgley, D. and Hutchins, C. (2004) *Abramovich: the Billionaire from Nowhere* (London: HarperCollinsWillow).

Nogee, J. L. and Donaldson, R. H. (1992) *Soviet Foreign Policy since World War II* (Basingstoke: Palgrave Macmillan).

OECD (2004) *OECD Economic Survey of the Russian Federation* (Paris: OECD).

Oldfield, J. (2005) *Russian Society and the Environment* (Aldershot: Ashgate).

Pesmen, D. (2000) *Russia and Soul: An Exploration* (Ithaca, NY: Cornell University Press).

Pilkington H. (ed.) *et al.* (2002) *Looking West? Cultural Globalization and Russian Youth Cultures* (Pennsylvania: Penn State University Press).

Pilnyak, B. and A. Tulloch (translator) (1975) *The Naked Year* (New York: Ardis).

Politkovskaya, A. (2004) *Putin's Russia* (London: Harvill Press).

Putin, V. (2000) *First Person: An Astonishingly Frank Self Portrait by Russia's President* (London: Hutchison).

Rahr, A. (2000) *Wladimir Putin: Der 'Deutsche' im Kreml* (Munich: Universitas).

Read, C. (2001) *The Making and Breaking of the Soviet System* (Basingstoke: Palgrave Macmillan).

Reddaway, P. and Orttung, R. W. (eds) (2004) *The Dynamics of Russian Politics: Putin's Reform of Federa-Regional Relations. Vol. I* (Lanham, MD: Rowman & Littlefield).
Remington, T. F. (2001) *The Russian Parliament: Institutional Evolution in a Transitional Regime, 1989–1999* (Newhaven, CT: Yale University Press).
Remington, T. F. (2003) *Politics in Russia* (London: Addison & Wesley).
Ross, C. (2004) 'Putin's Federal Reforms', in C. Ross (ed.), *Russian Politics under Putin* (Manchester: Manchester University Press).
Sakwa, R. (2004) *Putin: Russia's Choice* (London: Routledge).
Sandle, M. (1998) *A Short History of Soviet Socialism* (London: University College of London Press).
Schumpeter, J. A. (1934) *The Theory of Economic Development* (Cambridge, MA: Harvard University Press).
Service, R. (2000) *Lenin: A Biography* (Basingstoke: Macmillan).
Service, R. (2003) *A History of Modern Russia from Nicholas II to Putin* (London: Penguin).
Service, R. (2004) *Stalin: A Biography* (Basingstoke: Macmillan).
Sharlet, R. (2001) 'Russia's Second Constitutional Court: Politics, Law, and Stability', in V. E. Bonnell and G. W. Breslauer (eds), *Russia in the New Century: Stability or Disorder?* (Boulder, CO: Westview Press).
Shaw, D. (1999) *Russia in the Modern World* (Oxford: Blackwell).
Shevtsova, L. (1999) *Yeltsin's Russia: Myths and Realities* (Washington, DC: Carnegie Endowment for International Peace).
Shevtsova, L. (2003) *Putin's Russia* (Washington, DC: Carnegie Endowment for International Peace)
Talbott, S. (2002) *The Russia Hand: A Memoir of Presidential Diplomacy* (New York: Random House).
Taubman, W. (2003) *Khrushchev: The Man and His Era* (New York: W.W. Norton & Co.).
Tompson, W. (2003) *The Soviet Union under Brezhnev* (Harlow: Longman).
Tompson, W. (2004) 'The Russian Economy under Vladimir Putin', in C. Ross (ed.), *Russian Politics under Putin* (Manchester: Manchester University Press).
Volkogonov, D. and Shukman, H. (ed.) (1998) *The Rise and Fall of the Soviet Empire: Political Leaders from Lenin to Gorbachev* (London: HarperCollins).
Vujačič, V. (2001) 'Serving Mother Russia: The Communist Left and the Nationalist Right in the Struggle for Power, 1991–1998', in V. E. Bonnell and G. W. Breslauer (eds), *Russia in the New Century: Stability or Disorder?* (Boulder, CO: Westview Press).
Webber, M. (1996) *The International Politics of Russia and the Soviet Successor States* (Manchester: Manchester University Press).
Webber, M. (1997) *CIS Integration Trends: Russia And The Former Soviet South* (London: Royal Institute of International Affairs).
Webber, S. (1999) *School, Reform and Society in the New Russia* (Basingstoke: Palgrave Macmillan).
Westwood, J. N. (2002) *Endurance and Endeavour: Russian History 1812–2001* (Oxford: Oxford University Press).
White, S. (2000) *Russia's New Politics* (Cambridge: Cambridge University Press).

White, S., Rose, R. and McAllister, I. (1997) *How Russia Votes* (Chatham, NJ: Chatham House Publishers).

White, S., Gitelman, Z. and Sakwa, R. (2005) *Developments in Russian Politics 6* (Basingstoke: Palgrave).

Wilson, E. (1994) *Shostakovich: A Life Remembered* (London: Faber & Faber).

Witte, J. and Bourdeax, M. (eds) (1999) *Proselytism and Orthodoxy in Russia: The New War for Souls* (Maryknoll, NY: Orbis).

Yeltsin, B. (1990) *Against the Grain: An Autobiography* (London: Pan Books).

Yeltsin, B. (1994) *The View From the Kremlin* (London: HarperCollins).

Yeltsin, B. (2000) *Midnight Diaries* (London: Weidenfeld & Nicolson).

Index